DEC 1994

# THE FORCE

# THE
# FORCE

## DAVID DORSEY

RANDOM HOUSE
NEW YORK

Library of Congress Cataloging-in-Publication Data
Dorsey, David
  The force / David Dorsey.
     p.   cm.
  ISBN 0-679-41030-9
  1. Thomas, Fred.   2. Thomas, Kathy.   3. Sales executives—Ohio—Cleveland—
Biography.   4. Sales personnel—Ohio—Cleveland—Biography.   5. Xerox Corporation—
Employees—Biography.   6. Selling—Office equipment and supplies—Ohio—Cleveland.
I. Title.
HF5439.32.T5D67   1994      93-37272

*Book design by Tanya M. Pérez*

Manufactured in the United States of America on acid-free paper
98765432
First Edition

TO MY FAMILY

# ACKNOWLEDGMENTS

I would not have been able to write this book without the support of my wife, Nancy, my children, Matthew and Christin, and my parents, Gene and Rita Dorsey, and the cooperation of Xerox people both in Cleveland and in Rochester. I want to thank several people in particular: Chris Pulleyn, who allowed me to be a freelance journalist while I worked for her; Dan Okrent, for aiming me down the path that led to this book; Chuck Verrill and Liz Darhansoff, for seeing the possibility when it was only a three-page letter; Harold Evans and my editor at Random House, for giving me the contract and nurturing the project; and Richard Todd, a brilliant man and a great friend, for his patience and wisdom. Thanks also to the Todd family for their endless hospitality—and to Walt and Tim for not laughing as hard as all the others did when this book was still just a dream.

*With the roundabout logic of emotions, he felt that the worthiness of his life was bound up with success.*

—JOSEPH CONRAD

# CONTENTS

# AUTHOR'S NOTE

This book is a work of nonfiction. It is based on my experiences during a year I lived with a group of top Xerox salespeople in a suburb of Cleveland, Ohio. I went on sales calls with them. I attended their staff meetings. I joined them on their company vacation in California. I followed them home and shared dinner with them and listened as they bickered about their unsatisfied dreams until the early morning hours.

My purpose: I wanted to write an American success story. I wanted to tell in vivid terms the story of how a top salesman— along with his team—attains certain goals over the course of a typical sales year, and what impact this effort has on the personal lives of the people involved. With the permission of Xerox Corporation, and with few restrictions on my ability to move freely and observe, I listened, I watched, and I participated.

During my stay in Cleveland, one man and his wife began to emerge as the heart of my story: Fred and Kathy Thomas. As the year passed, I found myself just as compelled and fascinated by what was happening in this couple's life as I was by the usual measures of business activity—number of orders, summaries of revenue to date, percentages of plan. The soul of this book emerged over a plate of cold sirloin after midnight in a Cape Cod home west of Cleveland as much as it did in the district's conference rooms and the offices of customers.

I went to several corporations with my proposal to write about the life of a top salesman. Xerox responded most enthusiastically to the idea and sent me to the Cleveland district, where, the company claimed, it was getting superlative results under the leadership of a man named Frank Pacetta. I was eager to see what this level of success entailed.

Xerox Corporation itself has become a legendary success story. It enjoyed a turbocharged ascendency in the sixties, when owners of Haloid stock became multimillionaires after Haloid became Xerox Corporation and marketed the single most successful commercial product in the history of American business—the photocopier. At the start, Xerox had the good fortune to risk everything on a dry copying process rejected by every other company its inventor approached, including IBM. Chester Carlson's device created a universal demand for something people didn't even know they wanted—a quick, hassle-free photocopy. Currently, that nagging little itch for a copy has grown into a "document" market estimated to be worth roughly $80 billion in annual revenue. Xerox claims, at present, less than a fourth of that market.

In the sixties and early seventies, selling Xerox copiers was, according to company mythologists, an endless party to celebrate Accounts Receivable Unlimited. The company could do no wrong during those first two decades. It was the Ed Sullivan of corporate America. Like Sullivan—a wooden impresario who achieved greatness almost despite his seeming ignorance of how revolutionary or pedestrian his show was becoming—Xerox could hardly keep pace with its rising fortunes. Yet for all its insight and courage in wagering its future on the office copier, Xerox didn't know how to market its research on personal computers and its invest-ment in other advanced technologies, developed in its California labs. It didn't seem to know the difference, so to speak, between the Beatles and Topio Gigio. Like Ed Sullivan, the company couldn't fail—at least not until the Japanese gained access to Xerox patents and started their own variety show in the seventies, and Xerox began to lose market share.

Now the company's serious competitors, both international and domestic, number more than a dozen: Kodak, IBM, Canon, Ricoh, 3M, Minolta, Oce, Savin, Konshiroki, Pitney-Bowes, Panasonic, and others. In its battle against all these other manufacturers, Xerox has followed what has become a commonplace path in American corporate history: A once-thriving American business loses share to the Pacific Rim, gets scared, adopts Total Quality Management practices, raises productivity, and begins to win back business. The way the Cleveland district sells copiers illustrates how far Xerox has been willing to go in this comeback effort.

During the year described in this book, Fred Thomas heads the major accounts team, one of the most important of eight sales teams in the Cleveland district. The people on Fred's team are a fraction of the five-thousand-odd employees in the entire Xerox sales organization. The district itself ranks in the middle of sixty-seven sales districts throughout the corporation, with an annual sales goal in excess of $30 million. That goal represents a much higher number than ones typically given to other districts of comparable size; it is equal to the goals set for bigger districts anchored in cities like Atlanta and even Chicago. Year after year, the company has demanded great things from Cleveland—and people like Fred Thomas are the reason the district hasn't failed in its efforts.

Several years ago Fred's team exceeded its budget, as they call their sales goal, by a higher percentage than any other sales team in the company. During that year, this performance ranked Fred Thomas as the corporation's best sales manager, which meant he was ranked at the top of a sales organization often regarded as the best in the world of business.

From our first encounter, Fred and Kathy Thomas understood my intentions perfectly and cooperated completely. They wanted readers to understand and vicariously experience their ordeals, both good and bad, at work and at home. The other people I've described here cooperated in a lesser degree. All of them understood the ground rules: I told them I wanted to write about their lives, insofar as they would disclose themselves to me willingly. Names of companies and individuals who appear in this book as customers have been changed.

# THE FORCE

# YES

*1.*

FRED THOMAS WAS early, but he felt late. Every morning, before the sun came up behind the trees, he pulled his Mazda RX-7 into Freedom Square Drive and parked behind the Xerox building. This glass box, shiny and elegant and rather small, sat at a distance from the highway in a quiet little wooded park. Fred's commute into Independence, just south of Cleveland, killed almost an hour every morning. He bolted into the building.

Waiting for the elevator in his suit and pinpoint shirt, he looked like any other white-collar worker—pressed, starched, and fragrant. Yet there was something special in his face, a sort of edgy amiability. He had a perpetual readiness to be amazed at his own success. He had dark crescents under his friendly eyes, graying hair, and a handshake with the craggy heft of a pipefitter's grip. He looked athletic, with a low center of gravity, a man

who could uncoil a lot of distance in a golf shot. He was handsome, though not tall, with the slight paunch one might expect
in a forty-one-year-old sales manager. His face was cocked, like
a mousetrap, ready to snap into a smile. He handled this smile
with nothing more than his lower eyelids, his mouth hardly
moving, his eyes doing all the work. He used it in varying degrees with everyone, until he got home in the evening, when he
was eager to remove it.

On the fourth floor, as the elevator opened, Fred's day began,
like a horse race, with the yawning of a gate. He entered the maze
of his still-vacant office and zigzagged past the cubbyholes for the
sales reps. These cubicles, each no roomier than a library carrel,
offered no privacy, just a desk surface, a filing cabinet, an overhead
shelf. The whole place looked sleek and fresh. Everything felt
carpeted: floor, chairs, partitions. Walking through that bullpen,
Fred arrived at his own undecorated office, with its metal desk,
telephone, window, and—luxury of luxuries—a door he could
lock. He bit into an apple, devouring skin, pulp, juice, seeds, and
core, flicking the stem into his waste can.

At seven-fifteen, his day was old already. He walked down the
hall to the corner office where Frank Pacetta glanced at his mail
or talked on the phone, sitting behind a wide desktop on which
two small American flags were planted, instead of ballpoints, in the
penholder. His pinpoint shirts were so heavily starched, the cuffs
looked brittle enough to shatter. Pacetta was younger than Fred.
He was fiercely thin, all muscle and sinew and visible bone structure, with a receding line of dark hair. He weighed maybe one
forty-five, and when he moved he pointed his toes outward, as if
he wanted to scoop the entire world through the gap between his
legs. Physically, he looked slight. Emotionally, he could fill a room.
He was the most intense human being Fred had ever known.

Usually Fred opened the conversation with tentative humor. His older daughter wouldn't let him hug her when he left for work. Unbelievable, wasn't it? "I told her I'll die, and she'll regret how mean she was to me. She said that wouldn't happen." Pacetta hardly listened, but soon his mind snapped into focus and he realized Fred Thomas was standing in his doorway, smiling. Every morning, he needled Fred: "Put your helmet on, Freddie. It's a war out there. You look like Bozo. What happened to your hair?"

Pacetta had an infant's attention span. After more than three sentences, his eyes darted away. He began his usual morning pep talk: It was a pivotal month. The nut cutter. They couldn't fall on their swords this month. They launched this thing successfully. They were going to come back at it with a vengeance. They were going to be all over it. It was going to be a wild ride. Buckle up, bitch.

Pacetta used lines like these every day, every week, every month. Fred never wearied of them—it was the *way* he chanted them, the loopy sort of Dr. Strangelove energy behind his pep talks. An outsider, a nonsalesman stumbling into this world, might find it hard to comprehend Pacetta as anything but an amusing nut, like certain stand-up comics who are said to spend their winters on the stage and their summers under the care of Swiss experts in pharmacology. At first Pacetta seemed like someone whose eyes occasionally glazed over as his tooth fillings picked up transmissions from Somewhere Else. On principle, Fred didn't trust anything Pacetta told him, because there was always another level to it, and then another, and another, with nothing solid at the bottom. Yet Fred liked the way his boss turned every conversation into a game. It made life unpredictable. More than once, Fred had seen him weep on cue, before the entire district, like a fund-raising evangelist. It wasn't real, and that's what made it fun. Pacetta never lacked energy. He never stopped selling. He never stopped wearing masks. It was all an act, and Fred was amazed by it. He liked to wind himself up with the force of Pacetta's artificial energy.

After these impromptu morning meetings, back in his own office, Fred usually felt restless, off-balance. "Do I look like Bozo? He looks like a rabbit in his car. The little squirrel. He's like a little chipmunk driving around in that car." Pacetta was about thirty pounds lighter than Fred. Fred knew he could take him with a couple punches. Broken nose notwithstanding, Pacetta might like it—he'd be pleased by his own ability to make Fred snap. They'd laugh about it together, and the next day they'd cruise through the region and close three big orders, just riding the backwash of energy from the scuffle. Fred got exactly what he wanted from this brief encounter—another hit of Pacetta's slightly unhinged intensity. First thing in the morning, it was better than black coffee. Now he was ready to sell.

Over the past decade Fred had built a reputation as one of the brightest stars in the sales force, a force considered one of the world's best. Three years ago Fred Thomas was recognized as the most successful sales manager at Xerox. In Cleveland he's become one of the district's most valuable players, and he feels the pressure of that reputation every time he drives to work, every time he chases a number through yet another change of seasons. This year he's chasing the biggest number he's ever faced, and every month he gets a little closer to it—though not quite close enough.

Every month Pacetta tells him he'll do it. Other sales managers dare him to do it. His reps are more reluctant to commit themselves. And Fred—he says he'll never even sniff the prints of this animal he tracks from week to week, and month to month. In March, it's going to be a disaster. In April, a train wreck. In May, a meltdown. They nod. They don't even hear him anymore, not when he's in this mode. It's his condition of creative discontent about everything in life—his voluble and inescapable anguish about every call his people have yet to make, every voice-mail message he has yet to answer, every deal that's still undone. He wants people to place bets on how far he can push both himself and his reps before one of them cracks and does something worthy of tabloid coverage. It's his act. People laugh at Fred, no matter what he does, because he is a man surprised by his own good fortune. He can't quite believe he's really smart enough, skillful enough, to keep winning year after year. He has an underdog's awe at his own abilities. He disarms envy and resentment, he keeps people liking him, because he's genuinely baffled by what allows him to keep doing so well.

In front of a customer, though, he plays a subtle game. People consider him a natural salesman, one of those fortunate few who can sell without seeming to do anything but what comes easily and genuinely, a man who makes people like him and then buy from him because, by the time he's done with them, they don't want to make him unhappy. They want to take care of him. They feel as if they've become his mother or his father. They can't bring themselves to disappoint somebody who has spent five hours or five months looking at them across a desk with the expectant, defenseless eyes of a child or a puppy. When it works the way he wants it to work, they hardly realize they've surrendered to him. He sells by seeming to do little more than what he does when he visits casually with one of his closest friends.

At times, when everything goes well, he wonders why he gets paid. It doesn't feel like labor. What does he do? He calls on people. He gets them to like him. He talks to them through the smoke. He smiles and seduces and persuades and entertains, and then he solicits the cursive name on a line. Aside from this ink on a page, what has he teased forth into the world? He gets paid for building this thing called a deal, yet it amounts to nothing you can see, smell, hear, or taste. All year long he chases what amounts to little more than a moment of truce or surrender. A carpenter smells the pine he saws. A mason tries a brick wall with his boot. An assembly-line worker scratches his name inside the housing of a copier. But those who sell that copier—where's the body and aroma and signature of *their* work?

Fred Thomas sees a number on his W-2 tax form, a line telling him how much he earned the previous year; usually it's close to six figures, and this gives him a little feeling of warmth. Or he sees himself golfing in Palm Springs. That's the prize he'll win if he gets into President's Club this year, if he *makes trip*, by topping his sales goal. He feels about Palm Springs the way others may have felt about Canterbury or Jerusalem or Mecca. One man's prize is another man's pilgrimage.

Yet even this trip isn't the heart of his effort. What he makes, what he builds, is a certain consummation, a certain confluence of two smiles. He puts months into a deal, pushing and pushing until the customer nods. It happens, and then it's gone. It all comes down to one word. He lives for one thing: to hear another human being say *yes*.

It's June, and he hasn't heard that word enough. His year is nearly half over. He feels he's running out of time. This year the district goal tops twenty million, higher than ever. Fred's team is one of seven in Cleveland. Everyone gets part of the burden, yet it seems he's been stuck with more than his share this year. In the past few years, as head of the major accounts team, he's become the district's point man, the star. Now, on occasion, the younger reps are starting to outshine him, and he likes the comfort of backing gradually out of the spotlight, the relief of no longer feeling the need to show everyone else the way to do it.

This year he feels he ought to *hide* from the spotlight. His results haven't been reassuring. His team is behind the curve. Every morning in June, Fred wonders: Where are his reps? Out on a call? Closing a deal? On the golf course? His career depends on them. Why aren't they here before he gets in? Why don't they let him ride with them on more calls? He has half a dozen reps, and he needs to push four of them—Bruno, Diane, Larry, and Nancy—to a new level. He needs to interrogate, inspire, berate, humble, and praise them. He needs to hound them until they let him join them on a sales call.

One of the traits he finds most endearing in his reps is how far he can push them before they menace him. A rep who once threatened to shoot him still works happily for Xerox in Cleveland. When his other, less volatile reps lose control, he says *Good reaction,* and they're flattered. After work they go out for a drink together. Some of his reps love him, but more often than not they want to see as little of him as possible. They call him the Fly behind his back. They duck into the rest room when they hear him coming. He helps them close deals, doesn't he? Does he hear any complaints when his nagging puts money into their pockets? How else is a manager supposed to make an impact on the hundreds of deals his reps hope to close before the end of the year? He picks a few crucial targets, a few big deals, and aims himself at them. This year, many of those deals require months of work—from cold calls to proposals to demonstrations to studies to more proposals, spiffing the deal as it goes along, and finally the closing calls. All the way he keeps pushing, asking to travel with his people, begging to see customers. It's in everyone's best interest. They're all paid a salary, with commission and bonus to reward performance. The sooner they close the sale, the more they make.

When he calls them into his office, he does some of his best work. He seats them beside his desk and begins to question them.

These sessions can be like interrogations of criminal suspects— intimidating, acrimonious, sarcastic—or they can be like little bursts of Bach counterpoint—balanced, intelligent, luminous. More often than not, the reps listen and watch Fred with amazement. How can this man know so much, in such detail, about every tiny deal they've got cooking? A hunted look comes into their eyes: He has it all in his head! A hundred deals! Is there nowhere to hide? He asks them precise questions about intricacies of the financing, the location, the timing, the internal approval process, the delivery date, the discounts, the leasing, always showing them how much he knows, often suggesting ideas on how to proceed, supporting them, thinking them through the deal, encouraging them, shifting their motors into a higher gear, and then sending them out into the hallway with new hope and new ideas. Yet, usually, Fred doesn't feel he's doing his job until he sits in front of a customer, along with one of his reps or by himself, closing a deal.

So far he's been on only a few closing calls this year. Things don't look bright. In January his team sold only two percent of this year's goal. By the end of February, it hit five percent. In March, it topped sixteen—and so on, dragging toward summer. Where's the spirit? Where's the energy? What are these people thinking? June is crucial. If he can finish well by the end of this month, he might dare hope for good things in December. It's a steep hill they need to climb. In this recession, people question every penny. They cling to their jobs. They wince when another salesman walks through the door. Now is the time to act, not after the end of the month.

Of all people, Bruno Biasiotta ought to let Fred ride with him. Why, when Bruno arrived, couldn't he come into Fred's office and tell him what was up? No big interrogations, no long agonizing strategy sessions, just a little five-minute update on what was happening at Bell Publications. It might turn out to be an important deal for Fred's year, and especially for the month of June. Fred wanted to know where it stood.

Yet Bruno didn't feel obliged to keep Fred posted on his progress every two or three hours. He wanted to control his accounts. He knew when to close his deals. He wanted to do his own work, without leaning on Fred—and with good reason. Of all Fred's reps, Bruno least needed help. Clone five other reps off a string of Bruno's chromosomes, give them each a telephone and a bag, and Fred could have coasted through the year. If Fred liked, he could've said hello to Bruno in January and then touched base with him at the end of December, without much disappointment. He admired Bruno's air of smooth, easy confidence.

Bruno's black hair stood straight up on his head, in the current pincushion style. Usually, he wore a double-breasted pin-striped suit and Italian wing tips shiny as patent leather. He had a young, handsome, rounded baby face. With that face, he seemed incapable of threatening anyone, which is not to say it was a face without guile. In his late twenties, he had the air of a Florentine prince in flannel and silk and gold, someone whose ancestors might have had a taste for brocade and ermine—a man who could get presumptuous and casual with a customer without seeming vulgar. Bruno lived in a three-hundred-thousand-dollar house in the suburbs, earned six figures every year, and did it all by virtue of his green card. He had come to the United States from Monte Cassino as a child and never bothered to get his citizenship. Bruno couldn't vote, but he could sell.

Fred appeared in Bruno's doorway, smiling. He told Bruno he wanted to visit Bell Publications downtown, see if he could force this thing to happen before the end of June. Bruno said it would happen, but not in June. Fred's team was struggling, and this deal would pull them through. Bruno told him not to count on it. He told Fred to let him handle his own accounts.

Fine. Maybe Fred could help Diane Burley. She was more cooperative than Bruno, and she listened when he suggested how she might handle a deal. Usually she had a cheerful word when she came into his office, dressed in something costly, sleek, and fashionable. He liked Diane. He enjoyed his time with her. She enjoyed *his* company too—in other words, she didn't invariably try to slip out of the office when she heard his footsteps thumping across the carpeted bullpen.

She was black, single, beautiful, a few years younger than Fred. She attended the ballet and an occasional play and tinkered with an unfinished autobiography, which she locked in her dresser drawer. If Diane was seated in a restaurant near a smoker, she made a production of moving to a distant table. Occasionally, she asked for a new table more than once during the course of a dinner, sometimes while entertaining one of her customers. These maneuvers amused Fred, though he wasn't sure any customer liked to migrate from one table to another between the clams casino and the eggplant Parmesan.

Diane was having a good year. All the elements were in place. She could count on a whole slate of orders. She didn't really need Fred's help at this point, yet he offered her the pleasure of his company. Could they travel together? No. Not right now. It was all she could do to keep up with all the deals she was closing. Some of them were ripe, just dropping into her lap. One day she brought in six big orders—it was one of those times when everything seems to click. There wasn't much Fred could do to get incremental business from her in June. So he couldn't complain. She was doing what she promised to do. He left her alone. He seemed to have no other choice.

As a last resort, Fred approached Larry Tyler. Normally, Larry tried to stay as far away from Fred as possible. He was the Mystery Man. Larry could stare Fred in the face and promise wonders, without flinching. But would he follow through, or was he just blowing smoke? Fred didn't know where anything stood in Larry's territory until they got in front of his customers. Once they got out on the road, Larry couldn't hide a thing. This time Larry didn't avoid him—he didn't hesitate to invite Fred along on several calls at Gladstone, Inc.

Now he was on the road. This was where he felt most at home—knocking on doors, shaking hands. Some people said the profession of sales was something you did after failing at everything else. It was something no person would *choose* to do. Yet the qualities that make a good salesman also help make civilization possible—friendliness, courtesy, service, determination, tact, insight, cunning, and persuasion. When Fred hit the road again, he felt his own life open out into this web of emotion, intelligence, and playful guile. On the road, he took heart. Now maybe he could push a deal over the edge to that decisive moment when the customer said *yes.*

Every time he rode with Fred, Larry held the wheel of his metallic-blue Camry with one hand, smoking a panatella with the other. Sometimes he wore a tattersall shirt, a designer tie with a brown-and-blue pattern, and a pale blue suit. Larry seemed young for a man pushing fifty; he had a taut stomach, a narrow kinetic face, and the eager eyes of a barely restrained terrier. Sometimes, in front of a customer, Larry looked as if he wanted to be scratched behind the ears. No one would guess he had married at the age of twenty and carried photographs of four grandchildren. He combed his thin hair back off his high forehead and kept his mustache cropped. His blue eyes looked sly, narrowed in thought.

Larry liked to play tough. He liked to ask his customers if the

Kodak rep had wept in front of them yet. Larry didn't scare easily. He had tenure at Xerox. His wife had her own housecleaning business, Busy Brooms, and some years she earned more than Larry, providing him with a financial cushion. Larry moved among the Xerox managers the way a cat steals through a house at night with something alive in its teeth.

Most of the time Larry acted obsequious with his customers and his boss, as if he'd do anything gladly, go to any lengths, to please them. He carried a small bag of peppermint candies with him, to freshen his breath after a cigar on the road. On sales calls he reached into his coat pocket and handed out sweets, as if he were training his customers to play dead. Sometimes he tossed pepper- mints into the air and forced customers to catch them. But Fred didn't reach into the air when Larry tossed him a candy. Fred didn't believe Larry's act any more than he believed Pacetta's.

When they were on the highway together, Larry reached into his pocket for a peppermint, but Fred didn't eat them. Usually he was working on a mouthful of chewing gum already. In the car he and Larry played a guessing game with the candy. Fred asked Larry to tell him, again, how many calories were in these things. Larry told him: Twenty-three. *Really?* Thirteen. *More than that!* Fifty-two, then.

Every time Fred asked, Larry faked a new number. Larry had no idea how many calories the peppermints contain. Fred played along, believing nothing. It was a private joke about the nature of selling, the way people smoke each other with numbers, the way they play a poker game every minute of the day. Fred was always looking for a hidden level of meaning in everything Larry did. When Larry was startled by something Fred said, he seemed too startled. When Larry jumped to his feet and rushed back to his desk to make a phone call, he jumped a little too eagerly. Fred knew he was getting what he called the New York Nod from

Larry—just another feigned act of obedience. Inviting Fred along on this call was just another New York Nod.

Larry's assessment of this deal was brief: It was percolating. She was wiggling around on him, though. Fred told him never to leave her alone. When he talked to Larry, he liked to chew five sticks of gum at once, the words squishing through his teeth. He knew it would annoy Larry. They needed to know where her emotions were every day. He wanted to talk to her. Larry warned him not to talk with his mouth full.

Nell had permed dark hair and was wearing black jeans, a pink blouse, and a necklace of small Florida seashells. She had an honest, open face, not the seasoned, flinty look Fred hoped to see. He wasn't sure she was the sort of person who could force this deal to happen. She looked too nice. Nell was on their side already, and she wanted the machine, but she looked too sweet to sell the idea to her own boss. Every time they drove back from Gladstone, it seemed as if he'd accomplished nothing. When was it going to happen? Where would they get the orders they needed? Where would Fred Thomas finally make an impact?

In the evening, usually after the dinner hour, Fred escapes to his home in Avon Lake. He and his family live in a new and immaculate suburb, less than a quarter of a mile south of Lake Erie. Every house in this neighborhood cost hundreds of thousands of dollars, and all of these homes seem inhabited by young families, whose laughing children are seen on sidewalks, in yards, running in and out of doorways. Tall trees were left standing everywhere by the developer, giving the new homes a marbling of shadow and sunlight across bluegrass, blacktop, and brick. These houses, all new, fit in snug curving rows along winding roads; you can find a recreational facility with a pool or tennis court a short walk from almost any home. It's a deeply appealing world of proportion and balance and fresh paint in which every house has curb appeal, a flawless-looking tract, smelling of cut grass and cookouts.

From the street, the Thomas home—not large by neighborhood standards—looks even smaller than its twenty-seven-hundred square feet. It has a Cape Cod façade; the upper windows are all in back. Fred loves his house. He could live in contentment here for the rest of his life.

He has a dream of homecoming. He envisions walking into the kitchen. One by one, his children hug him—in this dream they are still so young that their arms barely circle his knees and they press their cheeks against his legs. Then his wife, Kathy, kisses him, hands him a vodka tonic, and listens sympathetically as he describes his day. Together, they commiserate and laugh and eat. After a certain hour—maybe eight, maybe nine—his family fades into the distance of other rooms, leaving him to watch a game. For three hours or so, he hears no other sound throughout the house and sees no other human face. His collie sleeps quietly at his feet. At last he is alone. This is his dream of perfect recreation: a few hours of idle solitude at night. But he rarely gets them. Usually, still in his suit, he rushes from work to the Little League baseball diamond to help coach his son's team. Or he joins his teenage daughter for ice-skating at the Winterhurst facility. Or he runs a few miles at the health club, working off his tensions.

When he's lucky enough to drive directly home, he arrives in the kitchen after everyone else has finished dinner. He finds Kathy there, cleaning up. She is beautiful, slim, fair, with fine blond hair cut in a bob; she is shorter than Fred and about the same age, and has a confident, almost tomboyish walk. Her blue eyes regard him now with a mixture of curiosity and quiet reserve. She has the habit of standing in place, wherever she happens to be in the room, giving no ground, listening but saying as little as possible. She says nothing as he walks through the door, opening with a dire assessment of the day. If she can help it, she doesn't say anything Fred might consider an expression of doubt. As he eats his belated meal, she manages the children—Kara, Kylene, and Christopher—who pass through the kitchen and family room like busy commuters.

When the dinner is done, Kathy retreats to the tiny den off the living room to watch Larry King while Fred stays in the family room to review his stock market report on the other television. Later, close to midnight, long after Kathy and the children have gone to bed, Fred may get half an hour of peace, maybe more. Yet he hardly notices it. Instead, he sits in the kitchen, phone in hand, and leaves voice-mail messages to each of his reps. He's exhausted. He's anxious. He's swamped with work. He is making things happen even at midnight. He's proving how effective he can be, and his face wears the look of a man absorbed in the flow of his work. Soon enough he'll relax. But first he needs to finish one more message before he goes to bed.

2.

WHEN SHE MET him in high school, Kathy thought Fred was wonderful. When he phoned her, or wrote letters to her, or took her out onto the lake to neck in a rowboat—when he showed her how to sneak into the Cedar Point Amusement Park without paying, getting away with something, and gleeful to be able to share the experience with *her*—he had an unpretentious charm that attracted her and seemed hauntingly familiar, comfortable and comforting. He was a romantic, a dreamer, a man who could be moved to tears by certain movies or stories or locker-room prayers. And he had warmth, a quiet and friendly amusement about his life. He was accomplished in everything he did, yet he always had an air of humility, the diffident and buoyant hopefulness of an underdog constantly grateful for his own good fortune.

When he was around her, there was always a hint of worship in his eyes. He acted as if his life revolved around hers, as if she were the most important human being alive, the most attractive, the most interesting, the most worthy of his love. He seemed willing to do anything for her. Half the time she felt as if he were, in an emotional sense, kneeling before her. As if he had to look upward to catch a glimpse of her and therefore saw her in a flatteringly foreshortened perspective, as if he longed only to raise himself up to her level, if not raise himself up *through* her, with all the influence she might have on him. Nobody else, no other *boy*, seemed this humble. He cared about her feelings and wanted to make her happy.

This surprised her, in a way, because she wouldn't have expected Fred Thomas to be so modest, so emotional, so quick to value another person more than he seemed to value himself. He was popular, a varsity player, well known around the high school, and he certainly didn't need to attach himself to only one girl. He was good in all sports—basketball, football, and especially baseball, which he loved more than any other game. He played them all well, and these rapid waters of success in his life seemed to enliven everything the two of them did together, freshening their affection for each other.

Fred came from a successful middle-class Lebanese family, though his Anglicized name divulged nothing of his ancestry. His father, Naif, worked as both a barber and a laborer, and his mother, Mona, was a nurse and office manager for a local doctor. He had a twin brother, John, who competed with him in sports. Kathy could see Fred inherited from his family the qualities a man needed to become successful—a hunger to work and a craving to win.

Yet she found herself drawn to him because of something else, a magnetism and warmth she felt in him. It didn't take Kathy long to realize why Fred's particularly winning charm seemed familiar. At his best moments he resembled her father, James, a salesman of industrial machinery. Her father lived a comfortable life, a life without visible stress; he had a happy marriage and a steady job that allowed him to include his wife in dinners and cocktail parties when he entertained his customers. It was a life of order, stability, and affection. Her father never appeared to be out of control. Conflicts never broke him. Anxieties never overwhelmed him. Compulsions never mastered him. The safe world of her childhood seemed to emanate from the quiet, restful center of her father's personality, which acted as the rudder of their collective fate, the guiding force behind his successful labor in the outside world and unwavering love at home. Instinctively, she recognized the same kind of force in Fred—that he had an easy way with people, the kind of genuine charm her father put to such good use.

When Fred first saw Kathy walking past him, as he and his friends backed their car into the McDonald's parking lot, he thought: *Funny walk.* She was lovely, with gleaming blond hair and blue eyes and an attractive sort of cheerful confidence. She wasn't tall, wasn't glamorously beautiful in a threatening way, but she *was* beautiful. She looked almost Californian with her sanguine vitality. Would she be interested in *him?*

The next day he spotted the same slightly nervous walk in the high school cafeteria, the walk of a girl who knows she's being watched. He wavered. He wondered what to say. He didn't even know her, but he knew he wanted to date her. He asked one of his friends to tell Kathy he wanted to meet her. On their dates, she was smart enough to cut him a disconcertingly skeptical look now and then, as if she was really thinking about what he said, analyzing, jumping ahead, giving attention to his words. That could be risky—Fred didn't want to be analyzed *too* well—but he was flattered by the attention, just as she was flattered by his solicitousness. Even better, after all her careful listening, she was *still* interested. She liked him. She responded to him. It was everything he wanted from another human being—affection and response. Her love made him feel worthwhile.

When Fred went to Bowling Green State University, where he tried out for the baseball team while he got his education, she followed him to college. By the end of their schooling, he realized he didn't have the skill to become a professional player. They were married, and Fred joined Xerox as a salesman, a dozen years after the company was founded—America was still in Vietnam at the time. For twenty years he remained at Xerox, building a long history of success, both as a salesman and as a sales manager. What was true of him in high school and college was true of him in business: Kathy's husband knew how to win.

In the earliest years of his career, Fred grew close to Kathy's father. The two men felt a kinship, that common emotional warmth Kathy recognized from the start. James became a sort of spiritual father for Fred. They would go out together in the evening and sit beside the lake, drinking beers until early in the morning. Fred gained wisdom about himself in those years before Kathy's father died. During the times when everything worked perfectly for Fred, her father would tell him he was riding a crest. He'd come down, but it would always come back. It was a force. That's what selling was. He didn't have to be smart. But he had to have that quality, that emotion. He had it.

Fred knew what her father meant. That force gave Fred's emotions an urgency, an electrical quality, a certain torque. He'd felt it most strongly as a young man on the gridiron, diamond, and court. When it was operating, this force conveyed a feeling of euphoria and power. He judged everything he did by how much it moved the needle of his emotions—and other people's emotions—toward this same feeling. It was less an emotion than a state of charmed confidence, when it seemed all he had to do was walk into a customer's office and the customer would roll over and say yes. It was the way he felt when he dated Kathy, sharing it with her as a way of persuading *her* to say yes. Successful human relationships were all based on the same thing—a continuous pull of emotional attraction. When he had this feeling, everything flowed, everything clicked, everything felt the way it did when he found his golf club's sweet spot on the first tee.

Fred was enthusiastic and delighted about almost everything. He laughed at himself. When he and his brother, John, went to work for Xerox in Toledo, fresh out of college, they wore pin-striped suits to work every day, suits they'd worn for years. After half a year, they bought Gucci boots and gray suits with white piping that ran through all the seams, as if every hem were supposed to be visible to people a block away. They were serious, intense, and at the same time ironic about everything. *Wow*, they thought, *are we going to impress the guys at the office. We're the Rhinestone Cowboys*. Fred's naïve exuberance disarmed people. People trusted him because he allowed and encouraged them to feel superior to him. He put himself beneath other people in order to win their trust and affection—an honest show of respect for another person's greater intelligence and skill. His feeling for other people *was* genuine, and it also happened to be useful. In Toledo, they called him Lieutenant Columbo. He didn't have the rumpled raincoat or the old Peugeot or the dog, but he did have the sly, disarming façade of bemused curiosity and enthusiasm covering a relentless sense of purpose. He appeared to be muddling through. All the while he knew instinctively what he was doing.

Fred was genuine. In Toledo he went around the office chanting, "I am honest, I am honest, I am honest." He had charm, not charisma. Kathy's uncle, Uncle Jack, was a flashier kind of salesman. Uncle Jack was Scottish, buoyant, and loud, and he took charge. He could walk into a bar and have everybody listening to his jokes. Fred could walk into a bar and nobody would notice. By the time he left he would have three signatures in his pocket, but even his customers would hardly remember what came over them. By nature he was a salesman, not a master of ceremonies. He was quiet and self-effacing and amiable, and yet persistent. People bought from him because they trusted him. They responded to him the way Kathy responded. One and all, they took pleasure in giving this decent guy what he wanted. They enjoyed saying yes—especially when it meant they might get a rest from the pleasure of seeing his smiling face in their doorway every other day.

Fred liked to feel he was a little different from most other salespeople. He liked to keep himself apart from the crowd. When Fred and Kathy moved to Cleveland, they refused to buy a house in Hudson, a costly eastern suburb where Frank Pacetta lived. It didn't appeal to them. Most of the other sales managers who lived near Pacetta in Hudson were living single-income dreams straight out of the fifties. They all lived in the same tract of oversized homes so new you could almost smell the latex paint. In June and July the wives met at the neighborhood pool during the afternoon. The husbands joined them for impromptu cookouts on their backyard decks. Hudson was like an extension of the office, and Fred wanted no part of *that*. He wanted to preserve the integrity of his home life. But as the years passed, the office claimed more and more of his time. Fred became more serious, less amused, about his work. Often, his creative discontent at work spilled over into their time together at home. Both of them wondered where Fred would go next, after twenty years with the company. Was he making progress?

For that matter, was Kathy making progress? After getting a master's degree in education and teaching for several years early in her marriage, Kathy made a decision to stay home with her children and devote herself exclusively to her family. She felt it was her duty to invest herself in her children's lives, at least until the youngest was well into grade school.

For almost two decades this has been her choice, and her days are, typically, the days of a mother and a homemaker. She goes to the automatic teller machine and shops for essentials. She helps her children with their schoolwork and their sports. She shuttles her family from one place to another. Each of her days resembles every other day. She keeps fixing meals, shopping, going to the bank, and doing all the other things she's been doing for twenty years of marriage. She suspects there may be more to life. Kathy wants to talk with Fred about her own life during their evenings alone together, but she knows he'll be preoccupied about his own day. Isn't it obvious to him, though? Her children are all in school now. She's coming back into possession of her own time, her own life, after almost two decades. She has much more freedom during the day, and it's making her reflect about how she wants to use it.

She's coming to realize her happiness depends on her own efforts, her own interior life. She attends church every Sunday, without him. She finds the atmosphere intelligent, tolerant, the silences filled with an energy she doesn't experience at home. And when she's alone, she comes up with plans to enlarge her life but rarely feels the need to let Fred know about them. In one of these scenarios, she imagines selling an idea for a television game show to Merv Griffin; she doesn't know how, exactly, she can arrange such a deal. Still, she has ideas about the game. She knows how it will work: The game show will split married couples apart, and they will be questioned by a panel of guests. The object will be to identify which husband belongs with which wife. It's called Matchmate.

In a more realistic view of her future, she wants to resume her career as a teacher. She knows how to get her name in front of the right people. The path is clear: start substituting in one of the local school districts and eventually apply for a full-time job when one opens up. She doesn't talk with Fred about either of these plans, because she knows how he'll react. In theory, he wants her to work. He'll enjoy having the additional income to help them pay the bills. But she knows he's troubled by the whole prospect of her independence. After twenty years, they've grown accustomed to a certain kind of partnership, and at times he fears she's pulling away from him.

## 3.

THE MONTH WAS coming to an end. Fred needed to push himself over the top with a single deal. With a sense of foreboding, he faced his biggest problem—Nancy Woodard. She had the worst territory in the entire district—the one no one else wanted—and was forced to call on nonuser accounts, customers who avoided Xerox because of disappointments in the past. After trying for six months to enrich this patch of arid topsoil, Nancy was beginning to realize she wanted more recognition. She told him maybe she wasn't right for this job. Maybe earlier she was successful only because she had a good territory. Could *be*, Fred wanted to say. He didn't expect her to write much, if any, business this year. If she wrote any orders, though, he wanted her to do it *now*.

Nancy was tall and physically strong, bigger than Fred, and had clear and unflinching blue eyes—a woman whose great-grandparents had tilled the Pennsylvania soil. She appeared in Fred's doorway wearing her trademark red suit, a white blouse, a gold chain around her neck, and a big diamond on her finger. That gem was more than a wedding announcement. It was a way of fending off management. She wasn't about to keep working all her waking hours. She was determined to do her job in less than ten hours per day, Monday through Friday. As she put it, "I refuse to impale myself on the Xerox sword."

She had been married to Gary Woodard in May, and she had a life now, a husband, along with a new regard for moderation. Fred couldn't comprehend how Nancy had time to pass around photographs of her wedding. She liked to chat about it. They served chicken instead of steak so they could afford the photographer. The wrong cake was delivered, but it tasted even better than the one they had ordered. They sliced it up and froze what was left. The bar tab ran into the thousands.

Fred figured her out: She was in love with being in love. In anticipation of being Gary Woodard's wife—in other words, a woman with a life—she had taken the two-year nonuser assignment. A tough tour of duty, but not too tough. It had a substantial, guaranteed, risk-proof salary. All other reps and managers were paid partly on commission. After seven years on the fast track, Nancy could arrive at a reasonable hour, go home at a reasonable hour, and enjoy a more than reasonable paycheck.

In Fred's view she didn't need to make her budget. She played ambassador, mended fences with enemy accounts, sold next to nothing, and yet never paid interest on her Visa card. Fred knew she had a chance for a big deal at Crockett Lang. No way was she going to get it in June, no matter how badly he needed it, because *she* didn't need it. Where was the incentive? The end of June was here, and she didn't seem to care.

Fred didn't want her to breathe without asking his permission. Understandably, this made her feel a little claustrophobic when she was in his presence. She told people Fred was one of those guys you love to hate. Love him or hate him or both, she tried to keep her distance and her cool. Every day in the office he watched her smile and pluck off her earring as she raised the phone to her ear. She looked calm and accomplished, even though she had wept at her last one-on-one meeting with Fred. He had slipped a letter of corrective action into her file because he had asked her for a written update on all her accounts every week and she had failed to provide it. In response, she mouthed off about quitting. He thought: *Make my day.* Secretly he hoped: *Now prove me wrong and bring in some orders.*

As often as possible Fred called Nancy into his office and started working on her. He used his Fred Flintstone voice, a grating horn that rose into a squeak of astonishment and then, two seconds later, dropped into guttural undertones of choking despondency, all of these notes issued through the tired little aperture of Fred's perpetual ironic smile: *I'm really worried. My career is over. It's over. I'm worried about that too. But this year really worries me. Know what? I'm the problem. I'm too organized. That's my downfall. I'm going to unorganize myself. I'm going to start running around like a chicken with its head off. This is how I'm going to un-organize myself. I'm going to start going out on calls with everybody. I can't wait to travel with you. See this calendar? That was one hell of a month. I was all over the world, and we had a great month. How about we call on Crockett Lang?*

Nancy laughed, but she told him no. Fred knew she was playing a game, protecting her customer. Maybe she was dragging her feet on the deal, sandbagging, postponing it until later in the year so she'd have at least something to show for herself in the second half. He didn't let up, though. He flogged her until she wanted to screw her business card to his forehead with the words *Get lost* scribbled on the back. In return, she kept avoiding him. She didn't want him to do this same thing to her customer. The Crockett Lang deal was in the most delicate stages of negotiation. She didn't want anything to upset the process. As she told Fred, her customer was a big softy. She didn't want Fred to be mean to him.

So in desperation Fred assembled a meeting in one of the conference rooms: They knew how far behind they were this year. Take a look at the numbers. The year was almost half over, and they weren't even near the halfway mark. They'd never make trip this way. He paused for emphasis. He wanted everyone to feel the stomach acid dripping. He wanted to build a feeling of obligation. He wanted them to feel guilty. He wanted them to want to do it for *him*. He wanted them to want to make *him* happy. That's what selling was, wasn't it? Making your customers happy? Making your boss happy? Making other people want to make *you* happy?

"Two minutes. I'm gonna preach. This has been the funnest, lowest-key month I've ever been in. If you're not tired at the end of the day, you didn't take yourself to another level or do something extra. That's what we're asking. I've been very, very lucky. I always have the special people on my teams. We're the crème de la crème. But don't be afraid to ask for help. If you want me to be the bad guy, ask. I want us to be tired, exhausted. If you aren't tired, you haven't gone the extra mile."

In the following days nothing happened. With every passing hour Fred became more and more depressed about his month and his year. A few days before the end of June, he happened to be at his desk when the phone rang. Before he picked up the phone, he thought: *Right now, the way my life's been this month? Calm down, Fred. Be ready for bad news.* As soon as he heard Nell's voice, calling from

Gladstone, he knew. "That's what I thought. Yeah." He turned his thumbs down. "Yeah." (Sigh. Another sigh.) "Hmph. Yeah." (Sigh.) "Right when I heard the president would be involved, I knew this wasn't good. Hey, he's the president."

Fred hung up. He stared at the phone. *That's over. The pain is done. Hey, no one got killed. I went to the wall on that one.* One bad year, it was all right. It was only a trip to Palm Springs.

There was still time. He couldn't give up. At the final series of June meetings of sales managers, all the managers gathered around the long conference table. There was a tripod tablet at one end. Usually Fred chose a seat as far as he could get from the head of the table, where Pacetta sat. Fred yawned and acted sleepy, made faces at some of the other managers. Quietly, people warned each other not to make eye contact with Fred. When Fred recalled something from his early years as a rep, the other managers said, "Take us back, Fred. Give us some history." This got a good laugh. A lot of laughter, at every meeting, was at Fred's expense, and he loved it. Yet Fred was paying attention, even when he clowned. His coffee cup, after an hour and a half, was still full. In college he'd been so intense about studying that he ended up highlighting every line in every textbook he read. When he was done with a book, every page was tinted a jelly-bean yellow.

During these meetings Pacetta was so impatient that he couldn't stop moving. He was in constant, compulsive motion, like a sufferer from Tourette's syndrome: squeezing his nose, jotting himself a note, straightening his tie, rubbing the side of his face with his fingertips, running his fingertips up and down his nose, biting his knuckles, sliding his thumb under his chin, raking his fingers across his forehead, banging his fist lightly against his lips, biting the nail of his little finger, adjusting his eyeglasses, crossing his arms, and finally coming to a state of repose. But no. Fifteen seconds later, the nickels and dimes rang in his pocket as he twitched his leg.

At every meeting, once everyone finished making projections of how much equipment they expected to install, Pacetta stood and faced them. He told them it was the most important day of the year. But then, with Pacetta, it was *always* the most important day, or week, or month. Why? One, it was the day they were in. Two, they were right on the edge of making it happen. Assume the worst. Assume the guy wouldn't have the equipment. Assume the truck dropped it off and the rep wasn't there. Assume the building wouldn't be open. Assume the electrical receptacle wouldn't work. This wasn't a game now. This was real. It was a clear grand for each of them in bonus if they made profit. Better'n a sharp stick in the eye.

The managers joked among themselves. Had they taken everything into consideration? What about dew point? Wind chill? Humidity? The orbit of Mercury? They filed out of the room, jumpy and preoccupied.

After this pep talk from Pacetta, Fred was ready to do anything for his boss. Where was Nancy? Where was the deal at Crockett Lang? Nancy was his greatest worry and his only hope: not the most encouraging mix of characteristics in a rep. No one else could save him in June. He needed the Crockett Lang order and he needed it now. He wanted more, too. He wanted to be there when it happened, to be the man who pushed the deal over the edge and *forced* it to happen. He wanted to be there for the close, when they heard the *yes*.

Nancy certainly didn't seem able to do it on her own. Maybe she did well in the past because she handled cream accounts. Did she ever consider that? Now she had to sell, really sell, and she didn't like it. Now she needed to face people who despised the company. It was easier to thumb through her wedding album, wasn't it?

Late in the month, Nancy walked into Fred's office. Fred didn't even look up from his notebook. He didn't want to hear another word from her. On her tablet Nancy circled a long list of machines at Crockett Lang—big, lucrative gear. She held the tablet up to Fred's face until he looked at it. He gave her a blank stare. He didn't seem to understand, or else he didn't believe.

"What I'm trying to tell you is, he got the okay," she said. "As soon as I'm out of here, I'm going over there. He's signing."

"No," he said. "Really?"

"Fifteen Kodak knockouts."

Fred didn't know what to say. "This is two years' work. This is going to be put in the national newsletter. You should feel good."

He was elated, and yet a little disappointed too. It had happened without him. His team would top its budget for the month, and he had made an impact—on the early sales calls at Crockett Lang, certainly. But he wasn't there when the customer said the final *yes*. He wasn't there to close this deal. However, he might still have a chance. He realized he would have to connive to get the orders onto the books for June, for Pacetta's sake. When his reps got orders, Fred got credit, but Pacetta wouldn't get credit toward *his* June goal until the machines were actually installed. Fred was proud of how he succeeded every month in getting most of his orders installed, when other managers might have been satisfied getting the orders, with or without installation. So Fred pushed Nancy to push Crockett Lang to take the machines before the end of the month. His own happiness wasn't enough. His month wasn't finished until Pacetta smiled. And this would give him a chance to get in front of her customer and close him for the installation.

When they got into Rodney Brown's office in the Crockett Lang print shop, Fred refused to sit down. He was too excited. He stood inside the doorway, while Rodney sat at his desk, looking up at the two of them. Brown was thin and wiry and had brown hair, glasses, and the preoccupied manner of a graduate student in mathematics, polite and unassertive, but tenacious. He wasn't soft. He looked stubborn.

"I don't know if I want to do that. Our docks are not very big. Putting a brand-new machine and letting it sit there—"

"We've done this a lot," Fred said.

"Not at Crockett Lang you haven't. What would be the advantage?"

"We could secure the equipment for you."

"But they're going to be all over the place."

"What's good about that is that you don't have to find just one spot for them," Fred said, turning an objection into a nominal advantage. There was no hesitation, no time to think. When Fred was watching the Lakers on television a few nights earlier, he'd noticed how the joy of basketball was in the way a player faked his defender. *That's what I do,* Fred thought. Fred wanted his customer to feel superior enough to become overly confident in his own shrewd insight into Fred's more, well, spontaneous approach. A customer who felt superior would feel more in charge, and Fred wanted his customers to feel in control of the deal. A customer who liked him was a customer who'd buy from him. Fred's disarming enthusiasm worked for him again and again. Oh, so they didn't have one place to store these machines? Didn't they see! That meant they could put them all over the place! Wonderful! He'd have to tell Mrs. Thomas all about it when he got home!

"But I've seen our loading docks and—"

But they could find places all over the building! It was perfect!

Nancy had by now produced the forms. She looked at Rodney

and said, "I just need to know exactly where you'll be putting the machines." It would have been a routine question if Rodney had agreed to the installation. But he hadn't. Rodney would be accepting the machines, without actually saying yes. It was classic. You assumed the sale. You didn't ask if he wanted the machine. You asked if he wanted two of them, or would three be better? But Rodney didn't fall for it. Fred and Nancy drove back to the district without permission to install the gear. Nancy knew why. She and Fred had pounded the Crockett Lang people into submission, never letting up. The customer finally drew the line. He signed the order, but he wouldn't take the machines.

Nancy told Fred her customer was sick of hearing his voice. She felt like crawling in there and crawling out. She'd dreamed about that moment. But now she was embarrassed. It took all the pleasure out of the moment.

So Fred phoned sales headquarters in Rochester, and he promised them the equipment would be installed in June. He didn't have the installation agreement yet, but he was sure he could get it. It was the only way to get the orders onto the books for that month and have the equipment delivered to Cleveland, just in case they *did* get an installation agreement from Crockett Lang at the last minute. He didn't intend to give up on the installations until the last minute. He did it to please Pacetta. He would go to any length to do that, hoping Pacetta would be just as loyal, in return, when Fred needed help in the future—but mostly because he liked and respected Pacetta, mostly because he wanted to please the man.

When Pacetta heard the news about the Crockett Lang orders, he burst into Fred's office. He smacked both palms onto Fred's shoulders, kneading and squeezing. Pacetta was giving him a massage. Fred squirmed under the pressure and got out of his chair, embarrassed by the massage. Later Pacetta took Fred's head in his hands and planted a smacking kiss above Fred's eyebrows. Fred winced. When they heard stories about this kind of thing, people who didn't work with him sometimes wondered if Fred had signed up with the Mafia. Pacetta was nothing like anyone Fred had ever seen. What guy would come up and give him a massage? Pacetta was playing a game all the time. He was a lunatic. He wasn't right in the head. Fred believed that's what made him so good. He felt something both pleasant and unpleasant in this encounter. He hated to admit how so much of his emotional energy derived from this horseplay. Just this sort of thing, the artificial and melo-dramatic kiss on the brow, was what got his engine churning for another day of work. He'd come to depend on it. He loved it. He hated it. He used it. In moments of reflection, he wondered if he wouldn't prefer to work in another sort of environment someday.

As it turned out, he and Pacetta tried every maneuver to get the signatures they needed for the Crockett Lang installation, but they ran out of time in June. The equipment arrived and sat in the warehouse, undelivered, and was installed in July. The orders got onto the books, and Fred got credit for them when he needed it—yet he felt he'd let his boss down, because he didn't do what was necessary for his boss to get credit for the orders in June. He'd won the game, he'd done his job as a sales manager, but he felt embarrassed. He felt as if he'd let Pacetta down. He felt as if he'd failed. Getting those installations for Pacetta was the true measure of his dedication as a Xerox worker and the greatest indicator of his ongoing victory as a salesman. He vowed never to let Pacetta down again this year.

By the end of June Fred's team has attained almost half its annual goal—about ten percent short of where Fred would like to be. They still have six months left to top their entire annual goal by at least twenty percent—which is exactly what they need to do for Fred to win President's Club and the trip to Palm Springs. Yet Fred is reasonably pleased with the June results—at least it gives him a shot at making up the rest in the time left to him.

Now's the time to escape. At the month's climax, Pacetta rents a tent and hires some caterers and buys some entertainment. He wants the rigors of June to melt into the frenzy of a party. For some of these people, these moments are their greatest reward. It's always something different. Will he take them for an afternoon of bowling and go-cart racing? Will he pay for an afternoon of golf at a little nine-hole course south of town? Will he arrange for an overnight ski outing for the entire sales staff in upstate New York? Will he fly the managers for a weekend in Las Vegas? Will he bring everybody up to Put-in-Bay for a bash? Will he have the next recognition meeting at the Thistledown racetrack? Will he bring in a heap of barbecued spare ribs during the all-day management staff meeting? He'd done all these things since coming to Cleveland. (Whether he could make a profit or not, after spending so much money, was a question on everyone's mind at the corporate level, though few people in Cleveland cared about that.)

Every month or so, he arranges for some kind of blowout or boondoggle or minor feast—something, anything, to fill the air with a sense of cash flow and easy abundance, to make everybody feel they're getting something for nothing, getting more fun out of the job than anyone else can possibly get from a corporate job. It's free. It's all on the company's nickel. Pacetta loves to spend the company's money almost as much as Fred loves to make it.

Pacetta becomes someone else on these occasions. He wants people to know he came of age in the sixties and early seventies. This starched martinet who looks like an MBA with a couple of actuarial tables in his back pocket knows by heart the bulk of Joni Mitchell, the Who, Cat Stevens, The Band, Crosby, Stills & Nash,

Jimi Hendrix, and the Jefferson Airplane from late evenings twenty years ago in college, when he played *Blue, Tea for the Tillerman, Who's Next, Surrealistic Pillow,* and *Electric Ladyland* at night in his college dorm in Dayton. He slips a few lines of rock and roll into every conversation if possible, sometimes quoting songs in such an understated way that few people realize the provenance of his words. He tries to make his own words form a seamless motivational thought by mixing in a few lines from, say, Robbie Robertson: *I expect results, gang. You've got to have your tongue hanging out. Pullin' in to Nazareth, feelin' 'bout half past dead.*

Pacetta wants people to speculate on what he might have smoked in his twenties as well as what kind of power he might wield once he hits his forties. Every message seems to be devoted to this contradictory vision of himself: *We're going to crush it, but you've got to give it everything you've got this month. Why are we doing this? Because we have to. Knock-knock-knockin' on Heaven's door.* (Translation: Stick with me, even if you think I'm a jerk. When I leave this place, half of you will have your towels wet from crying. The other half will say, Fuck *him.* He did this. He did that. Either way I'm putting money in your pockets. I'm just like you. I'm no corporate stiff. I'd rather be singing Bob Dylan.) This is the wishbone image of himself Pacetta projects every time he speaks to a crowd or takes a glue sniffer's snort of his Magic Marker, rolling his eyes back into his skull so that nothing but the whites show, or pantomimes masturbation while talking with a corporate vice president, which he likes to do when he has someone else in his office. Sometimes he even rubs the phone against his crotch.

It's all a game, an act, and when people forget it's all a welcome sort of bullshit and start taking it too seriously, they find themselves calling it Forced Fun. Pacetta pretends to be a maverick, a rebel. In reality, most of the time, he's corporate's puppet—he's selling more and more copiers every year, doing exactly what they want him to do. When he arrived in Cleveland four years earlier, people were so frightened of him, one rep refused to come into the office and had to be fired by certified mail. He needed to be the drill sergeant. It was the way business was done now. Business was an act of war. You didn't earn your wings until you proved how close to the edge you could push your people. When he held a kickoff meeting one year, he showed slides of Pearl Harbor. This week we go to war! Put your helmets on! Yet he kept pushing his act over the edge, pushing reality into a dream, turning the drill formation into a session of slam-dancing. By the end of that meeting, a food fight broke out, with projectile ribs and chicken wings and egg rolls, and some hapless fellow came onstage and told everybody they would have to leave if the air didn't clear of food immediately.

The green-and-white striped tents go up in the parking lot behind the building. The barbecues are lit, the beer chilled. Chicken, hamburgers, sausage—the smells waft through the back door. The corporate bean-counters will wail, but to hell with them. They don't want the district buying disposable cups for coffee, let alone spending this kind of money on a party. But as Frank put it, you have to spend money to make money! The stereo speakers crackle into life. Occasionally, at parties like this one, it *could* be the way it was a couple years earlier, with Pacetta at his most unearthly, making people question how many hallucinogens he'd ingested in college. Now, after seventeen years with Xerox, he's still reliving his college liberations, as if he'd just discovered alcohol and music and sex.

The crowd gathers quickly, the young women at their own table, and at the other tables the former school athletes, eager to dispatch the hamburgers, start this contest, and show these people who can really *sing*. Two of the youngest at one table taunt each other, laughing: "I'm going to kick your ass up there. You don't stand a chance, dickhead." Pacetta loves it. He loves conflict. As if it really matters who can sing Creedence Clearwater Revival more persuasively.

Two karaoke monitors are mounted so people at the tables can see the music videos and follow the lyrics on the television screens. Another screen is stationed on the ground, tilted up to face the singers, serving as a TelePrompTer. One by one, teams of singers do Tone Loc. They sing the Beatles. They sing Huey Lewis and Bachman-Turner Overdrive. When the night reaches its peak, Pacetta draws a crowd around him: Escape! Escape! Be young again! Lose your minds, people! Lose your minds! We're going to do it. We are going to bring home the bacon. Tomorrow it's going to happen!

Pacetta's so arrogant he believes he can, say, convince people to pay admission to watch him floss his teeth. If you aren't susceptible to Pacetta's camp charisma, you don't last long in Cleveland. Fred never admits he's impressed with the show. Looking restless and pained, but smiling, Fred says: "Oh, give me a break. Whip me, Frank. Whip me." Whenever the crowd cranks their arms and barks "woof, woof, woof, woof," Fred thinks: *My number's up. I'm too old for this.* Even so, as the evening lengthens, Fred begins to nourish himself on the energy. He drinks beer. He extinguishes a cigarette on his tongue to amuse the beautiful young reps on other teams, with their smooth, lucent faces. But it's nothing like the parties of the past. In those years the Cleveland district wasn't happy unless the management of the occupied establishment banned them from returning. Now the parties end in a different sort of ritual. At the old parties everything fell apart. At these celebrations everyone comes together.

The end is always the same. People gather in the Huddle and sing—welcoming anyone into the circle, winners and losers, rookies and veterans. Sometimes they link arms. Other times Frank stands in the middle, raising one fist straight into the air, like a black pride salute, and the throng gathers, straining on toes to grab either Frank's arm or the arm of someone who has managed to touch Frank. One way or another, through this laying on of hands, Frank makes himself the axis of their world. In this formation—an image straight off the cover of Pearl Jam's first CD—everyone sings Steve Winwood as they finish the last of the beer: "Bring me a higher love, bring me a higher love." Or if not a higher love, at least a higher entertainment budget. After enough beer, the younger people find a certain novelty and energy in this performance, where they turn their lives into a dream of MTV solidarity, an assertion of the way they want things to be. As always, Frank is acting, but he knows many of them, in this drunken moment, feel as much emotion over the metaphor of his raised fist as they will feel about anything in their careers. It may require a certain quantity of bullshit to achieve that electrical current, but once it's achieved, it isn't forgotten, no matter how staged its origins. It's a way of saying this small group of people have certain things in common that no one outside the circle can understand. If you aren't black (the wisdom goes), you can't know the meaning of black, and if you aren't a Cleveland district salesman, you can't know the meaning of Pacetta's phallic fist. It's us against the other—the competitor, the corporate watchdog, the customer. It's one man's vision of the force of selling, and he sells this vision to all the rest of them every minute of the day.

Fred shares in all this artificial emotion. It makes him uneasy, though. He wonders: Is this it? Is this all his life amounts to? Yet he doesn't know where he needs to go, what he needs to do, to find something more. He doesn't even know what he might find. And once he gets there, will anything he does for a living ever be quite this much fun? Who will be there for him, giving him the energy he needs to get up in the morning?

# THE GAME

*1.*

W HEN A SALESMAN begins, he's a Nobody. He knocks on doors. He hands out business cards. He waits for people who never return his phone calls. He isn't sure he exists in the world. It's an experience of intense invisibility. He feels rejected, unloved, a loser. That experience, a universal experience in sales, creates a lasting dread of failure, a fear of being unworthy, an outsider, an outcast. As one young recruit put it, you learn early that before you even walk through the door, they hate you for what you are—a salesman. It was depressing to drive around office plazas, knocking on doors. It could get worse.

One Cleveland rookie called on a seedy westside residence. Inside, two young women were publishing a television newsletter. When he arrived, the young rep found three weeks of garbage piled on the front porch, two rusted cars on blocks, two huskies

dozing on the cars, thirty cats searching the grounds, dirty under-
wear on the floor, and two women, one large and one small. It was
depressing just being there, let alone trying to get money from
these people. The big woman wanted to order a copier. She
wanted it in the basement, sitting above a few inches of water. Oh,
and by the way, she said, they'd just declared personal bankruptcy.
Could she have it delivered at night? Why? Because they had a
crack house next door, and if the neighbors saw the thing being
delivered, they would break in and take it.

Another time a rep made a house call in Youngstown. The
customer asked the female rep whether she minded if he removed
his shirt and slacks before their next meeting. He said he believed
in what he called bodily freedom. He published a newspaper for
nudists. She laughed. The next time she arrived, the buyer was
naked. Another customer kept an unattached, dry toilet in the
corner of his office and required every rep to sit on it before he
would consent to speak. You want to talk, buddy, you got to take
a seat.

You learn sales is a struggle to survive in a guerrilla theater,
where it's hard to distinguish the friend from the enemy, the
predator from the prey. Even in major accounts, customers try to
sucker you. You offer them a free trial of a machine and they take
it, getting three months' free usage and then returning the machine
without so much as a thank you. Or they string you along and then
dump you in favor of a dealer who shaves a few dollars off the
monthly fee. The cunning ones stall you until December, when
they suspect you'll be more willing to lower the price by giving
away your commission. They make passes at you over lunch, or
tell you how certain other dealers will slip them a personal check
for a thousand or two under the table. In many deals the sales rep
risks becoming the victim and the dupe. What many buyers want
is something for nothing—a meal, a machine, a little mind game

of domination. They want to force the salesman to give them a better deal than they deserve.

It isn't just about money. Every sales call is a struggle to control emotions. Everyone engages in this struggle, all day, in almost all individual encounters with another human being. It happens especially in the way buyers and sellers square off—in the way a customer faces parking attendants, gasoline jockeys, bellboys, waiters, receptionists, and merchants. These little acts of commerce are, in a capitalistic society, one of the primary forms of human encounter. A simple act of equal exchange. And yet every time it happens, both people, the buyer and the seller, wonder how much of it is real. Is the smile real? Is the handshake? Is the deal honest? Is the exchange equal? Is there anything genuinely human and spontaneous in the encounter? How much, exactly, can one person trust another? A good buy, a good deal, appears to be an act of friendship. It makes both the customer and the salesman feel like winners. But are they? Neither of them will ever know for sure.

A sales call reminds you of the mystery of another person's heart, the transience of human love and affection, the selfishness often concealed beneath acts of apparent generosity. In a sales call, even if only subliminally, you're reminded about how much you want to be liked, and yet how little you know of what other people say when your back is turned. If a salesman seizes the opportunity this presents, if he realizes how easy it is to manipulate a person who needs to be liked—in other words, all people—then he can make large sums of money, because he understands something terrible about human affection. No one knows with any certainty whether any act of friendship or love is real or simply a calculated ploy to get something from someone else.

This is a truth most people try to ignore. It's a truth that sends people into monasteries and chapels and cabins on secluded ponds.

Yet if you can face the universal reality of this emotional insecurity and not flee from it, then certain doors will open to you, simply because you understand how much other people need to be liked. The price you pay for this wisdom, though, is the likelihood of becoming a cynic, a manipulator.

If you sell, you learn ways of handling emotion, other people's and your own. If you reduce the job to a game or a war, a sale becomes a trick, a score. The idea is to stay in control, to be the puppeteer and not the puppet. The idea is to turn your customer into a friendly opponent—and often that's the way a customer wants to be treated. He needs a thrill, too, just to stay interested in *his* job.

Some of the game's tricks are simple and harmless. You learn to use another person's first name as often as possible in a conversation. If you sell copiers, you learn to lose your way in a building and stumble into the copier room as a way of introducing yourself without looking too predatory. You learn how to walk into an office, place a business card on a stranger's desk without a word, and then walk away and phone the man two days later. As you get more experienced, you adopt more complicated techniques for making the customer believe he's getting what he thinks he wants. You stay in control of the emotional game with winning moves and maneuvers, simulating friendship, forcing the deal to happen, making the customer feel satisfied.

In the *grease* sale, a rep relies on financial incentives to speed the deal along. These can be anything from discounts and low initial monthly fees to nothing more than a day of golf at Firestone or an evening on the town. In the *slam* sale, time pressure comes into play to close the deal, on top of short-term financial incentives. In Fred's speciality—what might be called the *puppy-dog* sale—the rep applies all these pressures in a subtle, almost indiscernible way, building a relationship with a customer over the course of several months, if not years, and then using all these techniques at once to get business, but without ever making it seem as if the financial incentives, the entertainment expenses, the time pressures, are anything but the natural evolution of a spontaneous human companionship. The pressure's all there in the history of the deal, and it finds expression in a customer's nagging sense of obligation, a feeling that represents the final flowering of those weeks and months of building a calculated friendship. The friendship is used to box the customer into a corner where he feels he can't say no without feeling like a fool.

When Pacetta told people to wear helmets when they went on sales calls, he was telling them to play the game, fight the war, against the Pacific Rim and the domestic companies. He wanted them to know they were vying with the buyer, too. Fred's team, the major accounts team, was a place where you could try to hide from that sort of battle with a customer. It was a salesman's heaven—studies, dining, entertainment, flights to Dallas and Chicago for product demonstrations, all of it building toward the district's most lucrative deals. In major accounts you built long-term professional relationships with customers. You faced fewer rejections this way. Working in major accounts helped a rep forget how people loathed and mocked salesmen.

Diane Burley wanted to stay as far away from battle as possible, which is why she treasured her companionship with Libby Jones at Crawford Manufacturing. Diane achieved with Libby what many reps achieved, in a much less permanent way, with their best customers. It was like a marriage, an alliance of trust. Her role on Fred's team was Diane's chance to forget the miseries of cold calling. She loved the security of her territory, the feeling of importance it gave her, the sense of being Somebody.

Diane believed she'd developed something rare and secure in her partnership with Libby. It *was* a remarkable bond. Like Diane,

Libby was black, single, beautiful, in her early forties, and as proper as a Daughter of the American Revolution. Diane cultivated a closer relationship with Libby than any other rep had attained with a customer in the district, and it paid off. Diane's relationship with Crawford was the kind of bond a rep worked years to build, coming up through the early years of cold calling and smaller accounts.

When Diane calls on Libby, everything is pleasant and personal. The Crawford headquarters is a rambling two-story complex with halls as cheerful and clean and bright as the greeting cards it manufactures. Libby welcomes Diane into her cubicle, where a quotation attributed to Martin Luther King, Jr., is displayed on the wall: Believe in the magic of your dreams. She wears an expensive muted suit, which looks as if it could have come straight from Diane's own costly wardrobe. As Diane seats herself beside Libby's desk and produces the order forms, without a word about the business at hand, they discuss what Libby plans to wear to a fund-raiser for the United Black Fund of Greater Cleveland. Libby hands Diane a photograph of the outfit.

"Just a little skirt and top," Libby says.

"Just a little skirt and top! I hate it when you say that. That is not a skirt and top. That is a dress, a two-piece dress, silk, with a peplum top."

She hands the photograph back to Libby and quietly fills out the order forms.

"That doctor I'm really interested in? My doctor?" Diane says.

Libby looks straight ahead, not making eye contact.

"One of the other girls at Xerox went to him, and he always asks her about me. I was going to invite him to Nancy's wedding. I haven't dated him yet. I'm going to marry him. I made a list of things to talk about. This is my closing line: *How would you have reacted to that invitation?* I don't ask him if he would have gone. Then he could say no or yes. I want to have a conversation."

Open-ended questions and closed-ended questions. It's a technique straight out of the book. In her personal life, Diane is selling. On sales calls, she's getting personal. There's no telling where one world ends and the other begins. At this point Diane hands the order forms to Libby, who proceeds to sign them. Not a word passes between them about the business. It's as if the act of buying and selling isn't happening. It isn't a game, a contest, a war. It's a friendship. The more routine the business becomes, the less it threatens the friendship, and the more solid the friendship, the more Diane can expect business as a matter of routine.

Her friendship with Libby resembled the kind of consulting partnership Xerox wanted all its reps to attain with their customers. Yet Diane was taking it beyond anything the corporation envisioned. In Fred's eyes, she was getting too close, making the relationship more important than the business. Fred didn't trust it. He wanted to pull Diane back out from under Libby's influence. He wanted the relationship to be less personal. He wanted Diane to start taking control of Libby's emotions. He had a plan. Actually, it was more like a plot.

In a wooded office tract south of Cleveland, a man named Evan wanted a new copier. He worked at a small company, Citadel. He wasn't giving Xerox a hard time. When Evan saw the 5100, a light flickered in his eyes. The video control panel! The speed! The two-sided capability! Where do I sign? This man, Evan, knew exactly how much money one of these machines could save his department, how much more work his people would be able to do with it. That wasn't his motivation, though. He wasn't under pressure to buy it. He didn't *need* it, exactly. He wanted it. He liked the look of it. The feel of it. He was dazzled. He looked ready to fill out a purchase order on the spot. It made Fred's heart ache, just thinking about the way that machine would get him another step closer to California. What were they waiting for?

There was a snag. Evan's company was owned by another company: Crawford. Evan couldn't buy anything without permission from someone at Crawford: Libby Jones. If she didn't want Evan to have a new machine, then maybe Evan wouldn't get a new machine. She was one of the district's most faithful customers. Over the past few years, she'd populated the offices of her company with hundreds of Xerox machines. No one wanted to upset Libby. Fred wasn't sure Libby objected to the Citadel order—she hadn't yet committed herself on it. So this was where things stood: Evan was waiting patiently, longing for his new copier, and Libby was sitting on the fence. It wasn't yes and it wasn't no. It wasn't even maybe, as far as Fred could tell. The deal was in limbo. No one wanted to close it.

Diane didn't want to talk about it. Libby was her best, most loyal and most trusting, customer. The last thing Diane wanted to do in life was upset Libby. Day after day, Fred reminded Diane of the deal, asking her what was happening, trying to prime her for his plan, his *plot*. So what exactly did Fred have in mind (as if she really wanted to hear about it)? With a conspiratorial air, Fred outlined the whole thing to Diane. To break things loose, he wanted to make Libby feel she was getting away with something forbidden. He wanted to offer her a credit of ten thousand dollars toward her account if Evan leased the machine on *his* account. A credit like this was supposed to go to the buyer of the machine, yet Fred proposed they offer it to Libby without mentioning anything about it to Evan.

"You make her feel she's blowing one over on Evan," Fred said, giving her the smile, using his breathless voice to evoke the same confederate smile from Diane. It didn't work. Diane was smiling, but she wasn't smiling *the* smile. She didn't want to manipulate her customers that way. She blinked her eyes rapid-fire, the way she did when she got nervous. She didn't think Libby would like it, and she didn't want to put her relationship with Libby at risk. No problem. Fred backed off, for now. Diane didn't want the relationship to go south on her, and neither did he.

## 2.

IT'S GOING TO be a night downtown for both of them, an escape from the grind. Fred and Kathy intend to spend the entire evening at the Flats, a redeveloped waterfront lined with dance clubs, bars, restaurants, and arcades. Fred's in the master bathroom brushing his hair, making brief eye contact with himself, playing both customer and salesman in this particular negotiation with appearances: "I don't know. A black sweatshirt with black Dockers? I look like Gary Player." Kathy's in the kitchen. A Norman Vincent Peale paperback—a staple of Kathy's reading—lies under the telephone, with a flyer from her church as a bookmark. Kathy has told Fred she wants to start teaching again, but she hasn't made much progress yet. He responds to these announcements with vague interest, the way he might respond if his daughter said she wanted to play lead guitar for Alice in Chains when she grew up. He wants Kathy to work if it makes her happy. They could use the money. Enough. No more talk about work on this night out. This is their escape for at least an evening—there's no point in spoiling it before it starts.

First they drive to the cash machine. It's time for Fred to

unwind and relax. It's time for him to do all the things he doesn't get a chance to do while he's at work. Now he can drop the smile, the air of congeniality. Now he can cut loose and be genuine—and, as usual, Kathy just happens to be the first person in his field of vision. As he pulls up to the ATM, Fred asks if she went shopping today. Yes. *What for?* Food. Some clothes. *How much?* Not much. *Was there any money left in the account?* Yes.

Fred worries about remaining solvent—he's obsessive about it. Early in the summer Fred brought home a check for approximately five hundred dollars. When he handed it over to Kathy for deposit, he added the sum into the checkbook register, turned the page, wrote the new balance on top of the next sheet of the balance log, and then subtracted the entire five hundred. They hadn't spent the money, yet Fred wanted to nullify all visible traces of it. The money was still there. But they would operate as if it weren't. It was behind-the-scenes money. That's what Fred called it. This bogus balance was Fred's idea of personal finance. His premise: Pretend the balance was low and they would both spend less. In the same way, on the job, Fred manipulates himself by predicting the worst—it is another version of his purposeful discontent, a way of acting as if things were worse than they are, if only to stay motivated at the highest possible pitch of emotion. Good emotion, bad emotion—it doesn't matter, as long as he feels something that keeps him moving. He doesn't want to relax, or get lazy, or take his success for granted.

Kathy has an answer: "Win the lottery, Fred. You've bought two lottery tickets every week for twenty years. You'd think pretty soon you'd win."

He has no desire to leave the company. He wants to stay there. But is there a place for him at Xerox? He just wants to sell. Larry told him to get out of management, get back into sales. He doesn't know. He used to be so tough, one rep had to get a month's disability after working for him one year. Those were the days. He doesn't feel effective. He isn't what he was a year ago, two years ago.

She believes it is all because he doesn't get enough sleep. He is tired all the time. He doesn't buckle his seat belt because he knows there's a chance he'll be injured and get laid up for a few months. There are other ways to get rest. Like going to bed at night.

They drive to her sister's house, where they plan to meet two other couples before they head for the Flats. All summer the dry weather has threatened to become a drought. It's had a strange effect on the foliage. Two months early, certain leaves are changing—maybe because of the drought, maybe because of the cool nights—and many trees are streaked prematurely with gold, orange, red, and ochre. It's still the height of summer and yet everything hints the year is about to end. Fred and Kathy can see their breath in the air at night, and a wool sweater wouldn't be uncomfortable, though neither thought to wear one.

The Flats, their destination, sit in a narrow valley downtown where the Cuyahoga River flows into Lake Erie; the two halves of the city perch much higher, on either side of the river. Blackened iron relics of Cleveland's abandoned industry stand above and around the soundstages and boardwalks—the iron grillwork of mechanical cranes rises hundreds of feet into the sky above the open-air restaurants, music drifting up through the exposed girders. Far above the entire complex an unused iron bridge spans the river.

The Flats are considered the heart of Cleveland's nightlife. You can find college-level bars and dance clubs where the waitress, if she likes your eyes, might sit on your lap while she takes your order. You can find pretentious restaurants across the street from the Circus, a show bar where the dancers wear nothing but

G-strings. You can find neopunk nightclubs with as many secret balconies and passages as a Palladium-style Manhattan club. You can watch expensive hookers stroll the boardwalk outside Coconuts, or catch a Cleveland Browns linebacker ordering beer while playing a game of pool at Jillians. In the summer, you can hear Bob Dylan or George Thoroghgood or John Mellencamp in the bandshell at Nautica. Anyone can find amusement here on almost any night of the week.

Along with the two other couples, they head for Jillians, where the billiard tables are lined up like infirmary beds. The women find a table with a view of the river, and the men make their wagers and choose their cues. For three hours they play, sometimes inviting the women up for a game, but otherwise taking a break only to eat their chicken Parmesan sandwiches and order beers and shots.

A toadlike man with wide jowls leans against the wooden rail, watching the game, whispering tips to Fred. Toward midnight, Fred thanks him for the advice. "Hey, us older guys have to stick together," the man says. Fred smiles and shakes his head and thinks: *These things always happen to me.* But it's true. The others *are* almost ten years younger. He feels a little out of place as he watches an older woman in a sequined skirt shooting pool at the next table with a man her age she met at the bar. It's odd to watch them play, to see how much care this lonely woman takes with her hair and her makeup, seemingly unconcerned by how much older she appears in this crowd. She looks slightly bizarre, so markedly different from the rest, but then how does *he* look, with his graying hair, to the lovely college women with cascading blond hair, the ones who just passed through Jillians on their way to Coconuts? Does he belong in the Flats? Not the way Pacetta belongs, not the way reps in their twenties belong—and Xerox hires people directly out of college, so the district always looks predominantly youthful. The truth is, in other lines of work the most seasoned salesmen are his age, salesmen approaching the peak of their powers, who are rewarded financially for their maturity and knowledge of human nature. Fred is entering that stage—he is just crossing the threshold of his prime, his most productive years, his forties. The way his company hires people, it seems as if the reps in their twenties are considered the standard. Yet he's reluctant to make a move, to leave behind the benefits and security and world of experience he's built for himself at Xerox, and so he tries not to think about what he has to do, how he might have to sell himself to people higher in the company to make the kind of leap he has to make, to find a greater level of fulfillment in his life. He's not sure he has the audacity, the slick and easy assurance he'd need to make a good impression on the corporate types.

When the last black eight ball drops into its intended corner pocket, the women announce they want to go dancing. The men want to have another drink at a sports bar in the Power House, a short walk from Jillians. One of the wives suggests Howl at the Moon. Fred doesn't like the sound of that—it sounds like a place packed with kids in their twenties. The men agree to give it a try and they all stand in line to pay the three-dollar cover. When they finally enter the bar, the rowdy scene startles them.

Two men are onstage, singing and playing the pianos, and almost everyone there—at least two hundred people, all of them on their feet—is singing. It's a huge live-music sing-along. Fred and Kathy and the others order a round of beers and begin singing selections from Crosby, Stills, & Nash, Jackson Browne, and the Doors. This is strictly a place where oldies are sung—no Pearl Jam, no Arrested Development, no Nirvana, no Lightning Seeds, no Spin Doctors. It's a place that reminds Fred of Pacetta's parties, where the managers recall the lyrics and the younger ones lip-synch uncertainly on songs popular about the time they were born.

By the end of the evening, the singers demand a volunteer from the audience for a lesson in sign language. They lure a slightly flustered girl up from the audience and ask her to stand directly behind their sign-language instructor on the stage. She watches as he goes through the motions of his invented semaphore—and when the lyrics reach the word *man,* he grabs his own crotch. When it's her turn, the girl—standing directly behind the man with her arms extended in front of him—hesitates to grab the young man's crotch, holding her hands above his zipper. The music comes to a stop. The traditional Howl at the Moon chant begins throughout the room and grows in volume: "Bitch! Slut! Whore! Bitch! Slut! Whore!" Finally, she relents and digs her fingers into the performer's pants and the crowd goes wild with cheers.

On their way back to the car, Kathy begs Fred for a few minutes of dancing at Coconuts. No, they need to get back home. It's time to go. She tells him they never get downtown anymore. They never dance. He doesn't want to dance. He is too old for this whole scene. It is one-thirty in the morning. He doesn't go dancing at one-thirty in the morning with kids waiting for them at home. Besides, it's a six-dollar cover, and he doesn't want to pay the cover when the dance club won't stay open more than half an hour after they get there.

They were all like this. Everyone in the district. Always seizing control. Kathy was tired of fighting to break through Fred's endless resistance to letting go when he was with her. She knew he relaxed when he was out with people from work, with her brother-in-law, with his friends from Toledo. But often—not always, but much of the time—when he was with her, he seemed obsessed by where he stood in relation to the year and where *they* stood in relation to the clock. His insecurities seemed to torment him when they were together, always reminding him of the things left undone, the money left unearned, the children left alone. When he was in that frame of mind, Fred might say he couldn't justify the expense of six dollars for half an hour of dancing, and yet it was never the money that mattered, it was simply his way to resist surrender. All day he submitted. All day he made other people happy. At night, he didn't want to submit, didn't want to please anyone but himself. With Kathy beside him, he didn't want to capitulate. It was the same kind of power struggle, at work, at home, at the Flats. But why? Why was he so afraid to surrender to her now, when he had surrendered to her so willingly in high school and college? Why, in the first place, did he have to look upon it as a surrender?

Did every expression of her own desires in life need to be a threat to Fred? Did he have to see every genuine emotion as a sign of growing independence? Was he *that* afraid of losing her? Some-how, Kathy's presence seemed to make it impossible for Fred to just open up and let go the way he did with the others—which was why she resented his after-work visits to the Flats, as rare as they were, with people from the office. She didn't worry so much that he was getting himself into trouble. She envied his companions because of the candor and laughter he shared with them. With them he was willing to spend money and emotion and time. He was willing to let go. When he was with her, he clenched his fists around all those things and wouldn't unclench them.

Instead of dancing they drive to Kathy's sister's house. They stay an hour, talking and joking, sharing another drink. During the hour they spend there, Kathy laughs long and hard. She loves double-dating this way with her sister because Fred hardly ever makes her laugh so freely when they're alone together. She craves deep, soul-nourishing laughter, the way it brings back memories of the early days of their marriage, when Fred was more consis-tently lighthearted. At last, in her sister's home, Kathy finds the relief she's been seeking, though she wishes she could have found it on the dance floor with Fred. When they are together now, Kathy doesn't see enough of that nameless quality, that charm, she'd recognized two decades earlier in Fred. Does she need to buy a copier from him to see that look of delight and easy warmth dawn in his eyes again when he gazed at her?

3.

DIANE BURLEY'S MOTHER died when she was three, and her father disappeared soon afterward. Diane was left in the care of her overworked grandmother. As a child, she never owned a new bicycle, and the shame she felt over the hand-me-down bike she rode seemed to epitomize the privations of her impoverished youth. The bike was a buttercup yellow, recoated with a flat house paint.

She married young, but the marriage lasted only a couple years, followed by two years in divorce court. Her husband didn't understand Diane's aspirations—the way she wanted to raise herself up to a higher level through her work. Now she wanted to find what she called her six-figure man, somebody who understood her passion to become a new human being through the force of her own efforts, someone who earned enough money to know he should wear his darkest suit for dinner at the Four Seasons in Manhattan. Somebody who slept at home every night. Somebody who would help Diane complete the personal and social transformation she was achieving in her life through her job at Xerox. Her job, ironically, was both the source of that ultimate fulfillment and the greatest obstacle in her way.

Her boyfriend, Kenny, left her one night after he walked into her house—he had his own key—and found her sitting on the floor with a large proposal spread out around her knees and on the furniture. He took one look at the room, spun around without a word, and left. He never returned. He told her later he blamed Xerox for their breakup. She wrote him a farewell poem and had it published in the Personals column in the *Plain Dealer:* "There comes a test of love, when two hearts feel alone—a fleeting sense of truthfulness—the desperate need to run . . . to live a life of emptiness, familiar life again."

Libby Jones seemed to care about Diane. She wanted Diane to find a good husband—to find for herself, maybe for the first time in her life, a secure role within a happy family. One day, as the two of them ran laps together at an eastside college track, they planned a dinner Diane wanted to host for her friend the doctor. To help prepare for the doctor's arrival, Libby agreed to come to Diane's house early. When that evening arrived, Diane had everything planned: long candlesticks, bone china plates, china napkin rings in the form of bows, marinated T-bone steaks, wild rice with mushrooms, green beans almondine, freshly baked dinner rolls, and pound cake with lemon sauce. She wore her closing flats, a pair of shoes she liked to put on any morning she expected to close an order. They were black, and on the toes were a pair of broken gold hearts pierced with lightning bolts. Libby brought two bottles of Chardonnay and roses for the table. The only snag: the doctor refused to eat the dessert Diane had made. He subscribed to the notion that some black women could ensnare a man by mixing certain ingredients into a dish. Maybe it was just a superstition, he said, but he didn't need any of Diane's sorcery to make things more intense.

When it was over, Diane felt her relationship with Libby was based not on studies of copier usage, lessons in materials management, proposals and financing and product features, but rather on the mysteries of human propinquity, the magic of what Libby and Diane saw of their own lives mirrored in each other's face—the glow of true friendship. With one meal, she managed to juggle her entire world, personal and professional, into a state of tenuous harmony. She was selling in an almost unrecognizable way, reducing her partnership with Libby to the ultimate essential, a state of emotion. A Coltrane saxophone riff could get so far from any recognizable melody you could forget what song initiated it, and by those indirections it worked in a more dizzying way than a mere repetition of a familiar theme. Like Coltrane, Diane played the low notes with her date and the high notes with Libby, and all those notes seemed to stray as far as you could get from the recognizable phrases. In her view, she was taking selling into a register beyond the acknowledged score.

For his part, Fred couldn't help but stick to the score. He was wondering if any of this friendship would pay off with a sale at Citadel. He continued to ask her about that deal. Fred wondered how much maintenance needed to be done on that relationship. How close could a customer get to a buyer and still maintain a separate identity? They were as close as Siamese twins already. Diane told him she planned to spend a weekend with Libby at Chautauqua Lake in upstate New York. Maybe she could bring up the Citadel deal then. Fred couldn't see how Diane's relationship with Libby could get any closer, unless they actually joined themselves at the hip.

He didn't mean to belittle this friendship. It was a lucrative accomplishment. Diane wasn't risking anything, though. Maybe she *was* taking the art of selling into new frontiers, but the whole arrangement was too cozy for Fred's taste. Diane wasn't taking command of this partnership. When you sold, you took control of other people, you motivated them to do things they wouldn't otherwise have done—all the while making them feel as if *they* were in control. It seemed Libby was the true leader in this relationship—she didn't just feel in control, she *was* in control.

The weekend turned out to be surprisingly awkward. Libby brooded about missing her boyfriend. She grew withdrawn and pensive and, worst of all, silent. Diane kept trying to think of things to do. They found a place to buy maple syrup and cheese. They toured a mall. They bought fresh apples, and finally they attended a livestock auction. Libby and Diane at a livestock auction—the idea was so absurd it was obvious how desperate they were for something to do together.

In Chautauqua, Diane discovered how much her professional relationship hindered the personal one. If Libby hadn't been her customer, Diane would have said she wanted to stay longer at a certain store in the mall, a place she had been waiting to get to all day. But Libby was weary and insisted they go back to the cottage. Diane's resentment over it wedged another excuse for silence into their conversations; she could see how her friendship with Libby would end in these silences as long as they continued to deal with each other as professionals. There would be limits to their candor. If nothing else, the weekend showed both of them how lonely they could be, even when they were together.

Finally, without asking Diane's permission, Fred decided to go directly to Libby. He found an excuse to make the call himself— the administrative people upstairs ran into a billing problem with one of Libby's purchases, and he could discuss it with her. During the discussion, if he had the courage, he could bring up the Citadel order. He wanted to bait Libby, see if she would bite at the ten-thousand-dollar credit she could get by giving Evan permission to get his copier. It seemed too much of a gift to resist.

Fred was wearing his favorite tie. It had a pattern of autumn leaves against a navy background, the leaves melting into a field of blue, green, rust, and white, with all the flat, refreshing exactitude of a serigraph. It was only a necktie, yet it made him feel persuasive. As Pacetta put it: *Dress good, feel good, sell good.* Anything was worth trying, as long as it might spark a confident emotion. He was back in the driver's seat, literally, and he loved it.

During the meeting Fred clarified the billing problems within the first ten minutes, and then they talked briefly about a routine deal Diane was hoping to close with Crawford. Then Libby got personal. It was the only part of a sales call she loved. By now Fred knew, as the conversation drifted, he would never bring up the Citadel deal. He was as timorous as Diane when it came to forcing Libby into anything. He felt ashamed of himself for being so easy on her. He didn't really want to endanger Diane's relationship with Libby any more than Diane did.

Fred told Libby he was burned out. She knew what he was saying. She had some advice. To stay calm, she liked to visualize a triangle with a blue flame in the middle. She listened to motivational tapes in her car. She did breathing exercises. Fred could do that, but he'd probably start thinking about a blue logo instead of a blue flame. He'd be meditating on the Xerox trademark.

"When you're golfing, after you've hit the ball and you're walking up to it, you're thinking about Xerox."

"That's true."

"That's terrible," she said. "This book I'm reading talks about the child within you—"

"I go home. I rush and eat. I listen to my voice mail. I do work. I take my daughter ice-skating. I go out in the field."

"But you're no good at home."

She told him he had to find the little child within himself. No way. He had three kids in the house already. He didn't need to fish around for another one inside him.

"That's what my wife says. But I do play with my children," he said.

"She's not needed anymore," Libby suggested.

Fred laughed at Libby's therapeutic way of leading the conversation, but he was startled at the way she'd pinned him down.

"I give her time."

"Yes, when she's asleep and you're asleep. You need to get in touch with the child within you and take time to—"

"I'm going to have a heart attack," Fred said, bringing the conversation back to the more comfortable and familiar emotional terrain of crisis and illness and death.

"You look good, Fred. You won't have a heart attack."

Libby looked away from Fred with an expression of hopeless amusement. It was an expression that, at one time or another, passed across the faces of his reps, his customers, his boss, his wife, his children, his insurance agent, bank tellers, as well as various parking attendants, cafeteria checkout girls, traffic cops, golf partners, cocktail waitresses, and crossing guards. In other words, it was an expression of resignation worn by anyone who tried to influence this man's behavior, failed, and quickly recognized the idiocy of trying.

"That tie is nice, Fred," she said.

He beamed. Now the conversation was back on a safe track.

Fred began to understand why Diane found it so hard to push Libby—she was as shrewd and calculating as they were. Libby knew how to take control of a conversation and broadcast exactly the right emotional tone into a small air space to make him feel rude if he led the conversation into something as painful as the Citadel deal had apparently become for her. If anybody was to get Libby angry—and that might indeed be useful—it ought to be Diane herself. Why should Fred experience that discomfort? After all, it was Diane's account.

. . .

He had no one but himself to blame on the Citadel deal now. He'd gotten himself in front of the customer—something he'd been yearning to do every day all year—and then he'd been as shy as a rookie. Did he ask her a decisive question? Did he push her to say yes or no? Did he close her for anything? How could he complain about any of his reps when he found himself just as reluctant as they sometimes were to face the truth about a deal? He could have turned it into a closing call, but no. He let the cup pass. If he kept doing that, he might as well take up another line of work.

He wasn't making an impact. He needed an unqualified success. Always, he needed to prove to himself that he could close a customer. He longed to drive through the sunlight again, see the smokestacks along the river, feel the weather's warmth on his face. Every day during the summer he troubled his other reps for a chance to travel. He had an idea how he could give Nancy a hand with one of her nonusers.

He told her she needed to open up Akron Automotive. What did he want from her? Did he want her to show up at their door with a raincoat on and nothing underneath? There was only so much she could do with the nonusers. Did she mind if he called on Akron Automotive himself? She told him he could do whatever he wanted.

On the road Fred looks as if he's ten years old again and has just won a Shetland pony in a box-top contest. He's back in the saddle. In Akron, he meets Jay Cook, who heads the company's print

operations. Cook is quiet and benign and pleasant, with small eyes
that seem to shrink in merriment when he smiles. Fred wonders
how this man could refuse to let Nancy call on him. Like Fred, he's
unassuming, unpretentious. Fred likes him. A man who keeps a
large spare tire leaning in a corner of his office is not, in any
categorical sense, a man to be feared. He listens closely when Fred
speaks.

"We've just changed vendors for convenience copiers," Cook
says.

"Which vendor?" Fred asks.

Talking with a customer, at the start of a conversation such as
this, Fred imagines himself walking on his toes across snapping ice.
He looks at Cook with undivided passion, aiming every ounce of
awareness at Cook's face, making Cook realize he doesn't want to
miss a word, doesn't want to say a thing to upset his customer,
doesn't want to offend Cook in the slightest way. He wants Cook
to feel like an executive vice president. He uses Cook's name as
often as possible. He employs little phrases to soften even his most
innocent questions: *if you don't mind saying?* He's begging forgive-
ness for past sins already in the phrasing of his questions. He's
making Cook feel respected, admired, honored. He's raising Cook
up to a height where the air tastes a little fresher, where Cook feels
more important than the people he serves at Akron Automotive.
He's showing Cook how much he wants to make Cook happy.

At the same time, Fred's question itself makes Cook feel a little
guilty. It's a perfectly reasonable, unthreatening question of fact.
Who was the vendor? But the implication of it lets Fred score a
small point against Cook. Fred says nothing more, nothing less,
but his open and smiling face speaks eloquently to Cook of what
the question implies: *I guess what we're saying is, it wasn't Xerox, was
it, Jay? I guess that's the issue here, isn't it? I'll need to know why it wasn't
Xerox. You might be hurting my feelings—but I'm prepared for it. I'm a*

*salesman. I'm used to rejection. Of course, that doesn't make it any easier, does it? And, of course, the customer is the only person who can make it easier on me—meaning you, Jay.*

"Minolta," Cook says, without much enthusiasm.

"Any reason why you didn't consider Xerox?" Fred asks, his fingers linked in front of him, elbows on the armrests. He makes sure there's no hint of rancor or even resentment in this question. Another simple request for a fact. But with each question he gets closer to forcing Cook into the position of having to tell Fred why he got angry with Xerox—and yet Fred's harmless, puppy-dog innocence, so manifest in his charming face, makes it harder and harder for Cook to get angry with Fred himself. Ideally, by the time Cook tells Fred what infuriated him, he'll feel so bad about making Fred suffer that he'll be ready to listen to anything Fred wants to suggest. Fred is making it impossible for Cook not to like him. He's making Cook feel a whole spectrum of emotions: anger, compassion, fear, sympathy, guilt, affection.

Cook hedges, avoids the issue: "I'm not sure. We went to six companies."

Cook doesn't have the courage to be open about it, so Fred lets it rest a moment and stalls. "Being in this business for twenty years, I know we have a tremendous product line right now, Jay."

"Yes. I'm familiar with that. But we have not had a good experience with Xerox."

Here it comes. It's just too easy. Selling isn't work. It's as natural as breathing.

Cook continues: "I was invited to a show earlier this year. I drove through a snowstorm, walked in, and they said, Sorry, it's been canceled. I was really uptight about that."

A rep with less experience might excuse himself and drive back to the district at this point in a conversation. A younger rep might face this remark as a defeat. But Fred recognizes it for what it is—a win, a sale in itself, the first surrender in what could turn out to be a series of lucrative surrenders. The man's biggest objection to Xerox has come out in the first five minutes of conversation. That's what Fred always tries to uncover—the deepest gripe. Once he spots it, he can work on it, get around it, soothe it, solve it.

"Were you invited?" he asks.

"It was supposed to be at one o'clock. Guy said it was canceled. I said, Thanks a lot."

Fred sighs and nods, full of sympathy, remorse, shame.

"That's an irritant. I can understand. I would feel the same way."

"That set the tone," Cook says.

"Wow. I'm going to apologize. For whatever it's worth. It's very embarrassing. It's too late to do anything about it, though. We've changed. You don't know it, and now you've got another bad taste. Which makes it hard. The thing is, if you talk to Xerox customers, ones who've come back to us, you'll hear a different story."

Now Fred begins to build the bond, the relationship, the common ground between them. One more push is all it will take.

"All I'm asking is, if an opportunity ever arises again, give us a chance. If your own machine is running perfectly, but you call and say you're not satisfied, we'll put in a new machine, no questions asked," Fred says.

There's a climax of silence. Fred knows how to exploit this silence and make Cook feel discomfited by it, push him into feeling obligated to say something, anything, if only to have something to pour into that silence. Sure enough, Cook is the first to speak.

"Tell you what," Cook says. "Shoot me a plan for a 5090."

"When do you want to make your decision?" Fred asks.

"By next month. Yes or no."

Fred pauses and then adds one last twist: "I'm going to go out on a limb on this," he says. "My boss might not like this. I'd like to give you a machine at no charge. I'm doing it in the worst way. I'm willing to let you get a 5090. Get it down here. See how you'd use it."

He's offering Cook a free trial of the machine. He wants to make it sound as if he has to beg permission from his boss for this immense gift, when all along getting a machine installed on free trial is a standard sales technique—he's begging for the chance to get the machine onto Cook's shop floor, but he wants Cook to feel that he's the one doing the begging for free use of the machine.

This is an old, standard sales technique: Dangle something desirable in front of a customer—a product or a favor or a pricing scheme—and then pretend you need to go back to the district and ask permission to give it to him, something you could do on the spot if you wanted. Make him want something, make him ask for it, and then make him wait a little bit for it. Make him beg. Make him pray. It's what a realtor does when she gets your signed offer for a house and then spends two hours talking with the seller after she gets his agreement, without telling you she's gotten the agreement.

In this case, though, Fred wasn't merely trying to force Cook into accepting a trial. He wanted to use a temporary trial installation as a way of gathering information on Akron Automotive's needs—as a way of starting a quality study—even if the machine didn't stay after the study was done.

Yet Cook knows better. The old sales techniques and tricks don't work as well as they once worked. Customers know how to break these codes. Cook knows what usually happens with a trial installation. You get a machine into a print shop and people start using it, and pretty soon everybody loves it so much they take it for granted. That's the point of no return. It's already sold as soon as they plug it in, long before any order agreement has been signed.

It's a nice offer, but Cook doesn't think it will be necessary. Fine. Fred has his request for a proposal. That's a major breakthrough, a sale in itself. Now he feels fully alive. For the first time in months, he's done exactly what he has yearned to do every day: sit in front of a customer and coax a *yes* from a pair of reluctant lips. He's closed Jay Cook for a proposal.

Nothing else is quite like the feeling this gives him. Coming back to the office, Fred feels in complete control of his world. Every victory along the way is a sale. When he enters the office, everything seems different to him—the quality of the light, the give of the carpet under his feet, the transparency of his own voice when he calls out the names of his reps. This sales call is an unqualified success. He's a salesman again. His quest, once more, is fulfilled. Tomorrow he will start all over, embarking on it yet again, but for now it seems heaven and earth click into perfect balance. He doesn't have a problem in the world.

*4.*

THE SLOPES AT Firestone Country Club looked uphol-stered in green velvet. It was a luxury just to sit with a whiskey sour and gaze at those viridian fairways, imagining how it would feel to take a divot into the nap of that spongy turf. Whereas the sun and drought had baked public courses into brown pastures, each blade of grass here looked as if someone had watered and fed it with an eye dropper.

As Xerox customers arrived, two beautiful female trainees, the district's newest reps, greeted and escorted guests into the club-house, where they were presented with souvenir golf balls, golf towels, and a Xerox umbrella. In the locker room, each customer found a hardwood locker with his or her name posted on it. Though it looked like rain, for the first time this parched summer, Frank Pacetta wanted to forge ahead with a full day of golf followed by cocktails and dinner in the evening.

As a highlight of the summer, he had organized the biggest client-entertainment event in years. It was a way of making customers feel slightly indebted, and money spent on them would usually find its way back to the company in a contract. People who scoffed at functions like this, people who said Xerox was buying the business by throwing money at its customers—often these were people whose firms couldn't afford to spend thousands of dollars on a day of golf. If it wasn't money under the table, if it was only a day of entertainment, only a day on the links, then it was acceptable.

Client entertainment was one of those underground industries woven throughout the economy the way the immune system coursed throughout the human body—physically unobtrusive, taken for granted, yet absolutely essential to the survival of the whole. Hotels, restaurants, airlines, watering holes, limousines, clubs, golf courses, theme parks, Broadway theaters, escort services—an endless number of enterprises survived by overcharging customers who willingly paid the price because they weren't really paying the price. They were expensing it, or they were deducting it—both dodges justified by claiming the money was all spent on customers or clients. In other words, it was a form of escapism that paraded itself as work. It was all funny money for the people who paid, and a windfall for the ones who sold.

Pacetta told people this particular outing would cost somewhere in the range of fifteen thousand dollars. It would come out of the district's profits at the end of the year, but who was counting? As Pacetta put it, you have to spend money to make money. Pacetta had invited close to a hundred people for the tournament, on a weekday—and Fred couldn't wait to tee off. He invited a few of his team's customers, and they would have fun together, talk about business as little as possible.

Fred arrived early, searching for Rob Onorato, one of the younger sales managers. Fred knew Onorato had planned to join Ron Nelson, his best sales rep, for a night downtown the previous evening, entertaining two customers from Canton, doing on a much smaller scale what Pacetta was doing at Firestone. Nelson was a weight lifter who worked out so religiously his body appeared to have about as much fat percentage as a rice cake. He looked as if both his chin and his heart were chiseled from granite. He boasted of being able to outdrink any customer—he claimed he started drinking competitively at the age of thirteen, possibly twelve (his memory was understandably vague). In certain moods, Pacetta was known to call his best reps Assassins, and Nelson was so good, Pacetta called him a Paid Assassin, presumably ranking him higher than a mere amateur killer.

Before meeting Ted and Ralph for lunch, people were advised, tongue-in-cheek, to coat their stomachs by eating a stick of butter. These two midlevel managers, who worked at one of central Ohio's larger manufacturing companies, were known to outdrink even the district's best. When Fred spotted him, Onorato looked as if he'd stepped onto a globe where the force of gravity was roughly double his home planet's. Everything seemed to droop: his eyelids, his arms, his lower lip. He stood inches below Fred, who himself could scarcely reach six feet by standing on his toes, so there wasn't much room for Rob to droop in a demonstrative way.

Rob explained he hadn't gotten home until after three that morning. He pulled Fred aside and described what had happened the night before. In the past, Ted and Ralph had set the tone for their relationship with Xerox on a visit to Chicago for a two-day product demonstration trip. They showed up at their Chicago hotel with an extra, empty suitcase. It became clear how they used that suitcase. It was empty on the way into the hotel but full on the way out. Ted and Ralph took all the liquor and candy from the in-room snack bars, as well as the shower curtains, the towels, the linens, the complimentary robes, entertainment guides, and anything else not fastened down. With it, Ted and Ralph established the terms of their deal, their requirements as customers: *You give us everything we can get our hands on for ourselves, personally, and we'll buy your machine.*

It was clear these two men would appreciate a night downtown. The drinking began at Shooters, in the Flats. Next they went across the river to the Circus. Ted and Ralph started grinning at approximately seven-thirty and didn't stop until they were halfway home, more than seven hours later. The dancers at the Circus came out in their negligible costumes—cowgirls and courtesans, French maids and milkmaids, tall and petite, top-heavy and svelte. Promptly, dollar bills emerged. It was customary, if you were sitting along the runway, to slip a dollar into the garter of the dancer who rested her ankles on your shoulders or removed your necktie and invented a G-string with it. If you wanted one of the performers to come to your own table for a private dance, you paid ten dollars. The four of them spent several hundred dollars at the Circus and then went back across the river to the Crazy Horse showboat, which took them out onto Lake Erie with a new troupe of dancers.

Around midnight, having docked again at the Flats, they returned to the Circus and started spending money in earnest. Ron and Rob ran out of cash on the showboat, so Ted and Ralph pulled out their wallets. These wallets had, as Rob put it, more secret compartments than James Bond's billfold. Ralph turned his wallet inside out, pulled flaps, and opened recesses to produce tiny green pills of paper. By unfolding these little origami puzzles seven or eight times, Ralph revealed that the little box of paper was actually a hundred-dollar bill. For the rest of the evening the alert bartender kept listening for key questions from their table: Change for a hundred? Could they break another fifty? So much money was slipped behind so many garters that by the time every other patron left, the management closed and locked the doors and refused to let the Xerox foursome leave. The dancers, it turned out, planned a special performance for them. One by one, the women filed into the room. Normally, topless was the rule. Now, some of the dancers were naked. At the time, it seemed a perfect way to end the evening, although Rob wasn't sure his customers would remember much of it. Then again, lapses of memory seemed not only justified but especially convenient, with those doors closed and the private show in progress.

An hour later, back in Ron's BMW, Ralph lost control of all muscles above his collarbone. His head flopped toward the driver's seat, and Ron leaned over, rolled down the window, and pushed Ralph's head toward it as a precaution. Ralph kept trying to pledge his love for Ron's black BMW: "Boy, thish ish a—man, I jusht love thish—I mean thish car ish—" At the end, when Ron arrived at Ralph's parked truck, their customer regressed to growls and grunts. Ted, who had a much higher tolerance for alcohol, volunteered to drive the two of them home in Ralph's vehicle. He promised to drive slowly. *Very* slowly.

After Rob finished his story, Fred found his golf partners and his golf cart, and they watched Pacetta move off with his group to the first tee. Pacetta played in a foursome with Gerry Faust, the famous former football coach for Notre Dame. He had been invited to speak briefly to all the guests before dinner. As the game progressed and the rain began to fall, Fred observed Frank and the others coming down fairways parallel to the ones Fred played. He heard Frank shouting instructions, wearing his purple Bogie Busters shirt and a pale lime cap. Throw your belly at the ball! Swing at it!

"Let's make some magic on this hole, Coach. You know what I'm saying? Hit it as hard as you can and let your natural abilities take over."

Faust laughed at Pacetta's mimicry of a golf-pro-as-football-coach. He swung at the ball and got all of it. It sailed up into the drizzle and plopped softly onto the green. He roared.

"Lookat 'is," Pacetta said. "Stick it, Coach."

"Put me down for a par right now," Faust said, his husky voice sounding like tearing paper. "Holy mackerel! Did you see that? I'm going to take up this game."

"You're an animal, Coach."

Fred's game didn't go well. The rain poured on his head and pooled in the bottom of his golf bag. All his grips turned slick as fish. He parred the first four holes and then his game fell apart. By the end of the eighteenth hole, he counted more than a hundred strokes. On the way back to the clubhouse, he steered the golf cart off the path to avoid the puddles, with his partner, a customer from one of the larger law firms in town, talking happily in the seat beside him, despite the weather. Once off the path, Fred decided it might be better to take a shortcut over a grassy hill.

At this point, Fred's world seemed to tilt away from under the wheels of his cart. Something slipped and gave, and then the world turned upside down; the three-wheeled cart tumbled over both of them, and Fred and his customer were rolling into the mud and grass, gazing up into the rain. For a moment, neither of them moved as the rain dropped into their eyes. Fred wondered what sort of sales technique could be used in a profitable way after having rolled a golf cart over the buyer. Was Dick all right? Yeah, muddy was all. Would they charge them for the damage? Was he all right? Did he think there was a prize for flipping the cart? Dick laughed. Fred was relieved.

Back at the club, as everyone assembled for drinks on the veranda, Fred went to the side door, avoiding the spectacle of a walk through the dining room. He found his locker, scrubbed the mud from his slacks and his face, and used the complimentary blow-dryers to evaporate the wet spots on his shirt. He wondered if you could expense a lawsuit. It was an accident, wasn't it? He'd been on the job. He could imagine the list on his expense voucher: coffee with Jim Salter, $1.56; mileage for two weeks, $126.00; attorney's fees and award for injuries and suffering on the eighteenth fairway: $351,476.00. He made a note to call his customer the following morning and offer to replace the man's torn slacks and ball retriever, with apologies.

Warm and dry in the dining room, Fred discovered dinner would be served in a couple hours, plenty of time to mingle and drink. The nongolfing reps began to show up and corner their customers for an hour of conversation. Finally, the meal was served, and afterward Pacetta introduced Faust.

"I'm not going to give you my money speech," Faust said, and the crowd laughed. "This is true. Everything I tell you is true. It's all true from now on."

Everyone laughed except Pacetta, who wore the expression he usually wore when someone else captured his crowd. It was a slightly disgruntled, infinitely bored look. Faust spoke about his trip to Lourdes, where he prayed for the fortunes of his football team at Notre Dame.

Later, Pacetta reminded people how much Faust had endured. He coached for Notre Dame when they were losing. But he didn't surrender. He didn't roll over. Faust had lived through Pacetta's idea of the worst hell imaginable—a highly publicized failure. Bank robbery, murder, an advanced case of leprosy—in Frank's mind nothing compared with the taste of failure. It was the ultimate horror for him, as it was for Fred. To Frank, Faust looked at that moment like a particularly noble, if slightly silly, example of courage. Faust had told Pat Elizondo he'd return to Notre Dame if they asked him. All would be forgiven, at least on his side of that imagined reconciliation. It would never happen, though. When you failed at that level, there was no way to backtrack and play the game a second time.

When Faust was done, Pacetta followed with gag awards for sliding down a sixty-foot embankment and getting into two sand traps on one green. Then he announced the bar was open again. A migration ensued. Fred watched Pacetta glance around the room. There was so much money to be made from these people, and he knew he could make it before the end of the year. They were taking the act of buying and selling and raising it to a higher level. It seemed no mere coincidence that every fireplug in Independence, Ohio, was painted in the colors of the American flag. They felt they were doing something patriotic while playing golf and drinking with customers. They believed buying and selling— the exchange of money, the coitus of commerce—was their republic's most intimate, life-affirming act. They had a reason to get up in the morning. Wasn't America great? They lived in a country where they could play golf during the week and get paid for working, because they *were* working. They were doing business. Sort of. Pacetta was spending thousands of dollars to make these people feel good, the way Ron and Rob made their own customers feel good at the Flats. On one level, the message sounded acceptable: *We love you so much we're giving you a day of golf and dinner.* On another level, it was real: *We're making you feel as if you owe us, big time, and we'll come knocking later this year. You can count on it.*

It's impossible to separate the bullshit from the reality. It's all part of Pacetta's phony histrionics—the drama, the competition, the parties, the operatic highs and lows of the sales cycle, the mind games. At gatherings, he appears to be a sort of game-show-host-cum-ayatollah, and then, in private, he keeps attempting to turn all casual conversations into the psychological equivalent of fast food. Everything is a quick and prickly encounter session: *Someday, I'm going to shave that beard off, Jeff, and see what you really look like under there.* He gives every gesture and word a purposeful spin. Why? To keep the gyroscope whirling. To put a spark and a twitch back into the surrounding emotional ether. Make them hungry. Make them weep. Make them angry. Make them fall in love with a number. Make them *feel* something, anything. Make them guess what he really means. An outsider couldn't help but wonder, Did anyone take any of this amplified heat seriously? Did it really keep things warm?

No, not exactly, because everyone recognized it as bullshit. But yes, they respected it, because it got results. By wearing the mask, by putting on an act, by turning everything into gleeful non-sense—in other words, by creating a culture of ironic phoniness that allowed people to do outrageous things, *as part of the act,* by pushing things to the point where you couldn't tell if it was a joke or it was serious—Pacetta was creating an atmosphere where any sort of clownish, eccentric, or cruel enthusiasm became accept-able, *because* everything was bullshit on the surface. Everyone accepted the act, hour by hour, day by day, and this gave Pacetta license to do things no one else could do. *It allowed him to get everything out into the open.* He kissed people on the forehead. He wrestled people to the ground. He hugged them and told them how beautiful they were, deep inside, where he could see their little hearts thumping so faithfully. It was all part of his Italian bit, his impersonation of a Mafia don as Puck might have pulled it off—all of it performed with this weird Billy Crystal lunacy woven into it. He was funny, crazy, but he wasn't exactly witty. He wasn't that subtle. His humor was always aggressive. The jokes were always slightly pugilistic, even the ones he directed at himself. It was more than a laugh. It was psychological assault.

Because his act was disguised as bullshit, it was a safe way of tricking everyone's emotions out of cover, teasing hidden feelings into the visible world, where he could take aim at the real and involuntary responses he wanted to evoke. Once he brought them to the surface, he could massage, heighten, and direct those emotions to a desired end. You could see the look in Pacetta's eyes when he made somebody snap or filled someone's face with gratitude: *Gotcha, baby! Now you're mine! Now I own you. And you thought it was just a joke.* For Pacetta, as for many salesmen, some people were to be treated with respect and genuine love, but most people were objects to be moved on a board.

By making all of his act ironic, a sort of continuous diet of jesting nonsense—which some people found themselves believing in those drunken moments when they lost touch with the deft, useful modulation of tone Pacetta achieved—he gave most people a way to safely mock and dismiss the act on a superficial level, even as they began to depend on the way it stimulated them on a deeper level. He made almost any sort of behavior acceptable. Nothing was embarrassing. Nothing seemed foolish or cruel or vulnerable or craven, because nothing was quite genuine.

Meanwhile, subconsciously, all these empty gestures and emotions—phony or not—were getting through to people. Like the sight of blood or the feel of a bass line in an Aerosmith track or the smell of Charles of the Ritz on a woman's neck, Pacetta's act stole past the frontal lobe and went straight to the limbic brain. When he said you were beautiful and special, you could dismiss it, but those words got through to you on a subliminal level you couldn't control. You responded autonomically, despite yourself. On a conscious level, life in Cleveland was like watching a movie or spending a day at Disney World. You knew it wasn't real. And yet, like those experiences, it went past your skin. Your blood pressure rose, your heart rate increased, and a certain sympathetic quiver began to ascend the rungs of your spine. People could laugh and dismiss the whole thing with a sneer or a bon mot, but all the while—and on a much more significant level—they were being manipulated, energized, driven to the edge. Despite themselves, they were responding. They were eating it up, and then finding themselves hungry for it when it wasn't there. It seemed the surface message in everything Pacetta did was something like this: *You can have fun and call it work, gang. You can escape the dull reality of work that most adult human beings face, because here, with me, you can be as wild as you were in college and still earn six figures every year.* Yet after a certain amount of time, anyone who worked for him realized it was just the opposite. He was saying: *Stay here long enough, and no matter what you do, no matter how much fun you have, you'll always be thinking about how it relates to your work. What was once fun will come to seem a necessity. You'll need it simply to get the energy to make a sales call the next morning. What was once merely a job will become your life. Stick with me, and—night or day—you'll never stop selling.*

5.

FRED STANDS IN the amphitheater's shadows, near the back of the room. New contests, for the last four months, are being announced, and along with them a new theme: Campaign for Excellence. The whole room is decorated with red-white-and-blue campaign bunting and crepe paper and confetti. Pacetta hands out cash for top performers, and everyone applauds. By this point, the little amphitheater is alive. Money never fails to electrify a room. Campaign hats are handed out, and noisemakers. For the rest of the year, whenever an order is logged, the theme song—"Happy Days Are Here Again"—will be played over the public address system in the office.

Fred likes to call these theatrics the fluff. He claims he's at a stage of his life where he doesn't need fluff anymore. He acts as if he hates it when the entire district becomes a fluff factory at the beginning of the year, or the quarter, or whenever a new contest theme is introduced. Yet he finds himself drawn as deeply into the theatrics as everyone else. When Palm Springs was announced as the destination for President's Club, somebody had the idea of creating a contest around the theme of "California Dreamin'." Recordings of the Mamas and the Papas were dusted off. The sales managers created a skit involving references to the Beach Boys. At a gathering to kick off the contest, Fred dressed in surfer attire, wearing a pair of sunglasses with the word *Wild* on one lens and the word *Thing* on the other. At another district meeting, one of the secretaries offered to type up proposals with only a day's turnaround for anybody who put the proposals in her box at an early enough hour. It was called the Oily Boyd Special, and she emerged into the amphitheater dressed in a chicken suit to announce the offer. It was endless. An unremitting current of cartoon-quality hype, day after day. As much as Fred sneered at it in public, he nourished himself with the energy, the artificial feeling, it created. He was hooked on it.

These empty theatrics and the primitive energy delivered within them found their way into the district's whole way of motivating itself. An acceptable level of nonsense became incorporated in the way the district structured the pace of its own sales year. Every few months a new theme emerged in the meetings, the parties, the contest, even the way the managers decorated the office. Early in the year, the managers decided to turn their lives into a horse race. The Cleveland Classic! Soon huge charts found their way onto the walls, with each rep and manager depicted as a jockey riding a horse. They pasted hydrocephalic photocopies of managers' faces atop little cardboard and papier-mâché cartoons of jockeys on horses. And these grotesque figures each week made their way across a paper track, posted to the wall inside the district office, to indicate how far along each contestant had come toward the finish line, the final number. At the end of the quarter all the people in the district met at Thistledown Racing Club, and Pacetta handed out toasters and microwaves to the horserace—er, um, sales contest—winners. It was silly. It was ludicrous. It was perfect.

The contests, the parties, the skits, the whole act—it turned work into a fantasy, draining away the monotonous reality of the daily labor, giving managers an excuse to post everyone's results on a wall. It was all out in the open. The very look and feel of the office became a constant pinprick, an endless emotional goad, pushing everyone toward greater results. You couldn't walk into the office without seeing your face or your name posted beside a number—and everyone could mock your failure or envy your success. The very walls themselves taunted and triggered emotions. The building seemed to be built not of wood and nails but of mirrors. Everywhere you looked, you saw yourself exposed as a loser or a winner, a Nobody or a Somebody.

Everything became a contest. At any given moment, at least ten contests were usually in progress: Fast Start President's Club, DM Club, DM Club Fast Start, Centralized Heavy Hitters, First Trimester Max Leaders, District Monthly Leaders, Dash for Cash, and so on. Everyone had a chance to win. And if you won at something, no matter how superficial the contest, you felt good. It was unavoidable. People wanted to win because in the sales contests Pacetta hosted he rewarded and recognized people lavishly, spending the district's money on prizes: microwaves, bicycles, and boom boxes. He mounted names and photographs of winners on the walls. He played God—and, as God, he had an obligation to keep an eye on everyone, note when they were doing well, and show them he paid attention to their lives. He was *aware* of them, almost as much as he was aware of himself. All the time, he stoked their feelings. Business management and sales—essentially, it was all the same thing: a way of motivating people to do things they wouldn't otherwise do.

In contests during the year, reps and managers competed fiercely for even the slightest of prizes. In one Thanksgiving contest, called Pix with Paul, the entire district labored to win a free turkey and the honor of standing side by side with Paul Allaire, the president of the company, in a color photograph suitable for framing. Those who didn't perform quite so well earned entrance into nothing more than a group photograph with Allaire. Losers weren't allowed into the picture at all. Some people forgot how silly it was and started to care about getting into one of those photographs. These pictures were one way of being watched and appreciated. They were paper trophies. And what *was* a trophy, anyway? A gold cup with handles, a gilt grail some people prized more than anything in the world. It was a way to control the ups and downs of your emotional life, a way to prove you were Somebody, at least for a year or two of your life.

Everyone battled for the rewards because they'd learned to play the game, to pretend winning mattered—*within the terms of the game*—in order to feed on the emotion it generated. Once you entered the game, once you began to play it, you had a chance to share in that emotion. That emotion was your fuel, your vehicle, and your destination, all in one. All the material rewards were there simply to generate a little more energy, another spurt of feeling, down the road.

Summer was almost over. Fred felt he was falling behind again, yet he felt energized by the district hype. By the end of August, his team had reached only sixty-six percent of its annual goal. If he was to get to Palm Springs, his people needed to sell as much equipment in the last four months of the year as they'd sold in the first eight months. So far, his team had reached only two thirds of its plan, and the year was almost three-quarters finished. He told his people he needed orders, orders, orders—as many as they could manage. Although he wasn't supposed to sell equipment himself and had no sales quota to make on his own, apart from his efforts to push his individual people over the top in their own goals, he was prepared to go out on any call with any of his reps, pushing to close orders that might lag into the next month, the next quarter, the next year. Yet there never seemed to be enough opportunities for him to travel with his reps, get in front of customers, help force deals to a satisfactory finish.

Fred decided to leave Bruno Biasiotta a voice-mail message. It was less effective than questioning Bruno face to face. Bruno resented it. Yet he responded promptly to his voice-mail messages.

Evidently, Bruno didn't feel his manhood could be threatened by a *recording* of Fred's voice. So, within earshot of Bruno, who was sitting at his desk a few feet away from Fred's open door, Fred picked up his phone and left Bruno a recorded message. They were listening to each other without being able to see each other, each pretending not to hear the other. For them, it was the most productive way to communicate.

"Bruno, this is Fred. Just a reminder. You owe me lunch for that golf match, and I don't forget things I win. Also, you need to call Bell Publications. Do it alone if you want. But let me know. I'm here to support you and help you, Bruno," Fred said, in a sarcastic voice, smiling into the phone, pretending to leave a message, knowing Bruno was listening from his office across the hall.

"I think I'll four-four-five that one," Bruno shouted to Fred from behind his partition, without moving from his desk, without picking up his telephone. By punching four-four-five, Bruno would erase the voice-mail message.

"I sign your expense reports too, Bruno," Fred shouted back, unable to see Bruno. "Bear that in mind."

Jim Salter worked in an office at the end of a narrow, cramped hallway just inside the entrance to Bell headquarters. He looked older than Fred, with thinning hair, a conservative suit, and a limp. He had the air of a man who had talked to thousands of salesmen, and he looked at everything with the double vision buyers develop when they realize how many levels of truth they need to plumb before they can feel even reasonably comfortable with a deal. Saying no gave him the kind of fleeting, repetitive sense of ease a smoker gets from taking well-spaced drags on a cigarette.

They were attempting to sell him a 5090, the biggest traditional duplicator in their line, an alternative to an offset printing press, a machine as costly as a lakeside bungalow. Weeks earlier, he told them, "It's just flat-out no, as far as the 5090." Everyone was trying to sell him copiers. He'd been in fifteen other showrooms. Salter loved the machine. It was obvious. They'd come down already on the price. They'd taken him to Chicago for a product demonstration and a dinner. So what was he waiting for? How much more could they do?

This deal was a major checkpoint along the way to a successful year for Fred. He needed to make this sale. When Salter talked, his wide blue eyes challenged them, daring them to say what he wanted to hear without offering a clue as to what it might be. Fred saw the desire in Salter's eyes—the man wanted to buy this box. Yet he was hesitating. He wanted his treasurer to look at the deal. Business wasn't good. No deal. Not yet.

The meetings with Salter continued. Each time they met with him, it was the same story. Fred told him Bruno was discouraged. Salter was unmoved. Bruno could be as discouraged as he wanted, but Salter wasn't going to buy just so Bruno didn't have to be discouraged. They were building a two-hundred-and-forty-million production facility. Bruno shouldn't get too discouraged. He shouldn't become a shoe salesman. They would buy the gear eventually. You don't always get what you want when you want it. You learn that as a little boy.

All along, Fred played the puppy dog, warm and ingratiating. When he got outside onto the sidewalk, though, Fred wanted to smash something, possibly some portion of Salter's facial anatomy. Fred had learned his share of boyhood lessons. He didn't need Salter's advice on maturity and patience. He needed the man's signature.

• • •

Fred asked Bruno to rewrite the proposal yet again, giving Salter even lower payments during the first year. It would make Salter feel like a bargaining robot, a stud. That's the way it was done—you "baked" extra charges into the deal at the start so that you could take them away during the negotiations, letting the customer feel he was bargaining your life away when all along you were just getting the price down to an acceptably lucrative level. You were giving away money you never expected to get in the first place. Bruno sent the proposal downtown and set a date for another call.

When they arrived, Salter limped to his seat. Bruno offered free leasing during the first year. It was a gift of cash flow, nothing more, nothing less. Those waived payments were baked into the monthly fees later on. But you didn't talk about it that way. You talked about getting free use of the machine the first year. Many customers didn't understand these methods of financing a sale, and so it was better not to go into detail. Others, like Salter, understood—and liked the way it gave them the appearance of a good deal in the first year or two.

Fred hated these financing tricks. He missed the days when the price of a copier was one number and nothing else. There was no negotiating. He was always thinking to himself: *Why do we do all this cat-and-mouse stuff with the customer? Tell us your requirements. Then we'll meet them. The customers force us to do these things. They want a lower price. The customer keeps squeezing us for a lower price. America is unproductive because it takes so long when you have to play these cat-and-mouse games. Why don't we take away negotiations? I liked the old days when there were no negotiations, no tricks or games or tricky relationships. We drag things out. The customer is dragging things out to get the best price.*

Salter was also the kind of buyer who probably knew how to make it look like a real bargain to his superiors. A lot of buyers didn't care where the money came from, nor how much they spent, as long as their budget would handle it and their superiors approved it. Salter was hard to figure, though. Fred couldn't tell if he was on Bruno's side and was simply too weak to sell his own management on a machine he clearly loved.

"First twelve months we pay the bill on that machine," Fred said.

Salter nodded, looking at the numbers, and he told them he'd get back to them. When they called on Salter the next time, he said he liked the price. Fred's heart was pounding. He could smell the order. He wanted to clamp his fingers around Salter's wrist, lift the man's hand, and place it on an order form. He'd done that once— picked up a customer's hand and laid it on the signature line. It worked *that* time.

"If it's a go, it'll be a go by the end of the week. I'll know immediately."

"So we can get back to you Friday," Bruno said.

"I'll call you," Salter said.

When he got back to the office, Fred felt invincible. This was the part of selling he loved, when he could feel it build toward a peak, when the rhythm of that crescendo became part of his week. He loved it when selling became a tactile thing, as it always did, triggering a faint tremor in his body.

Fred didn't give Bruno a moment's rest. Quietly he sat in his chair and eavesdropped, from his desk, on Bruno's phone conversation with a customer from one of Bruno's other accounts. It sounded as if something might happen, but Bruno wasn't pushing. Fred scooted his chair closer to his open door and started talking to Bruno while Bruno stayed on the phone. When he was happy, Fred felt capable of anything. He became the Fly again, rising from the depths of depression to the heights of enthusiasm in the course of a single day.

"When? When? When? When?" Fred whispered loudly enough for Bruno to hear, shaking his fist in the air. He wiggled his thumbs. "Is it a go? Is it a go? Bruno, is it a go? I'm getting excited. I don't know where I'm at. We'll write six hundred orders this year."

Bruno gave Fred a thumbs-up sign. Fred hooted.

"This month? Signed?"

Bruno mimed the words with his mouth, his hand over the phone's mouthpiece: "I don't know."

"Date. Date. Get a date."

"When do you think we can finalize these orders?" Bruno asked into the phone.

"You give him the date, Bruno. The date. The date."

"Next two weeks?" Bruno asked into the phone.

"Next Wednesday. Tell him next Wednesday. Give him a date. You give him a date."

"I'll call you next week and schedule something." Bruno said.

Why do that? These people didn't know how to close an order! What did Fred do? He ranted and raved. But it worked. Look at his W-2. There was proof that it worked. Next Wednesday? Ha!

Bruno was still on the phone, but Fred didn't notice. He was too busy adding numbers on his calculator, sitting with his head bent over his desk as he talked. Even so, Bruno heard every word. He never missed a word.

"We are going to crush it," Fred said. "Boy, my mind just doesn't stop."

At a meeting of the sales managers, Pacetta told them there would be no question of letting anyone hide in his own little patch of shade. Everything would be brightly lit, down to the last semicolon on the last proposal. At this particular meeting Fred's timing was perfect. He stood before the group and told the other managers, machine by machine, what his people were doing and how they would be able to use the new discounts, the end-of-year actions. His people wouldn't be able to change a punctuation mark on a proposal without his knowing about it. Frank grinned. Now was the time to become Big Brother with the reps.

"This is the role model. That's exactly my requirement. Done. See that? That's tremendous, Fred. You're on it. Fred's captured what I want us all to do. He's going to force it to happen." It was one of his favorite phrases: Nothing happens unless you force it to happen. It was the heart of old-school selling.

"There's nowhere to hide when they come in to see me," Fred said.

"You've taken all the fluff out of it. It's tremendous. That's what I want. I want us to know what's been done down to the gnat's ass."

In the office Fred stopped at each cubicle and purged whatever thoughts happened to cloud his consciousness, and if he couldn't find the rep at his or her slot in the bullpen, he wandered the halls until he found his victim, pinned the rep against a wall, and fired fifty or sixty words into the air. Within fifteen minutes he contacted each rep, discharged his ideas, and wandered on without farewell, doing the same to another rep, and then another. Finally, he returned to his office. He spotted Larry Tyler at a terminal, finishing a proposal. Larry was so busy, he'd made calls to four different people at one company before seven-thirty that morning.

Fred took his car keys out of his pocket and shook them at Larry. He told Larry to get off the computer and in front of a customer. Larry turned red but restrained himself. He wasn't going to snap. It was exactly what Fred wanted him to do.

Fred shadows and teases and buzzes his reps, never giving them an hour without accountability, looking for a chance to travel with them. As the summer comes to an end, the orders pour in. Larry, Diane, Bruno, start coming into Fred's office to post the smaller orders they're getting, and the numbers start to add up. Fred keeps pushing.

In the bullpen, Fred flits from one cubicle to the next, speaking in sentence fragments, using body language, making unintelligible noises of frustration, going from one rep to the next, summarizing the status of deals—one, two, three, four, five, on his fingers—cramming more information into one sentence than another manager can get into a fifteen-minute lecture. *I was down at Chillians the other night, we had about eight beers each and then six shots, oh, did we have a good time, but I can't talk about that—you missed it, Bruno, you missed it—I don't have to tell you—I mean, Bedford Telecommunications has to happen, Bruno, it has to hap—and unless you call them tomor—you should be in Sandler's face—I mean, today you shou—*

It's Salter, Fred. The name is Salter, not Sandler.

*When I see Mr. Sandler, I'll call him Salter. If I liked the guy, I'd get his name right. I've never gotten a customer's name wrong in front of the customer. And I'm never late. I may get lost on the way, but I'm never late.*

And Jillians, Fred? It's Jillians, not Chillians.

*I'll call it Chillians, Bruno. You don't have to tell me what to call it.*

And you don't have to tell me what to do with my day. I'm not a little kid, Fred.

*You wrote no orders last month. None. I don't want to talk to you. I beat you at golf. We need to hear some no answers so we can get to work. That's when the selling starts. We've got to stick our necks out on a limb. We do. We've got to run it up the red flag and see what happens. Quit hedging around the bush.*

The "song-and-pony show" was Fred's merger of "song and dance" and "dog-and-pony show." Bruno couldn't tell if Fred was joking when he mangled figures of speech, or if he considered it a tidy way of condensing two or three tropes into one, or if his brain simply short-circuited under duress. Maybe it was part of Fred's simpleton act, or maybe Fred didn't actually know what he was saying. Bruno could never tell, nor could anyone else. Fred knew this, and he delighted in their doubts. It disarmed people. It enabled him to do to people what Pacetta did to him—he hammered them until they broke, and then he did something simple, he mangled a name or a figure of speech so that they laughed and felt superior and kept liking him despite everything. He kept them liking him the way parents keep liking an errant toddler, crashing amiably through the tulips. He kept them crying and laughing at the same time, and it was both perfectly calculated and perfectly natural.

Fred told Bruno they needed Bell Publications before the end of September. They did everything they could imagine to win the deal. They spiffed the deal with as many credits as they could afford. As far as Fred could tell, Salter was sold on the machine. But would his superiors buy it? Neither Fred nor Bruno had any way to get to Salter's boss themselves, so all they could do was wait for Salter to phone them.

Though they didn't plan to stop at Bell that afternoon, Bruno invited Fred to go with him on some other, less significant calls. Once they got downtown, Bruno's beeper went off. Bruno reached for it, and read the digital message that appeared on the beeper's tiny liquid-crystal display. Fred wasn't paying attention, and Bruno said nothing—he simply tapped Fred's shoe with his own glossy brogue. Fred glanced down at the message Bruno was holding up to Fred's face: Bell Publications called. Without a word, they sprinted to Bruno's car and started driving, looking for a pay phone. They knew a gas station near the corner where Euclid intersected with a deteriorating, north-south street Fred couldn't remember. It had one of the drive-up telephones Fred liked to use.

It was a gray day, still hot and muggy in September. The rain began to fall. Clouds moved fast, swagging low across the lake, giving the whole skyline the quality of an unfinished sketch on gray linen, the tall office buildings melting into the blankness of the speeding mist and then reappearing in the gaps between clouds. When they arrived at the BP service station, Fred handed Bruno a quarter for the phone call, an unusually generous gesture. Bruno got Salter's secretary.

She told him Salter had just stepped out. Was it going to be good news? She said they were getting the 5090. When Fred saw Bruno's smile, he knew. Bruno hung up the phone and they both rolled up their windows. It was as if nothing had happened. But as soon as the windows were sealed, Bruno and Fred turned to each other, smacked their palms together in a high five, and let loose. They shouted, yelled, screamed, all within the airtight enclosure of Bruno's car. If anybody had seen them, they would have wondered if Fred or Bruno had just won the Big Game.

By the end of September, Fred's team reached almost ninety percent of its annual budget. With three months left in the year, Fred seemed virtually assured of making his annual nut—and yet he was still worried. A hundred percent wasn't anywhere good enough, according to the terms defined by the corporation and his own past performance. He needed twenty percent more than his annual budget to find himself flying to Palm Springs—and that was the only measure of his success he'd been trained to accept.

One time, coming back from Bell, Fred and Bruno talked about the future. Bruno was the one person on Fred's team who was almost certain to get promoted the following year. He was hoping to become either a sales manager or a specialist in high-volume machines. Bruno needed to feel he was advancing his career. His wife, Diane, was expecting their first child. He needed a good showing this year to get the promotion and make enough extra money to see himself through the expenses of parenthood. Fred wanted to help Bruno do well.

"Frank's going to put you somewhere after this year," Fred said as they drove past the steel mills in Bruno's Audi. "Maybe a high-volume specialist spot."

"That isn't challenging," Bruno said. "I told Frank if it doesn't happen next year, I'll have to look around. I wasn't doing it to put a bug up his ass. I was just informing him. I'd like to get into international marketing if I could."

"You don't want a desk job, Bruno. No matter how creative they get on that stuff, they always end up taking a calculator to it."

"I know that, Fred. The only guy who isn't accountable is the one sweeping the floor. Even he's accountable," Bruno said. "I'm not looking for a title to boost my ego. I want to develop myself. Holy shit! There's the new Lexus coupe! Check that out. At Xerox, there's politics with everything. There's politics when you make a phone call. There's politics when you get more supplies from the stockroom. There's politics whenever you take a piss. At Xerox, no matter what you do, if there's somebody who doesn't like you, you're screwed."

"It's that way everywhere, Bruno."

Where did Bruno get this self-assurance about his future with Xerox? Did he have some kind of Italian bond with Pacetta that guaranteed him advancement on his own timetable? Pacetta gave Fred all kinds of assurances but told him nothing specific, made no binding commitments. Bruno acted as if he'd been told he could expect more than Fred believed he could expect. He was taking a promotion for granted. Fred felt he could take nothing for granted with Pacetta. Fred had no idea where Xerox would put him in a year or two. No one was coaching him on where he might go and the training he might need to get there. Pacetta was always intimating that great things awaited, but Fred knew how much credence to invest in Pacetta's words. At this point, that's all it amounted to—just words.

6.

AUTUMN WAS INFILTRATING the air and trees, creeping south across the cold lake, clarifying the night skies. As the summer ended, the sky became a grisaille of haze. This Halloween weather would last through the autumn and into the winter. From now on, the city lived in perpetual dusk. Chicago, Gary, Cleveland, Buffalo, Rochester—an iron cowl hooded the Great Lakes littoral towns as the days grew short, cold, and wet. After hovering over Cleveland all summer, the drought departed, leaving behind only a memory of sunny brilliance in the color of leaves. Trees along the interstate became a tweedy screen of russet and orange with flecks of green and gold, a blur of peeling birches and grenadine sumac.

As Fred drove to work every morning, the scent of wet leaves filled the cramped and dusty interior of his worn Mazda RX-7. In Ohio the woods and wildlife seemed to enjoy a freedom he'd never know. Even in his office he could see the fletched tips of a blue heron's wings sailing over the grid of parked Toyotas, BMWs, and Volvos. In Independence, the larger birds, the herons, geese, and hawks, never appeared to migrate far from their hollows and warrens. The geese would fly in V-formation over the unkempt half acre of antique graves on Rockside Drive—the limestone obelisks and crooked slabs of pink granite visible from Fred's desk—but these birds would be flying north, toward his window, not south. They circled the roof and settled where they began, in the crescent of unmown rushes beyond Diane Burley's almond-beige Lexus. The same geese could be found there in July or October or December, just as Fred could be found in his own nest, four floors up, from one season to the next. The impulse to migrate had been bred out of his Levantine blood. Yet the urge to escape overtook him more and more often. He could see the district was going to change within a year, and he wasn't sure he wanted to work there after those changes occurred.

Late in the afternoon, Fred joins Bill Hookway, one of the district's specialists, at a little restaurant east of the city for a few drinks. They've just finished making a sales call, and Fred suggests they stop somewhere, maybe to share a basket of Buffalo wings. They pull off I-90 and drive up and down Euclid on a strip that reaches out into one of the older parts of town inhabited by a core population of eastern Europeans. When they don't immediately spot any decent bars in the obsolescent strip malls, they settle on a place called the Richmond Restaurant. When they get inside, they discover there's no bar, no lounge. They walk toward the back—the place is almost empty—and ask if they can order drinks. The waitress nods.

They find a table near a busing stand with rows of water glasses and silverware. Hookway orders a Manhattan, Fred a gin and tonic. They take one look at the menu and realize they've gone as far from the Flats as they can get. None of the usual appetizers here. No jalapeño nachos, no Buffalo wings, no mozzarella sticks or potato skins. Nothing but onion rings and fries. Finger food from another era. After the waitress takes their order for onion rings, she stands two tables away, polishing her shoes by spraying them with Windex and buffing.

Fred wants to know if Hookway feels the way Fred does about his work and his future. His creative discontent is changing. He still goes through the motions of panic with his reps, ending it with a smile or a click of his heels or a friendly joke. Yet that kind of discontent isn't what he feels right now. His anxieties aren't as purposeful as they used to be, and his discontent has become more corrosive. His fear is becoming real, and he wonders if Hookway feels just as apprehensive about the premises of the whole game itself—not just whether they will win or lose in any given year, but whether they should keep playing it the way they've played it for so long. He knows he's ready for a change, but he doesn't know how to make it happen. Does Hookway feel the same way?

By the time Hookway downs his third Manhattan, he starts to loosen up. His stiff graying hair is blown back off the forehead, and his glasses make his small blue eyes look even more like a hawk's. The aggressive angles of Hookway's face are mitigated by the vulnerability of his slightly rounded cheeks. Usually he talks in a rapid, quiet voice, hurrying his syllables, as if he suspects eavesdroppers. Many conversations with Hookway have this air of undertones at the water cooler. It's a salesman's favorite tone, a way of establishing a sense of almost illicit familiarity, a way of making the listener feel privileged and special.

Hookway's image is the exact opposite of Fred's. Fred is the disingenuous bumbler, the man who mangles customers' names and slaughters figures of speech and yet makes President's Club year after year. It's his act, and it works by making other people susceptible to him. Yet it limits him. He's afraid he'll become the prisoner of his own mannerisms. He tells people: I'm not smart. I just know how to get the job done. And then a day later, he reminds them: Remember, I'm not smart. He fears too many people believe him. Too few of them, Fred suspects, can see through the image and the smoke. Pacetta saw through it on the first day, but Pacetta is gifted and is not a Normal Man. Others higher up won't understand how someone with Fred's self-deprecating style can ever handle anything more than Cleveland major accounts. Fred always feels threatened by someone who appears as cool and corporate as Hookway. He's smooth, with no wasted motions, no chinks in his armor.

So Fred's a little apprehensive about how this conversation will go. He isn't sure what Hookway thinks of him—he isn't sure what anyone thinks of him, how many of them laugh at him behind his back—even after all these years. He's been on calls with Hookway, too many to count, but they've always been a little reserved with each other. Fred thought of him as an enemy four years earlier. Hookway was one of the inner circle when Fred arrived in Cleveland, in the months before Pacetta showed up—one of the four or five insiders who had direct influence with the previous district manager. He was one of the most competent of the few people who survived Pacetta's first year in the district. He lives in Hudson now. He has one of the huge, beautiful houses with backyards like a scene from *A Midsummer Night's Dream*, not far from Pacetta's home. So he's part of the Hudson group, the way he was part of the inner circle before, and though it doesn't give Hookway as much unofficial power as he enjoyed in previous years, he's settled into his new role with finesse. He knows his work. As a DocuTech specialist, he drives Fred's reps toward deals, nagging them as relentlessly as Fred does. As this brief conversation evolves over drinks and onion rings, Fred begins to feel affection for Hookway. It's a revelation to him how even *the* Bill Hookway is ambivalent about *his* career. It's a relief.

"How can I get to that level where there's a little relaxation?" Fred asks.

"Debbie looks at me: *Why do we need this? Why do we need all this stuff?* I'll ask you the same thing. Why do you have to have everything in excess of here? I was in a cabin last week and on this little boat, and that was all I needed," Hookway says.

"So put the For Sale sign out," Fred says.

"You've got it all, Fred. You do. But do you need all that?"

"But what happens if I leave my job? That's what I think about."

"I don't need what I have. This place puts all the pressure on us. But we don't need all this shit," Hookway says, sipping the Manhattan.

"My brother's wife has never *not* worked."

"Think about it. He's never there. I would work too, if I were her. I'd volunteer at the goddamn hospital."

Fred reflects on that. He knows Kathy would be happier getting out of the house when he isn't there. That worries him. She doesn't like him the way she liked him when they were young. What if she feels trapped in her marriage? What if she feels she missed out on life because the two of them dated almost exclusively in high school and college? What if she wants to escape her marriage, the way Fred sometimes wants to escape his job? He jokes about how he'll lose her if she gets a taste of independence. He tells people Kathy loves him, but she doesn't *like* him. He tells people he can't blame her, either, considering how his career consumes their lives, and he laughs. But under the laughter, he's worried. He wants her to go back to work, yes, but he doesn't want her out of the house. That frightens him. He doesn't feel worthy enough of her love sometimes, and she doesn't seem to realize how hard he works for her sake and the sake of his children—so he has no plea when it looks as if she wants something more from a marriage. But he loves her, and he needs her. He wants her to need him, want him, lean on him. He just doesn't know how to treat her—he's the first to admit it.

"You've changed. You've changed, Hook. Debbie's the best thing that's happened to you."

"No doubt about it. But I had to change. Because you kill yourself in this job." Maybe they would end up like Hookway's father, dead at fifty-four.

"You get older."

"But I've had everything I ever wanted. There's things more important than being in the office every morning. My dad put that in perspective."

"I've been a bear with my wife," Fred says. "You don't know the half of it, what's gone on between the two of us over the years."

Hookway talks about how he dreams of leaving the district and getting into teaching. He wants a job that will allow him to devote himself to his wife and their life together. Fred tells Hookway how much time he spends with his own children in the evenings and on weekends.

"You know, my problem is, I don't know how to play politics. I have a very limited vocabulary. I do. I'm as average American as you will find."

He just keeps waiting for Frank to tell him what to do next. He doesn't maneuver to get what he wants. He doesn't think he should have to do that after twenty years with the kind of success he's had. Somebody ought to be telling him now where he'll be going. Nobody knows he exists. Where will he go? Where will they put him?

On their fifth drink, the conversation winds down. Fred says he wants to stay in Cleveland, for the sake of his children. They're happy in school, with their friends. All he wants is a job where he feels like he does the work and earns the money. He doesn't want to manage people. He doesn't want to be managed.

"My goal in life is, when I'm fifty, I'm out of here. I'll be teaching business at Kent State or something," Hookway says. "You are a great salesman, Fred. Why should that be a problem?"

"Exactly."

"A title isn't what it used to be. It used to mean something to be a salesman in this company. Now you're expected to move up."

So where does a talented salesman go when he's getting older than the college students who get hired every year with no work experience? How does he stay as a salesman and yet still feel he's advancing in his career within his company? How can he change and yet stay where he is?

He doesn't want to leave his neighborhood, let alone Cleveland. His children are attached to their schools and their friendships. Fred feels he has no right to fragment the lives of his family for the sake of his career. Yet how could he stay in Cleveland *and* make an advance in his career *and* do it at Xerox? He doesn't think it's possible.

All the sales managers sat around the conference table. They talked casually about job candidates they interviewed the previous week. Fred feigned interest as everyone debated whom among the college students they ought to hire. It was mildly diverting to watch the other sales managers talk it over.

"This young woman was into I-love-humanity. I brought her into reality," Pat Elizondo said, near the head of the table. "I told her for someone who likes people a lot, she was going into the most selfish line of work there is. Her eyes filled up."

At the far end of the table, very softly, Pacetta sang a recent R.E.M. hit: "Consider this, consider this, the hint of the century."

"I want Elizabeth," Fred said. "She could get sick because she wanted to do so well. I like that. Lisa wasn't tough enough." (She stuttered.)

"Statistics show that people who stutter—" Pat said.

"She's being Jane Pauley now, folks," Pacetta interjected.

"—they show that when a person stutters, you hang on their words."

"I feel sorry for her," Fred said, about the stuttering job candidate.

"You feel sorry for her?" Rob Onorato said, smiling, across the table from Fred. Rob was short, overweight, and pink-cheeked, and he had the smile of a carnivorous cherub. He had an appetite for experience, for the salty iron taste of conflict, and he knew he could box a customer into a deal better than anyone else on the staff. He knew how to make Fred laugh. "You t-t-t-t-took p-p-p-p-pity on her?"

"Was there a superstar? Or should we see other people?" Pacetta asked.

"I thought Chris was pretty fiery," Rob said.

"Fire and ice," Pacetta sang.

"She'd work till her fingernails fell off," Rob said. This woman would rub the fur off a cat. "You want some killer instincts coming out. You should have seen my team last week. They were animals. It was beautiful. It was like raw meat in front of the lions. It's Pavlov's dog. That's all it is."

Pacetta took the opportunity to read the group some of his cherished management principles from *Leadership Secrets of Attila the Hun.* "I see it, Frank," one of the other managers said. "I see what you're saying." Pacetta closed the book and leaped out of his seat. Eyes closed, as if preparing to speak in tongues, he walked to the video monitor and pressed the flat of his hand to the screen. "Put your hands on the television, my children. Do you see it?" Pacetta was trying to get a laugh, trying to wake everyone up. Fred shook his head and smiled with genuine pleasure. One of the other managers did her nails. They'd seen this act before.

Rob wished all of them could have seen his people. "They were vicious. They were frothing. It was beautiful."

"Guys," Pacetta said, "Let's try to focus on one conversation."

As everyone else in the conference room studied the overhead slides, Fred studied Pat Elizondo. He knew where she was headed. It was obvious. She would take over the district when Pacetta got promoted. A few years as district manager and then on to a vice presidency. No doubt she had her entire career mapped out in her head. She had her five-year plan, maybe even her ten-year plan. She probably knew where and when she wanted to retire. This couldn't have contrasted more sharply with Fred's own career. He didn't want to move up in management—he wanted to be in a position where he could sell, where he could close customers again and again, sharing the feeling of abundance on both sides of the deal, when both the customer and salesman believed they were winning. If he rose into a spot like Pacetta's, more of his time would be consumed in the office and less in front of a customer, where he longed to be.

Within a company admired for the opportunities it gave women and minorities, Elizondo was lucky to be both Mexican and female. This caused more than a few smiles and nods among the white male sales managers in the district. Yet Pat earned her status as heir to Pacetta. She had a sterling record. She was the opposite of Frank in almost every way. Rather than push, she pulled results out of people. Pacetta was lean and angular; Elizondo had softer contours, a dark complexion, and lustrous eyes. She kept her hair short, and her skin looked as smooth and young as a teenager's. She was one of the shortest people on the staff, and she was constantly trying to lose ten pounds, no matter how hard she worked out. She had a disarming grin, and she never looked tired.

Like Diane Burley's, Pat's drive to succeed grew from the experience of her childhood. She'd grown up in Gary, Indiana, where her father, a Mexican unable to speak fluent English, was forced to take a job at a steel mill, beneath his education as an engineer. Pat was a member of a large family. To get attention at night she fell out of the bunk bed. She had vivid memories of waiting in the afternoons at the front window, with her sisters, for her father to come home from the steel mill; her mother would put on jewelry and Pat would run upstairs and bring down her clarinet and play Benny Goodman tunes for him. As it was for Diane Burley, her career at Xerox was a way of surmounting the privations of her childhood, a way of giving herself a greater freedom of movement than she'd known in her youth.

There was nothing wrong with Pat. She loved sports as much as the men did. She knew more about college football than either of them. But it wasn't the same. She had a master's in business administration. She was book smart, political. She was a different breed, as tough as Frank, but more naturally compassionate, more attuned to the new way of doing things. She was married to John Kitowski, a rep on the printing systems team. He was lean and wiry and had short blond hair, gray eyes, and a narrow face with skin stretched tautly over his cheekbones. If she took over the district, he would have to find a job elsewhere within Xerox, because he wouldn't be allowed to work directly for his wife. They lived in a three-story manse east of the city in Cleveland Heights, a house old enough to have ashtrays grouted into the bathroom's wall. They were both in their mid-thirties and had ruled out the possibility of children, largely because of what parenthood might do to their careers.

If Fred stayed where he was, Elizondo would be presiding over his future, so he paid close attention to her progress. It discouraged him to consider how perfectly suited Pat was to rise in the company—a minority woman with no children. He liked Pat, but she didn't surprise him the way Pacetta did. She didn't have Pacetta's phony staged lunacy, his knack for doing the least expected, most disconcerting, least appropriate, and most laughable thing at the most awkward moment. Watching Pacetta in one of his manic moods made Fred feel vicariously free. Frank understood and feared defeat as much as any of them, and still he wasn't going to let anything upset him enough to put him at a loss for words. He wore, at all times, his game face, never divulging what he felt in front of the players. He could fake his way through anything.

Fred didn't envy Pat her impending promotion. He had no desire to move up as DM and follow Pacetta's act. Nonetheless, though he liked Pat and she liked him, he wasn't delighted at the prospect of working for her. He'd become addicted to Pacetta's goofy unpredictability. On Monday, Pacetta looks as if he's about to contort his entire body into the shape of a fist. On Tuesday, he's a child, playing pranks on a woman who arrives from corporate headquarters to give a talk on ethics, asking everybody to scoot their chairs an inch closer to the podium every time the woman turns her face away from her audience, until the woman gives a puzzled look at all these people crowded up beside the lectern. On Wednesday, Pacetta recites Elvis Costello or Grateful Dead lyrics as he strides through the bullpen, twirling his body to the left, counterclockwise, every time he turns to his right around a corner, performing this seemingly drug-induced variation of a square dance he invented only moments before, if only as a way of making his little journey to the men's room more interesting. By Friday, he's back to his injunctions about the need for exhaustion and pain and hard work.

Fred didn't care what mood his boss happened to be showing— each of Pacetta's multiple personalities energized Fred in a different way. He told himself he loved Pacetta because they both lived for the drama of team sports, but that just begged the question, because then he'd have to explain the magic of sports. What he really loved was the way Pacetta never eased up on him, never stopped pushing Fred to make his budget, and thus helped Fred put money into his own pocket. Psychologically, if he needed, he could lean back and let Pacetta do the pushing for a while. What would he do without that tailwind? How would he get off the ground?

Maybe Pat Elizondo could do all these things too, in a minor key, but Fred knew it wouldn't be the same. Her cheerfulness couldn't have contrasted more sharply with Frank's funny, brusque exhibitionism. Frank liked to speak in his own gangster argot. He didn't fire people. He pulled the trigger. When he admired an especially ruthless sales rep, he gave the man the title Assassin. When he closed a deal, it was a Hit. Pacetta's act relieved the job of its monotony, infusing it with a Hollywood mobster romance to airbrush the brutal, impersonal, and often boring reality of business. But Elizondo would never be able to borrow from Pacetta's lexicon of murder, along with everything it implied about selling. Pat Elizondo wanted to break records as a sales manager *and* be a completely blameless person. Fred wondered what would be so interesting about that? There was something startling, surprising, energizing, imaginative—something, well, emotionally *beautiful*—in Pacetta's routines. Fred felt about the aura of danger and cruelty in Pacetta's act the way Butch Cassidy seemed to feel about the dubious ethics of his own career in train robbery. It was a small price to pay for the beauty of doing it the way he did it.

Fred had no doubt Pat Elizondo would be taking over the district within a year. She would bring a different style to the district, and she might change the business in ways that would leave Fred feeling empty and cold. Fred realized the old guard and the new guard would be changing places, as it were, in the hallway outside his office, and it made him uneasy. To the left of Fred's office, in the corner, was Pacetta. In the office directly to his right was Elizondo. Fred wasn't sure what would happen to him when Elizondo moved from her office into Pacetta's, leapfrogging over Fred's.

Fred felt he was riding backward in a stranded raft as the river flexed into rapids ahead of him. Everybody expected big things to happen after this year. Frank would leave for a better job, Pat would move into Frank's spot, Bruno would get a promotion—but where would Fred go? Fred knew he could stay where he was. But after twenty years, wasn't it time to do something for himself? Yet where would he go within Xerox? He would never become part of what he believed was the power structure at Xerox, the god-father-bagman system of careerism, except in his dependent relationship with Pacetta. A godfather would pick his minions, one by one, making a list of candidates for indoctrination. Those chosen few, when their time came, would be called into service at the corporate level, in a subordinate staff position, for a year or two of bagman duty. Through this process a godfather would build a loyal base of servitude within the company, a stable of dutiful people suitable for future subordinate positions. For the bagman, this period of hazing at the Big House would open doors to better jobs in the field and maybe a vice presidency, or better. However, neither Fred nor Pacetta wanted to endure the subservience of it. But where were they to go, if not upward along the traditional path, with more and more management responsibilities—the kinds of duties Fred hated? Yet this system was working on a lower level, because Fred had placed his fate completely in Pacetta's hands. Pacetta was his godfather. He hoped Frank would pull through for him when the time came for a change. But what if Pacetta left before he set something up for Fred? Would Pacetta bother to look back over his shoulder at the people he left behind?

Fred and Kathy sit at their kitchen table. The light shines down onto the dishes; the surrounding kitchen is dim, the pattern of its pale green country wallpaper hardly visible. Children play outside in the dusk. The refrigerator clicks and hums, but the rest of the house grows silent and dark, except for the occasional muffled sounds of Christopher upstairs in his bedroom. The family collie, Laddie, dozes in the family room, hardly disturbed by the volume of voices in the breakfast alcove.

Fred tells Kathy he would leave Xerox if only she could make enough money to support the family through the transition. He tells her his brother feels exactly the same way. He implies the men in his family are pawns of a system that forces them to do work they've outgrown because their wives don't make enough to give them freedom of movement in a two-income world. She knows better. She knows he loves his work when it goes well. She knows he feels safer when she's at home. She knows he *does* want her to earn a salary, but not if it makes her independent to the point where it alters the emotional balance of their lives. Despite all his talk of escape, she knows he probably wouldn't leave Xerox even if she earned a good salary. His brother, John, who lives in Toledo and works for Xerox in Detroit, is still with the company, despite all of his moaning, and his wife works.

"And what's John's excuse, Fred?" Kathy asks, staring at the center of the table, where pink slices of sirloin cool in their own juice on the serving dish. "His wife works."

"I'm not him. I have objectives and goals. What does Johnny have to do with my goals?"

Fred stands and paces behind his chair. He doesn't notice, on the desk behind him, under the telephone, the Norman Vincent Peale tract on positive thinking Kathy's been studying. It is one small, silent gesture in favor of hope and cheerfulness, in contrast to the tenor of many conversations at this table.

"You two have done everything exactly the same, all your lives. And you've both complained constantly about everything."

"I have goals, Kathy—"

"But what I'm trying to understand is—"

"Johnny loves being a manager. I hate management. He wants to be a district manager whether he complains about it or not."

Kathy knows this talk leads nowhere. She knows something has triggered it at work, but Fred never has the presence of mind to nail what's really bothering him, never seems to pay enough attention to his own tensions to trace them back to their origins. His discontent tonight isn't creative—she can tell that much. Her husband's tone has the note of genuine anxiety. Yet she doesn't know why. He could have told her: *Pat Elizondo's going to take over the district. It's not that I deserve that job. I don't want it. I don't want to work for anybody in Cleveland except Frank. It bothers me to know Pat might change the way things are in the district. I don't like the uncertainty. It makes me want to leave. Can you understand that?* Instead, he works off his tensions by bickering with her, telling her how he feels about his life without explaining why he feels that way.

Fred, on his side of the table, can't understand why his wife doesn't just play along in this conversational game. Why can't she let him come back to earth when he gets home? Why can't she let him vent his frustrations and calm down, decompress and then have a rational conversation around, say, nine-thirty? Even after twenty years of marriage, she hasn't caught on to the way his mind works.

As it is, these disputes have an inexorable life of their own. Each remark triggers a predictable retort in a dialectic during which, eventually, Fred will contradict each of his own assertions with an equally passionate reversal. He wants Kathy to have an income, but only if she stays home for the children. He wants the freedom of full-commission sales, but he also wants a regular, guaranteed paycheck. He wants to cut loose and tell her how tough his life can be. When Fred gets home, he wants to face no customers. He wants things to be real. He doesn't need to sell himself to Kathy.

"But you're just the same. You love—"

"I do not love it. I love selling, whether I'm selling paper bags or—"

"If I told you I had a full-time job tomorrow—" Kathy says.

"Gone! Gone! I would have taken the Kidder, Peabody job in a minute."

"Okay. Mm-hmm," she says, quietly, wondering if Fred will ever say anything completely accurate. Often she refuses to respond because the constant urge to correct Fred's assertions exhausts her, and silence seems her only defense against Fred's embellishments. "I worked for six years, and all those years you were just as dissatisfied. And you didn't leave."

She doesn't believe he wants her to work. She knows he finds it threatening, and yet he urges her to do it. He harangues because she doesn't have an income, blaming her for his sense of being boxed into a job where he'll risk everything, financially, if he tries to make a move. But he doesn't leave because Xerox gives him a sense of security—not because he's trapped in his job. She has a theory: Fred pushes her to get a job because he knows the harder he pushes her to do something, the more reluctant she'll be to do it. He's trying to take control of her by pushing her to do the very thing that threatens him the most. It's reverse psychology. And she has to admit it works. The more he pushes, the less she wants to become independent, the more she pushes back against the force of Fred's bullying. It's like a constant game of poker in which the bluffing is so complicated that neither player can quite sort out the apparent motivations: *If she's acting as if she wants to work, then maybe she really doesn't want to work, because she knows that if she acts eager to do it, then I'll be afraid and encourage her to stay home. Yet maybe she realizes I'll push even harder on her so she'll feel reluctant to do it, and therefore I want her to stay home and that's what she really wants to do?* A conversation becomes a hall of mirrors when the mind games grow this involved.

Kathy once used this technique herself. She grew so tired of the way Fred was pushing her to get a job that she acted more eager than ever to get out of the house, whereupon Fred promptly quit pushing and told her she ought to stay on top of things at home, which was exactly what she wanted to do at that moment. She wanted to resume her career at her own pace, not his. It showed her how ambivalent Fred felt about her emerging independence. Yes, he wanted the added income. No, he didn't want her to become completely autonomous and free.

She tries to keep their conversations from becoming a game, a struggle for control. She tries to be rational. She knows Fred's discontent is as essential to his life as certain minerals are to his blood. He thrives by indulging in it. It drives him upward. Yet when he comes home, he's on a binge. He believes the more he gripes, the better he'll do. Kathy doesn't welcome the odd sort of honesty this represents. She'd rather have him wear the face he wore when they were dating—the puppy-dog looks, the love letters, the naturally ingratiating manner he saves for his customers now.

The two of them have come far from the nights in high school when they laughed together, when Fred looked upon Kathy as a beacon—like the lights a sailor aligns in his sights to guide him into port. She was an embodiment of his hopes, and she responded with sympathy. He wants her sympathy and she wants to be appreciated—all they want from each other is the *yes* they gave each other freely in their teens.

Instead, when he comes home he tests the water, hoping for sympathy and friendship and support: Rough day today. We'll never make it this month. He wants her to draw him out, ask for explanations, probe his feelings, tell him how good he is and how many years he's succeeded. He wants her to tell him he can do it because she believes in him. Instead, she backs off. She doesn't know how many times she can keep hearing this kind of doomsday rhetoric when Fred comes home—even though she knows it's his way of keeping himself sharp, making himself expect the worst so he'll do his best. She doesn't fully realize at those times, when he's feeling genuinely discouraged, that he really wants her sympathy. But when is he genuinely discouraged, and when is he motivating himself? Fred himself seems to have lost sight of the difference. When, for that matter, will *she* get sympathy and support? She gets discouraged too. Why does she need to be the one who keeps doling it out, day after day, when she has her rough days too, when sometimes she needs support and encouragement just as much as he does? When will it be her turn to predict doom and have Fred there to coach her back into the game? She wants to be appreciated too. *Rough day today. We'll never make it this month.* This isn't the sort of appreciation he once showed her.

Suddenly Fred thrashes the air, his palms open, his fingers splayed, the gestures of a man unjustly accused.

"It has nothing to do with dissatisfaction. You're so stupid, Kathy. Can't you see?"

"What does it have to do with, then?" she asks, still gazing at the sirloin. Her eyes are motionless, unresponsive. It's as if she were looking for a visual anchor, something to make the world hold still.

"I've reached a level of earning power," he says. "I know what

I want now. I know what I can do. It has nothing to do with complaining. Those were just words."

"But that's what I'm getting at. There are so many *just words*."

"I've realized what I can do now. I know what I want. I want independence."

"Now, if you want me to have a full-time job, it doesn't matter, does it? I could be a cashier. For me to get back into—"

"A cashier! Why would you want to be a—"

"That's exactly my point. You wouldn't care, as long as I brought in enough money. For me to get back into my teaching career takes time and effort," she says.

"What if—"

"But—"

"Kathy, I'm in the middle of a sentence. What if you help me become successful? You wouldn't have to work, would you?" he says.

"Can I respond now?" she asks.

"Yes."

"Believe it or not, that was just what I've been thinking. But it takes time to get back into teaching. I've put my name in for substituting—"

"Have they called you?" Fred snaps.

"No."

"Have you called *them*? Have you bugged them?" he says, in the manner he uses when he hammers his reps. Have you called them, Nancy? Have you gotten back to him, Bruno? Have you taken it to another level, Kathy? Fred enters his professional domain. There's no way to distinguish between his job and his personal life, the soldiers and the civilians, the warriors and the wives. He's most fully himself during these moments. His tone, his stance behind the kitchen chair, his choice of words and the emphasis he puts on them—were they seated at the district office, no one would guess

Kathy was his wife rather than one of his workers. She certainly couldn't have been mistaken for one of his customers.

"Yes, I've called them," she says.

"Be a squeaky wheel, Kathy. I'll bet you I could get you an interview."

"Okay. Show me. Go ahead."

"They'll never forget my name. I guarantee it."

"Okay, Fred. Well, do it, then."

"If I was in your shoes, I'd have no problem calling them. I'd call them tomor—"

"Then do it!"

Suddenly Fred softens. He's accomplished his mission. He's forced Kathy to admit how much she might need him, to respond in a way that only vaguely resembled the way she responded when they were young.

"No. It wouldn't be right. I shouldn't be the one to call them," he says.

At that moment, Christopher walks into the family room. With the two rooms completely open to each other, the boy has walked directly into the conversation. He has curly hair, his father's dark complexion, and the still-rounded cheeks of a youth on the threshold of his teens, and he's begun picking up some of his father's mannerisms—some of Fred's facial expressions and footwork during an argument, turning on his heel and flailing his arms. Christopher wants to take his Nintendo deck to his room, and Fred nods. But Kathy objects. It violates one of her rules. Fred always wants every conflict resolved immediately, unless he is the author of it. Fred wants Chris out of the room, and he's willing to violate Kathy's authority to speed his son's exit. Kathy stands firm on her rules. So Chris stalks away, inheriting their anger, leaving the two of them with their silence and cold sirloin. They lose the thread.

"The only way I'll be happy is when I'm dead," Fred says,

grinning, trying to put everything into perspective. It's one of his favorite observations, and it amuses him whenever he says it. Now they start putting each other on. They are laughing, together, at Fred's act. She's amused. This is the way she likes it, the way she wants it to be again—intimate and ironic. She reminds him how he kept predicting his death at her sister's place. He spent the whole weekend walking around her house wheezing and whining about how he was going to die. He was in good shape. He could run for miles. But he was always on the verge of death. Why?

Usually, as the year gets closer and closer to the ultimate deadline, Fred becomes more and more obsessed with his health and his body. In previous years he became fascinated with the state of his organs, his skin, his nerves. One year he came to work for a Saturday sales meeting after staying out late drinking with his buddies. Halfway through the meeting he collapsed. He started to sweat. Pain shot up his arms. Pacetta and the others rushed him to the hospital. The doctor suggested he'd had a panic attack. There was nothing wrong with him, except maybe the overtime he was putting in on his liver. Maybe he should stay in the hospital overnight, just to recover from his hangover. Hangover! Was that all it was! The whole group had a good laugh, until Fred told them he needed to go home. He had a dinner planned with his wife. Pacetta told him to wait. He would call Kathy—he wanted to shock her. When she answered the phone, he told her Fred was hospitalized. She didn't believe it. She knew these people. It was a practical joke. He gave her the hospital's phone number and told her to call back, just to verify the story. Fine. He was in the hospital. So what? She knew Fred was out drinking the night before, and she was familiar enough with the symptoms of his hangovers. When he got on the line, she asked if he was going to be home for dinner. One last meal. How did that sound? Now, tonight, she is using the same dubious tone with him.

"I'm getting a headache. I really am. I'm getting a headache."

"That's because it's my turn to talk," she says.

Fred misses the wit, or ignores it, tactically. Kathy's smiling now, amused at her own remark, looking up at last from the shining table with the cold sirloin, the crumpled napkins. He suggests maybe he should take a break. Go to Toledo to visit his brother and their friends, talk about what they ought to do with their lives. Kathy remembers those wild years. She knows what sort of trouble Fred can get himself into in Toledo. One night, coming home from a party with the other salesmen, Fred ended up in jail after being stopped for driving under the influence. Officer: *Would you please put your right foot in front of your left?* Fred: *Sir! Yes, sir!* Officer: *Would you please count from one to ten?* Fred: *Sir! Yes, sir!* Officer: *Would you please put your right index finger to the tip of your nose.* Fred: *Sir! Yes, sir!* Officer: *Just do it, goddammit.* At the lockup, Fred was allowed the traditional phone call. *I have rights! I want the keys to my car. I want my phone call!* He called his brother, John, but it was no use. He reported back to his uniformed custodian: *My brother's drunk too.* He couldn't bring himself to call Kathy. An officer had to drive Fred home.

She asks him where he'll go in Toledo, once he gets there.

"I don't do anything on these trips, Kathy. Nothing. I hate trips. I'd rather be home."

"I beg to differ. On your Vegas trip, without spouses, there was a certain sum of money pissed away while I was shopping at T. J. Maxx," she says. He moaned about the trips until he went on them. He loved it once he got there. It was always the same. He moaned and moaned and then he loved Hawaii. And Florida. That time in Nevada.

"Once in my lifetime I gamble, and you drill me about it."

"I will always drill you," she says.

"And if you do, you will always get flack back. I didn't do anything."

"There were fifteen years in Toledo when you can't tell me you didn't do anything," she says.

"One short period. That's all."

Fred picks up the telephone to check his voice mail, and Kathy clears the table. As always, the conversation ends in stalemate. Because of his absolute adaptability, Fred's reps have learned to be skeptical and relatively calm in the face of Fred's mercurial words and gestures. But Kathy hasn't. One night Fred might threaten to leave Xerox, and then the next night he might say he loved his work more than he loved his life—and both nights he would be telling the truth. He's measuring aloud the heights and depths of his emotional seas, one night underwater and the next riding crests so high he can see the earth's curve, yet Kathy hears only equivocation and paradox in his description of the view. The voyage hardly seems worth the trouble if it has to be this way, day after day. After twenty years, she feels like a stowaway.

Fred wasn't alone. A lot of people at Xerox dreamed of escape. One young woman planned to make enough money to leave sales in her thirties and get a SoHo loft to begin her career as an artist. Another was getting a law degree on the side. Bruno dreamed of going to Italy. Pat Elizondo wanted to become a social worker. Diane Burley wanted to marry her six-figure man and retire. The escape plan was an emergency parachute, rarely used, but always available, just in case. Some actually left. And yet even some of *those* returned. One rep decided to quit the day he came home, picked up his dog, and, in a rage, tossed the dog—legs flailing—all the way across his backyard, over the fence, and into his neighbor's yard. The dog survived, but the rep's career didn't. He decided to sell cemetery plots. He hoped it would cheer him up. Now he was back working for Xerox again—one of the few allowed to return after jilting the company.

Kathy was sure Fred could find a new job somewhere, inside or outside Xerox. Xerox salesmen were reputed to be the best in the business. He could get a job anywhere. So why worry? Everywhere he went, he saw possibilities. He met insurance salesmen at parties. He saw articles about franchise fairs where he could learn about starting his own business. Even when he went to the Parmatown mall to get new heels on his shoes, he took a look at the shop and wondered if it was the sort of thing he could buy and run. No matter what he decided to do with his life, he would be selling something—that talent would always offer him a way out.

# QUALITY

*1.*

OVER THE YEARS, Fred had become a sort of cryptographer. He knew how to decode the meaning of a glance, a cough, an uneaten martini olive. He recognized the unconsciously eloquent quality of a person's posture, his collars or shoeshine or credit line. He joined one of his reps on a cold call and predicted what month he would close the deal. He faced a customer and within minutes guessed far more about this person than anyone put into words. A salesman who believed he understood how to control the human heart quickly began to lean on his ability to *read* people, as if human beings were V-8 engines built of plastic so that the pumping of valves and push rods and pistons could be seen clearly and understood by someone who had a mechanic's intimacy with the way a flywheel usually spins.

A conversation between two reps who thought they knew how

to read people might go something like this: So, whataya think about this guy, this little low-life purchasing manager with that face like an anvil? *No way. Drop a dollar on the ground, and he wouldn't pick it up. He wouldn't bend over for anybody. He'd know we're smoking him.* How about this woman with about twenty rings on one finger? *Three weeks, maybe four, and we'll get a trial in her print shop, no question.* That corporate VP with the Gauguin necktie? *Never in a million years. We'll take a bullet on that deal. Didn't you see the way he talked the ear off that woman and made us just sit there in the lobby? See the way he crossed his arms?*

A man confessed to things in the way he cleared his throat, riffled a contract, or postponed his last cigarette. When he sat in front of another human being, Fred was in his glory. A good salesman liked to do what Henry James said a good novelist does—puzzle into awareness an entire world of circumstance and character and history from a single glance through a doorway, a queasy handshake, an unintended word. He wasn't psychic. He was minutely observant.

This ability to wield such insight, to ride forward on the strength of intelligent conjectures about other human beings, went hand in hand with the emotional force of an old-school sale. Fred felt in control when he got out into the field with his reps and saw customers. He made people laugh, touched them, navigated the map of their faces and uncovered a path toward the sort of reaction he wanted to get. He jotted a few notes to himself in his spiral notebook, a few words about everyone he met. When he pulled it out later—this battered green loose-leaf composition book he bought at the drugstore for a buck or two—his future unfolded in a tangible way and he felt he could touch what he needed to do next, what his *reps* needed to do next. He loved to clear a trail through the world this way, making his way from one person to another, one on one, revealing to himself new horizons in the force of these provisional friendships. He was making progress. He was getting people to *like* him.

In this way, over the years, Fred developed an intuition, a gut reading, on how things would go for him in any given year. When he gazed into the pages of his notebook, he knew what to expect from his year and his life, because he knew how to read the people he met at dozens of companies around Cleveland. There was something deeply comforting in breaking the code of the human face, using these moves he understood, the familiar current of friendliness and pressure, the baiting and waiting, the whole dancing courtship of a seller's affection for his buyer until the two of them approached the altar and consummated that dance with betrayal or betrothal, or a delicate balance of both. It was all psychological, all emotional, all a way of taking control.


Fred knew how to read Nick Callahan. The man needed a friend. And Fred was going to be there for him. Fred knew how to be a friend. It came naturally to him. He liked customers who wanted to become close with a salesman, people for whom the benefits of the friendship might outweigh the importance of the deal itself. Nick Callahan was one of these people, though he acted as if just the opposite were the case.

Fred enjoyed dealing with Callahan. He was their buyer at the phone company. They liked each other, and Callahan was a worthy sparring partner. Like all close friends, they could insult each other for hours and take no offense. Fred felt bad for Callahan because he'd heard he was on his way out at Bedford Telecommunications. Nick looked as if he was in his early fifties. It was a disheartening age for early retirement. Too much of the man's professional life lay ahead of him. No matter how comfortable he'd be, Callahan would feel cheated of his prime. But Fred wasn't sure he believed the stories Bruno told about Callahan's impending exile—it might be a mind game Nick was playing, a ploy to get a sympathy deal before year's end.

When they got to Callahan's windowless office in the Bedford building downtown, Callahan was wearing a wrinkled white shirt and a creased paisley tie, and his hair looked grayer to Fred than it had in the past. Callahan wasn't big. He stayed slim, and he seemed hardened—he had the bearing of an ex-marine. Years ago he had lived in Manhattan, where he gained seventy pounds and lost his wife, who stayed in Cleveland. When he returned from punching his career ticket in New York, he simply quit eating. He ate nothing for weeks, and dropped the extra weight as fast as Mahatma Gandhi himself. He was still single. He was having fun, if you believed what he said about himself. Fred wasn't sure, though he'd seen Callahan's framed photograph of an intriguing woman in a pink dress who looked as if she had vivid memories of her prom.

"Point-blank, we are not going to do the low-volume machines all at one time," Callahan said to Bruno.

Would he buy any of the equipment they proposed?

"I'll do the ones it's cost-effective to do. I got beat up Monday morning because I'm not giving them savings. They're saying get rid of copiers."

Fred knew Callahan had ordered, not long ago, some Konica machines, and he wanted to make Callahan feel guilty. Management might have been telling Callahan to save money, but apparently he had permission to keep handing out money to Xerox competitors.

"Tell me something good," Fred said, reaching to curl his fist around an imaginary dagger sticking out of his back. "I've got a knife back here with those Konicas you bought."

"Xerox has screwed us for years. You get me into these big

deals—one and a half years later they come out with a program that knocked down rent so much that I lost two hundred thousand. I'm afraid I'll get screwed with just one vendor."

"We're coming back. We're winning bids now," Fred said.

"If I've got six copiers and all quality is equal, I'll take the lowest price," he said. In other words, the Konicas didn't cost as much.

"As long as my end user is happy, if it's reliable, it's less money, and you get the service, I agree."

"I'm not ever giving you all the business in your product," Callahan said.

"What if we can come back with a better package?" Fred asked.

"My boss threatened me this week. Tomorrow I'm deciding whether I'm staying or leaving this company," Callahan said.

Fred would believe that story after it happened. Fred tried to read Callahan's face. He didn't seem to be bluffing, but it was hard to tell. Maybe he should feel sorry for the man, maybe not. Better to wait until the ax fell and the head rolled. Fred wasn't thinking about the deal. He was thinking about Nick. That was the way he sold—by paying attention to the buyer's blood pressure and pulse. Bruno ignored Callahan's words and started to describe his proposal.

"I know what you want," Callahan said. "You want it before the end of the year."

"He's got a baby coming. He's going to know what life's all about," Fred said.

"We'd like to deliver a number of the machines by the end of the month," Bruno said.

Callahan ignored this overture. He didn't like to be pushed.

"And then a new machine will come out next year at a lower cost," Callahan said. "I know how it works."

"We really don't know. We can't predict what the company will do in a year," Fred said.

"Yeah, well, just give me another jar of Vaseline," Callahan said. He once controlled thirty-one thousand copying machines for AT&T. He knew the score. He knew what all these friendly overtures across a desk meant. And they knew he knew it was an act.

"I didn't work my ass off for nothing, Nick. I want the business," Bruno said. "We're going to give you a good deal."

That jar of Vaseline—it was a tough remark, but Fred saw the color in Nick's face after he said it. The man blushed at his own obscenity. There was a deeper layer of decency in Callahan you couldn't miss. How could Fred not like him—*really* like him, not just in a provisional and useful way. The poor bastard, holding onto his power, his sway, even as he watched himself losing his job. The jar of Vaseline was Nick's way of saying *Don't be salesmen. Don't bother. Because I know what you're doing. Hey, guys, go ahead and give me the shaft. I can take it. But don't pretend to be doing something else. You've been asking me to bend over for years now. What's one more year? Just don't act like I've got to look the other way while it's happening.* That was the tone Fred admired in a customer—the tone of a man who understood reality and didn't put on airs. Callahan was a guy who would join you for drinks after work at the Crazy Horse Saloon, and with topless dancers contorting themselves on the runway, he would talk about how tough it was to be a white male over forty in business, unless you were high enough up in the company to set the rules. Fred could commiserate with Nick. He could share a fraternal drink with him. Nick had no pretense, no act—except that he acted tougher than he was and didn't show how much he was hurting, except maybe in the telltale hue of his face. In his own way, Fred too was incapable of hiding his emotions from anyone. Kathy told Fred he was an open book.

Nick Callahan was a man who didn't feel terribly wanted. Fred recognized this. He knew how to leverage Callahan's insecurity to make a sale. He would be a tough sell on the outside, but Fred understood Callahan's sorrow, and he knew how to answer it. He could make Nick Callahan feel like a significant human being, if only for one last time in the man's professional life—he could give the man a sense of power. Fred had a hunch that Callahan might give them a hard time but he would also give them some business. If this was indeed his final year with Bedford. Secretly, he'd be looking for companionship, a little solace, a little attention—something to salve the burn of exile. Secretly, he might find himself responding, childlike, to any attention that made him feel a little more important, despite himself and all his worldly cynicism. That, too, was an act. No one could stay in control all the time. No one was completely immune to affection, calculated or otherwise. Fred could entertain Nick Callahan and give him the warmth, the attention, he needed. He knew this sale wouldn't depend on numbers or studies or the influence of anyone flying in from Rochester to lunch with some lofty executive. This sale would get personal.

2.

IT WASN'T SUPPOSED to work this way now. The rules of the game were changing. Fred wasn't supposed to force things to happen. It wasn't the progressive way to do business. The hype, the circus, the contests, the feverish competition, the parties, the tricks to get orders on the books, the artificial friendships with customers—all this emotional pressure from above, these incentives and maneuvers and games, were considered old-school selling. He was supposed to let his reps win or lose on their own. Business was supposed to work from the bottom up now, not from the top down.

You could imagine some corporate wheel in Connecticut, with a lockjaw slant on the vowels, making pronouncements about the business: *We've improved the quality of our operation. We empower our people. Each of our employees runs his own business. He or she figures out whom he or she needs to satisfy. He or she identifies what he or she needs to produce. And he or she runs his or her own little company—whether this individual is on the assembly line, out in the field, or up in the corporate tower. This is the quality way to do business. This is what we've learned from Japan.*

Sounds wonderful to Fred. He isn't sure his reps will know how to handle it, but he often fantasizes about a state of total *empowerment* for himself. He has a firm grasp on the basic amenities, although he doesn't have all the details worked out yet. Probably it would involve an office on a golf course somewhere. He could come in around nine, work half a day, and then determine when exactly to quit making phone calls—say, about three or three-thirty—and when exactly to tee off. But then where would the energy come from? What would keep him awake during the day? On occasion, he needs to see young people chugging beer in the parking lot. He needs to walk into his boss's office in the morning and emerge with grave concerns about the state of his own haircut. He needs to feel the energizing influence of Pacetta's swift kick. He needs to see his own smile, photographed and framed and mounted on the wall in honor of his election as sales manager of the month. He needs to hear people singing "White Rabbit" and trying to lip-synch the words they can't remember. He needs to make his boss happy by getting his machines installed before time runs out.

He can let his people go. Give them all the slack they want. He doesn't, after all, need to make trip this year, doesn't need to spend a weekend in Palm Springs. But would he feel like a good manager? Would he be making quite as much of that unique product he knows how to make, the final and irreversible *yes?*

Now's the perfect time to leave people alone. He can skate through summer and then scramble when the leaves and snow begin to fall. He can shuffle quietly through the bullpen with the best of intentions, minding his own business. He can sit in his office, and check to-do items off his Day Timer. He can try to alter the world by sitting still, like Buddha, radiating an aura of puissance and compassion through the upholstered partitions. He can manage by osmosis. He can let his little kingdom simply follow its own natural inclinations. Also, he can sign up for a frontal lobotomy. Many options in life are open to him. Not all of them strike him as the best way to proceed.

He *was* letting go of his reps, like it or not. On his own team, Larry Tyler knew how to elude Fred. With Larry, Fred was forced to be a progressive manager, not an old-school salesman. Though Fred hadn't had trouble riding with Larry to Gladstone, now Fred had a much harder time finding the Mystery Man. Larry kept himself busy, staying out of the office, making it hard for Fred to keep track of him. He wanted to close his own deals, and Fred had no choice but to allow him this privilege. If nothing else, with Larry, Fred had the satisfaction of knowing he was managing at least one of his reps—albeit unwillingly—the way it was supposed to be done. He left Larry alone, despite himself, and gave Larry enough rope to either hog-tie his customers or hang himself. Not until the end of the year would Fred know how Larry was putting the rope to use.

Larry liked to do things almost in spite of people who had authority over him. His father had always found fault with Larry's life. As a salesman for Simplex, his father hated IBM, his company's biggest competitor. So, with a degree from Notre Dame, as an act of defiance against his father, Larry hired on at IBM. Later, when his father entered the hospital for major surgery, Larry organized a blood drive among his co-workers at Big Blue. Unknown to his father, Larry kept his father alive using IBM blood, as it were—and it didn't strike him as funny until it was all over and he realized what he'd done. He'd turned his father into a Blueblood, of sorts. Sons rebel against fathers in strange ways, sometimes even in their acts of compassion.

Larry had known failure on a much larger scale than almost anyone else in the district. In his twenties, he earned a small fortune selling IBM computers. With his nest egg in the bank, he left and bought a recreational vehicle dealership, just as the Middle East oil crisis began. As gasoline prices skyrocketed, Larry's business crumbled. He lost everything he'd earned. Working his way slowly back to solvency, he took a series of selling jobs, which led him eventually to Xerox. After that experience, no prospect of failure at Xerox could unnerve him. No matter how badly he failed as a copier salesman, it would never approach the personal financial debacle he had suffered, the worst a businessman could experience. He emerged from it a stronger man—no one else could intimidate him, certainly not the younger people, these kids who didn't know the meaning of failure, who moved quickly into management at Xerox and had no inkling how a person's life could fall apart.

Pacetta was suspicious of Larry because he sensed Larry's independence—he was a rep who didn't crave Pacetta's sort of motivation. When Larry joined Fred's team, Pacetta warned him: He'll drag you down, Fred. When Larry attended Pacetta's karaoke parties and award-giving ceremonies, he looked around at the faces of the younger reps and he saw the exploitation in what

Pacetta was doing—taking these young people in their early twenties and addicting them to the short-term win, giving them a sense of drama they might never see again in their working lives. Larry's impression of the whole scene was dubious: Pacetta would use these people and then move on to his next assignment while the rest of them would be left behind with some photographs and some numbers indicating cash flow in their checking accounts and a yawning feeling of vacancy. He could imagine them, after Pacetta left and they went on to other jobs, haunted by memories of the drunken, collegiate pulse of Pacetta's celebrations. Their working lives might never be quite this much fun, ever again.

Larry didn't need that intensity. He enjoyed his work, and he hated supervision. He knew how to control his accounts, when to push buttons, which customers to fly to Toronto for a night on the town, and how much to expect from himself at the end of every year. He didn't need Pacetta, or Fred, to tell him what to achieve or how to do it. Pacetta could whip them all he wanted with this worn, old-school rhetoric in honor of the thirty-day chase. He told them patience was for people without budgets. But patience was the way of the future, when the sales cycle might be two years rather than two months.

Larry had a deal he expected to crown his year—a proposal to sell a DocuTech at Yeager Adhesives. DocuTech was the largest duplicator in the Xerox line, a digital device used as a traditional duplicator and also as a printer linked to a network of personal computers. Yeager was a classic, complicated Big Hit. The deal involved not only Larry but people from the printing systems team.

He knew how it would go down. He visualized fearful scenes in conference rooms, scenes in which Yeager people shrank from the information he presented to them about their own lack of efficiency—he had numbers, dates, and names. Presenting that information would be one of the peak experiences of his year. He could hardly wait to see the look on certain faces during those crucial meetings. He reduced the whole thing in his mind to those few calls giving him the psychological power he needed to pull it off. He would control the power of those meetings. It was a privilege rarely granted to a salesman, who was often little more than a supplicant.

Yeager itself was an obscure company. Larry had a deadpan way of describing the company. Yeager used pig by-products to make caulking, roofing materials, and sealants. They imported top-quality pig bristles from England. They shaved the pigs over there, which was good. Shaving was good. They didn't dip them in acid, as was done in the States. One could delve further into the product line, but he found that level of detail was usually sufficient. This is at least one example of what a modern postindustrial job could become: selling nondescript office equipment to a company that fashioned porcine by-products into useful gooey substances. Was it any wonder people were susceptible to a manager who could turn the job into a rock-and-roll and sports fantasy?

Larry's key strategy with Yeager was to devote several months to showering attention on certain people. Finally, with an assist from Pacetta—who became friends with Yeager's chief financial officer—these people released to him records of how much money the company spent on the printing of booklets, phone directories, newsletters, and manuals when these jobs went to outside printers. That printout of numbers felt like a loaded gun under Larry's arm. It would be his greatest argument for DocuTech, and his greatest power over the careers of at least a dozen people at Yeager. On those printing jobs, DocuTech could save the company hundreds of thousands of dollars.

Upstairs at Yeager he found Lamont Cox in a playful mood. Cox was a black man, muscular, with a trimmed mustache and a little thatch of beard under his lower lip, enough hair to fill a thimble. He was a heavy smoker, which gave his voice a resonance that rumbled across many square feet of tile and carpet. Larry sat in the small office, showing Cox his numbers.

Whenever they met, Cox tried to intimidate Larry into telling the truth: *I know when I'm being conned. I cut a rep off at the knees when that happens. You guys remind me of the Marine Corps. You consider yourselves invincible. But when you come in the door, you're in the real world. If you tell me the sky is blue, and I look through my window and the sky is orange, then you're in deep shit.*

It didn't mean a thing. Behind all the bluster, Cox rarely questioned Larry's numbers. Larry knew where each of Yeager's sixty-five copiers was located. He could envision the floor plan of the building, knew the operator's name and the copy volume for each machine. Over the years, by diverting a lot of work from those machines, in addition to the outside printing jobs, DocuTech could save Yeager millions. The operators of these machines, as well as their managers, would all feel threatened because they would answer to Lamont Cox. He would be in charge of the DocuTech, increasing his own influence at the expense of nearly a dozen other people. They would resent his ascendency.

Larry knew he had the power to threaten jobs. When you taught a customer how to work more productively with a new copier or printing system, you often put people out of work. Lamont knew it, and Larry knew it, and so did all the people whose purchase orders were listed on the printout in Larry's hands. Yeager was an exception. With DocuTech, Cox didn't expect to put anyone out of work, but he wasn't about to admit it yet. He wanted the fear to last.

Before Larry left Yeager, he got Cox to commit to a meeting of all the worried users. Larry expected it to be a key meeting. Everyone higher than Cox wanted the new duplicator. Now they had to bring the users on board—the people who could sabotage the deal by fudging numbers and creating mechanical problems. Though it didn't happen often, it was always a possibility.

On the morning he drove to Yeager for his crucial meeting, Tyler carried a sheaf of overhead slides, which, like a selection of indiscreet photographs, he would pull slowly out of concealment and lay quietly on the table before his opponents—watching them as they slumped into their chairs. He felt the joy a private detective feels as he returns to his client with the incriminating black-and-whites shot through a motel room window. Today he would appear to be what Frank Pacetta wanted from his reps: He would play the role of Assassin. Often, it was enough to produce the pistol and lay it silently on the table. No one had to fire anything, or anyone. It was enough to flourish the means. This was a quality deal, yet it offered him all the manipulative power of an old-school sale.

The meeting was billed as a roundtable discussion, which sounded very genteel, very dry. Yet Larry needed to convince this group that a DocuTech would be in their best interest. In other words, Larry planned to muscle them. Using quality procedures, he would force this deal to happen. These people could kill the installation. Each of them could create roadblocks, complaining about little problems with the new system, creating a lot of static. They might try to divert work away from the new system to print shops on the outside. They believed neither Lamont nor Larry could track their printing jobs. If this was true, then these people *could* with impunity divert work to the outside, away from the new system—but nothing was further from the truth. Larry needed to show them that he and Lamont Cox knew what these people did in their jobs. He wanted them to feel slightly violated. He wanted them to fret about staying employed. Most of all, he wanted them to realize they couldn't write a purchase order for an outside printing job without a record of it getting back to the people who would be deciding to implement DocuTech—without it getting back to *him*.

When Larry arrived at the conference room, Lamont Cox sat at the far end of the long dark table and beamed: "Larry!" His deep, resonant voice carried his ego into the hallway and adjacent rooms. His flannel suit had the sheen of wool fabric fresh from the dry cleaner's, and his dark skin shone under the lights. This was an important day for him, and he was Larry's wholehearted partner. Almost a dozen people filed into the room, silent, sullen, with the aggrieved reserve of schoolchildren filing into detention hall. No one would lose his job today, but the group didn't know this yet. They *did* know the new configuration, with a centralized printing facility, would make them responsible to Lamont Cox, and today they would get their noses rubbed in it. It galled them. They were angry.

Cox introduced Larry, who talked briefly about how much money the new system would save Yeager. He recommended they funnel all printing jobs to one centralized location—a print center. There was a wave of snickering around the table. Larry paused and glanced slowly around the room. He wanted to prolong this moment, before he produced his weapon. Finally, he lifted the transparency and placed it under the glass lens. As people began to recognize the numbers he projected onto the screen, the insolence drained from their faces. It was as if Larry had started to play a videotape, a little time-motion study, of their private work habits, as recorded on hidden cameras. The jobs weren't identified by user, but the transparencies implied Larry and Lamont knew exactly who sent which jobs out, where they were sent, and how much they cost.

He told them he'd gone through their accounts payable and looked at dollars spent on vendors. He told them he had an itemized list of expenses to vendors, describing printing jobs and who was involved in each of them. He expected to achieve much lower costs for outside printing, once the new Xerox system was installed. Larry's proposal showed which jobs would go to which printing vendor in detail.

Each of his listeners had the look of someone being frisked. His audience wondered how much *more* Larry might know about their daily jobs. He had delivered the first punch. That gave an advantage in every competition, from chess to fistfighting to nuclear war. Sales was no exception. After a few minutes, still stunned, they recovered some composure. One timid question rose from the group: Could he identify the users who sent out each of those jobs?

Yes, he could. He told them their top management had gone through the lists. These executives were surprised, unpleasantly, by some of the numbers. With that one sentence, Larry dominated the room. He elevated his job to the level of business management itself—he identified himself with the company's top executives. He wasn't selling these people. He was managing them. He was leading them around by the nose. No longer was he knocking on someone's door, begging for an order. Now he put himself into a position to open or close doors on *them*. The product, the sale, became entirely secondary. He had the initiative. He ruled, using nothing but the force of facts—he had power because he was revealing, not concealing, the truth about the value of this deal, which rested on a new understanding of the way these people needed to do their jobs.

He told them top management checked and verified the numbers. Was he proposing they do all their printing work inside now, on the DocuTech? No. They would have overflow, certainly. They couldn't do all their work inside. They still needed to send some work to outside shops at times. He told them the report wasn't meant to be an indictment, saving that tension-breaking line until now. It was time to start granting mercy. This was selling: Create tension, prolong it, play with it, savor it, and then relieve it. Larry mounted the next transparency. It listed all the people involved in document creation and publishing. Below it were Larry's recommendations on how many people should be used and where, in all different functions. Where seven people worked now, eleven would be needed eventually. They would hire, not fire, with this new machine.

Smiles blossomed around the table. Everyone was safe, for the moment. Yeager would hire people—it was just the opposite of what these workers feared. Gradually the character of the meeting shifted. It became almost a training session. There was nothing these people could do to stop this deal. They just needed to decide whether they would be part of the new operation—and it was clear that if they tried to divert unnecessary work to outside printers, management would prevent it. This meeting served as a warning.

Larry stood before a hostile crowd and used nothing but the truth to bend the will of a dozen people. There was nothing demeaning about it, nothing tricky. He used fact, not opinion, to move them. He projected incontrovertible numbers—Yeager itself had given him the numbers—and the crowd quietly held its breath. He forced them to acknowledge and accept the arithmetic. He was showing them how to do their own business more productively. He had called the meeting, making them feel he needed their permission to proceed, and yet by the end of the meeting he had showed them how, in a way, they needed *his* permission to be part of their own future at the company. He'd given himself power by doing his homework. He didn't need recognition meetings. He didn't need cash out of somebody else's pocket. He didn't need to see his photograph on a wall somewhere. He knew what he'd accomplished. Yeager was in the bag. The deal was done. He was Somebody.

3.

IN MANY WAYS, Larry Tyler's work followed the Leadership Through Quality model—a Total Quality Management program at Xerox, adapted from Japanese principles, in which customer satisfaction, not short-term profit, was ostensibly the supreme business goal. Almost every American corporation above a certain size is implementing some form of TQM program based on Japanese principles. The idea is simply a variation on the Golden Rule: Treat your customer as you would treat yourself. Give your customer exactly what your customer needs to improve his business or his life. Don't just sell a product, *satisfy a customer.*

In a sales environment, your mission is to genuinely care about the customer's needs, not simply pander to a buyer's feelings. In a sense, it's like the difference between prostitution and marriage. In one relationship, you offer temporary pleasure, on a personal level. In the other, you build a lasting relationship between two entire lives, two organizations. You do something for your customer that's beneficial to his business or his life—and to yours.

There *is* something deeply ironic about this whole program. Have companies gone so far astray that they need to tell their people to do the most obviously necessary things? Customer satisfaction! Customer satisfaction! Customer satisfaction! How many times do they need to say it? How many times can they invoke it on sales calls? It's like praising the wonders of oxygen to somebody who has no desire to hold his breath. What do the corporate people think the sales force did in the past—make people un-happy? Selling people things they didn't need? Well, as a matter of fact, in more cases than the company liked to admit, yes.

Fred sold for Xerox for many years when the only guiding principle was to write as much business as possible, as early as possible, by any means possible. They stopped at nothing; they did whatever it took to make their goals. When he arrived in Cleve-land, reps were bending rules to get orders and then forcing the company to accommodate the orders. Customers were unhappy. As the company molded itself to a whole new set of values, it brought in Pacetta to clean up the district. As a result, everyone in Cleveland understood quality—at least, everyone was going through the motions of serving the customer's requirements.

The core spirit of selling hadn't altered completely under Pacetta, mainly because the company kept pressuring the district to attain ever higher annual budgets. Under Pacetta, the Cleveland district tried to sell both ways at once. Pacetta promoted customer satisfaction, and yet when success was at stake, he encouraged high-pressure sales. Pacetta made the transition bearable for Fred because he allowed for both old and new styles of selling at the same time.

The TQM movement at first looks like nothing but a smoke-screen of bureaucratic paperwork. Each employee is trained in many processes: how to identify his customer, how to determine the services or products he produces, and how to devote himself to continuous improvement. For an engineer, this is a straightfor-ward task. You look at the products you create, and you measure how effectively they serve the buyer's needs. For the assembly-line worker, it's more subtle. He needs to envision the next assem-bly-line worker as his customer and then determine what he can do to make *his* customer's life a little easier—in other words, his job may be to please the next worker on the line. Every employee must identify and satisfy a customer, even if, for most employees, this won't be the actual buyer of the physical product. Finally, the program demands that every worker measure his effectiveness in this improvement process by asking the customer, through a mailed survey, to rate his level of satisfaction with the rep, the sales process, and the product itself.

Traditionally, the sales force has been the last to see the importance of the quality movement. In sales you find the most resistance to breaking down the image of the customer as an opponent, a mark. Sales thrives on competition, and often the customer can become the salesman's nemesis in the Big Game. Robbing a salesman of that vigorous sense of entering the championship playoffs every time he faces a customer takes a lot of energy and fun out of the daily routine.

The quality program asks each and every salesman to rise above manipulative techniques and look upon the customer as a partner, not an opponent. It requires nothing less than a compassionately intelligent approach to every customer's business. A salesman who relies on quality principles doesn't trick his customer into a deal. He works his way into a customer's confidence, but not to sell the customer something he doesn't need, not to force a customer to do something he wouldn't otherwise do. Once he establishes a relationship with that customer, he begins to learn, in great detail, how the customer does his business. The Xerox rep studies how documents are handled within the customer's business. He spends weeks gathering information on document flow and, in the end, produces a report showing specific ways a customer can save money, reduce employment, raise productivity, even before purchasing a single product from Xerox. Of course, the sales pitch eventually comes, but a genuine quality approach makes the sales pitch almost insignificant in comparison with the generous intelligence of the analysis that precedes it.

The whole program is meant to do more than just keep everybody honest. It's meant to raise the activity of the sales force to an ethical and professional level never before attained—a higher level. It's meant to transform the force into a team of consultants, partners, whose actions are governed by principles of genuine friendship and compassionate intelligence rather than gamesmanship or manipulative techniques. It isn't meant to change salesmen into saints, but it is quite serious about how doing things the right way will eventually result in greater rewards, years down the road.

It's easy to imagine the Perfect Quality Sale. It begins with a cold call on a hostile customer who uses a competitor's equipment—Canon, Konica, Kodak, whatever. After getting her foot through the door, the rep—by showing how professionally and intelligently she can handle the customer's problems—gets the customer to peruse a written proposal. The proposal is of such high quality that it lures the customer to the district office for a product demonstration. In the showroom, the customer falls in love with the new equipment. Meanwhile, as all of this happens, the rep invites the customer to attend a free series of seminars on Total Quality Management at Xerox sales headquarters in Rochester or at corporate headquarters in Stamford, Connecticut. The customer gets a taste of the product and learns how it can be used.

Once the customer is convinced Xerox has become a new company, with the customer's own best interests at heart, and with a new line of outstanding equipment, then the rep gets even more intimate with the buyer's business. The rep requests, and is given, permission to enter the company and study the way this customer handles documents—in his walk-up copier locations, in his centralized print shops, in the way he expedites large print jobs by sending them outside to other companies. After weeks or months of study, the rep returns with a detailed written analysis of how the customer handles his copying and printing operations, and how he can increase his productivity, with or without new Xerox equipment. The customer doesn't have time or money to do this sort of study himself. When he looks at the report closely, he's astonished at how much expertise and intelligence have been generously given away. Even without a purchase of Xerox equipment, this free consultancy will improve the way this customer does his job. He's free to bring the whole process to a halt, right now, without giving a penny to Xerox, and come away with something that might have cost him tens of thousands of dollars if he'd hired an outside quality consultant.

But he doesn't call it to a halt. He feels obligated to push further, and he's interested in knowing more. He asks for another proposal, and then another, and finally he allows the Xerox rep to install a machine in his print shop, for a temporary free trial, just to see how it works. After a month of free usage, he decides to buy the machine and return his old equipment to the competitive manufacturer. He signs a five-year lease for a pair of large duplicators. Thus, Xerox enlarges its market share, delivering a solid blow to its competition. Every one of these dollars is fresh. Every penny of this deal represents new revenue. More important, this deal has started the process of turning a first-time buyer into a long-term user. It has expanded market share.

In contrast to this ideal sale, most Xerox business takes place within companies who already use Xerox equipment. The reps keep returning to these faithful customers, asking them to lease new equipment as soon as, and often before, their old Xerox leases expire. In effect, the reps ask customers to extend their leasing fees further into the future, usually at a slightly higher rate than in the past, in exchange for slightly better equipment. A large proportion of Xerox business rests on this process of returning again and again to faithful customers and "churning" the equipment.

This isn't nearly as lucrative for the company as going into a hostile company and knocking out competitive equipment, but a large proportion of the company's annual revenue depends on churning. It's the company's bread and butter. Through churning, Xerox preserves its existing leasing revenue on an installed base of equipment, where it can continue to reap large profits through maintenance and supply contracts.

The trick is to keep faithful customers habituated to paying a monthly leasing fee rather than buying their equipment. Xerox and other copier dealers have trained customers to budget for a monthly fee rather than pay for the total cost of a copier in one big chunk. The customer commits himself to three or five or seven years of fees—in other words, he commits himself to pay the total of all those payments whether or not he keeps the copier for the duration of the lease. If he gets into a seven-year lease and becomes dissatisfied with the machine after four years, Xerox will do everything to make the customer happy—including a free replacement of the old machine with a new one—but it will not forgive the customer the balance of payments on the lease. One way or another, the customer will make all of the payments, regardless of how long he keeps the machine.

The leasing program habituates customers to making a payment for life. Once the customer has found a place in his budget for that monthly fee, it's a much smaller task to get him to increase it slightly in exchange for new equipment than it would be to have him come up with a hundred thousand dollars for the purchase of a new machine after having budgeted no money whatsoever for the purchase of a copier during the four or five years since he last bought one.

The automobile industry learned the leasing business from Xerox. Before leasing took hold, you bought a car by making monthly finance payments—until the debt was paid and you owned that little Cobra, with a hundred thousand miles on the odometer. Now, your car dealer has weaned you from any desire to own your car. With this new mentality, you never imagine yourself wanting to keep a set of wheels longer than four or five years—and why would you want to, with all the maintenance that little Hyundai might require? Once a customer finds a place in his household budget for the leasing payment on a new Honda Civic, it's easy to get him to trade up to a Prelude, because it means only a few dollars more per month. Neither Honda nor Xerox want you to think of ownership as the goal. If all customers bought their machines outright, the revenue stream would disappear. The whole point is to keep the payments flowing ceaselessly, and slowly getting bigger as the quality of the new equipment improves. In the process, nobody even expects to buy a piece of equipment that might last for twenty or thirty years, like, say, a Maytag washer. Obsolescence is taken for granted as technology changes and five-year-old machines begin to break down more and more often.

At Yeager, Larry Tyler used the new rules, the new techniques, to play the old game—to stay on top, in control, and to win. He probed until he understood what his customer needed better than the customer himself understood it, and then he used this information to force his customer to do business more effectively.

Fred and his team submitted to the new regime, the new regimen, in a similar way—and it *did* change the way they operated. Fred was an expert old-school salesman, a master at slam-dunking equipment on his own short-term schedule when he needed to do it. He understood how to spike the business, and by no means did the quality program nullify any of these skills. He simply annexed a new vocabulary, a new binder of paperwork, a new set of more sophisticated procedures around his old core of routines. He polished himself into a consultant. It wasn't entirely cosmetic, though. Often it was real. This year Fred and his people were going into companies, studying copier usage, coming back with bar graphs and charts and calculations of savings. They were showing the customer how to improve his business. They were becoming partners with their customers. They were letting the quality of the numbers alone draw the customer into the deal.

Without the quality approach, Nancy couldn't have won *any* business, because all of her accounts were nonusers. Her accounts didn't trust Xerox. They'd been burned. They were looking for trouble. Only a new approach could get Xerox through the door: *We won the Commerce Department's Malcolm Baldrige Award. We're experts on quality! We'll show you how to win it too.* Without this pitch, Nancy certainly couldn't have gotten as far as she'd gotten at Akron Automotive.

She organized and presented a study showing patterns of copier usage at Akron Automotive along with how the DocuTech would change those patterns. When she met with Cook she showed him how he could save his department and his company tens of thousands of dollars. Cook was impressed. It gave him a way to justify his purchase to his own boss. It was similar to the approach Larry Tyler used at Yeager—fact-based, number-based persuasion clean of tricky techniques. At her next meeting with Cook, he came to the most important issue on his mind immediately: What did she recommend as a backup machine? If they had one machine, and it went down, they were out of business for two hours.

He wanted *two* machines! Nancy was astounded. By asking this question, Cook showed her how far he'd come. She could see Cook respected her and the techniques she and Fred used to show him how much he could benefit from new procedures and new equipment. It sounded as if he'd made the decision to go with Xerox even before she arrived at his office. Often the decision to lease a machine happened offstage this way, in conversations where the Xerox rep had no influence. The rep met countless times with the buyer, but the decision was made later, in meetings between the buyer and his own boss. In this case, the deal wasn't signed, but the signature wasn't far away.

On many deals, reps and managers were turning the quality program itself into a sort of sales-promotion incentive. Fred's team offered their customers lessons in the Leadership Through Quality program, flying customers to Rochester or Stamford for free lessons on, say, materials management. They offered this wisdom as a premium to customers simply for letting a Xerox rep stick his shiny oxford through the door. Usually the potential buyers wanted to exploit these lessons on the spot. They wanted to taste all the rewards of quality management procedures: greater productivity, fewer jobs, higher profits. No problem. *And—oh, by the way, Jack—to achieve these things, it wouldn't hurt to acquire a new line of copiers or duplicators.* At this point Fred and his people would open the brochures.

On the surface they were consulting. All along they were selling. They were doing everything they'd done before—lavishing the favor of free knowledge the way they lavished a day of golf or dinner on a customer, making the buyer feel indebted. Quality was more than that, though. Fred didn't scoff at the indisputable heart of a genuine quality sale: Nancy Woodard going into Akron Automotive and keeping logs of how many copies were being run on the company's existing equipment—who, why, how many, and so on—and then using that information to show how much more efficiently the company could handle the same workload with new equipment. This was serious, genuine consulting, a giant leap forward from the kind of slinky emotional course of a grease sale. Her friendship with Jay Cook had much less to do with this deal than the impersonal force of her calculations.

The quality procedures were working in a different way through Fred's approach to Wellco, a company that manufactured heavy-duty ball bearings. This company had been a nonuser for years, though it wasn't assigned to Nancy Woodard's territory. Earlier in the year, Fred wrote a letter to the account, inviting them to make a trip to Stamford for a presentation on the wisdom Xerox wanted to share with its customers about Total Quality Management. He and Pacetta lunched a few decision makers, and they agreed to make the trip. Everyone was impressed with the presentation—it was thorough, and a few top Xerox executives made an appearance. The representatives from Wellco were flattered by all the attention, and they were convinced Xerox could teach them something.

Then the whole thing languished. Fred didn't hear from anyone for a month, two months. Finally, he called Al Brook, his decision maker at Wellco, and asked for a meeting. When they met at the company's offices, he and Brook laughed and talked for an hour. Fred could see Brook liked his manner—modest, solicitous, insightful. Fred showed an interest in Brook's own circumstances, how much experience Brook himself had in sales. During the meeting, Brook called one of his people, Sue Kelly, into the meeting, and by the time they adjourned, Wellco had ordered a copier. The order was, certainly, a payback for the trip to Stamford, and all the trips Xerox shared with Wellco about how to implement a quality program. Yet the eye contact, the shaking of hands, the sharing of idle jokes, the smiles and sympathy and friendly questions—the establishment of a friendship—that's what closed the deal. At the end of the meeting, Sue agreed to fly with Fred to Rochester for another quality presentation, this one a seminar on how to manage documents more effectively using quality principles.

The evening after this seminar, Fred took her to dinner and

they talked about sports. He did with her what he'd done with Brook. He broke the code of her personality, noting her little references to softball, finding out within a few minutes what kinds of experience they had in common, building a relationship, from the salad to the dessert. She liked to play softball with her husband, and she managed a girls' basketball team. He told her stories of coaching his son's Little League team. Whenever Fred started talking about his son, he liked to rattle on about the game: "Friday night, my son's Little League game. He's pitching. A girl gets up to bat. With a ponytail! She doesn't look like a big hitter. We're going to win! But no. He walks the girl. He walks the girl! We couldn't believe it. Our team loses. You know what? I don't care. Christopher did great." It was a fine meal. No one was at a loss for words. By the end of the dinner, after his continuous display of warmth and childlike exuberance, she liked him. The quality program got them to that dinner, but Fred's personality carried them through it. Nothing more would happen without this affection Sue felt for Fred. The upshot of the trip was an order for three machines.

At this point, Xerox had spent thousands of dollars on these people, ingratiating itself with a customer in the most legitimate way possible. Not only was Wellco getting value out of these flights to headquarters, but Al Brook was feeling important, becoming the point man in this campaign to tap Xerox wisdom on quality. Fred knew he needed to feel he was doing something significant for his company. After the proposal for the three machines was delivered, Fred got another call from Brook.

He wanted four copiers, not three. Then he paused and said he wanted to offer Fred a little Christmas present early in the year. Oh? They wanted a proposal to replace a hundred machines. Fred's personal relationship—his ability to read the buyers and push certain emotional buttons—is what won him the business.

But that wasn't all. Part of this relationship was built by the sense of partnership Fred established by sharing the quality wisdom with them. Like most other sales in Cleveland, this deal was halfway along the road toward quality, with a solid core of old-school selling.

4.

SOMETIMES, WHEN FRED worked late, Kathy sat at her kitchen table with a pad of paper. When Fred wasn't around she felt free to dream, sitting with a pencil and paper. One year she composed a Christmas song, and a choir of children recorded it so a local radio station near Toledo could play the song during the holiday season. More recently, sitting in her kitchen, she did mechanical drawings of a pen that would write by laying down lines of small insignias. This pen would create a dotted line of sorts, except that instead of dots it would print a row of tiny hearts or stars or asterisks. She was sure she could patent this product, if only she could get a prototype built. She was sure, as well, that her idea for the Matchmate game show would be a moneymaker if anyone ever produced it.

The money would prove it hadn't been a waste of time, but money wasn't the reason she did the things she did. She didn't think about the money she might make from these inventions as much as she enjoyed letting her imagination follow its own natural path and make its own discoveries. So, once she got past the concept, she didn't know what to do or where to go, and she began to lose interest in the project. As her creative steam lost pressure, it was the perfect time for Fred Thomas to enter the picture with a business plan. In a perfect marriage, a perfect partnership, this is exactly what might have happened. Yet when did he have time to be there to encourage her? He was too obsessed with his own goals to pause long enough to see how important Kathy's hopes were to her. He was dubious about her dreams. It would cost money to protect and push her inventions in the market. She would need to hire an attorney or a consultant to help her take it from concept to product, and that was where Fred always balked. She wanted to have some kind of creative role in the world, and each time she sat at her table with a sharpened pencil, she wondered if she might come up with an idea for something that might find a home in other people's lives, yet her energy flagged when she had to take an idea beyond the level of creative play.

Still, the Matchmate idea continued to nag at her. It seemed a matter of principle to push this concept beyond her kitchen table—and it *was* more romantic to imagine herself as an inventor than as a schoolteacher. She wasn't sure she took it quite seriously herself, but she couldn't escape the way it kept nagging at her. She had hopes for it the way Fred had hopes for the lottery tickets he bought every week on his lunch hour. On one of the days when her resolve and energy seemed renewed, Kathy drove to the library downtown. It was raining when she got there, and she parked across the street and ran through the rain up the steps and into the old limestone building.

Inside, she found several books about television game shows, and then she wandered through an underground passage to the stack of phone directories, finding one for Los Angeles, where she looked up Merv Griffin Enterprises. Several days later, back home, she called, but she discovered the firm didn't accept outside ideas. They had a staff who invented games. They didn't need unsolicited submissions. More and more it seemed that if she were to have an impact on the world—and maybe make Fred happy by making some money in the process—it would have to be through teaching.

Fred gave himself without reserve to his most immediate crises; therefore conversations about Kathy's life and her feelings seemed impossible for him. He wanted results, accountability. He wanted life to be an arena with winners and losers and a balanced checkbook at the end of the month. He wanted a woman to earn money and still be there for the children and the dog. In other words, no matter what Kathy ventured, little would be gained. Anything she did had to be done clandestinely, outside his watchful gaze, at least until it justified itself with income.

Kathy didn't want more money in her life. She wanted more *meaning*. She wanted more than anything—more than her game show, more than her teaching career—to do something beautiful, even if it was financially negligible. She wanted to volunteer in a hospital or some kind of hostel for inner city children. She wanted to help children who needed help, ones who lived in a world governed by drugs and violence. This hope had come to seem nothing but a selfish dream to her, and she was afraid to suggest it to Fred because he would never allow her the time away from home she needed to pursue it. Where was the money? Where was the reward—the equal exchange—for all the effort? When she faced Fred, she felt defensive about everything she did, even her highest impulses. Sometimes it seemed the only time she could reflect intelligently on what those impulses meant to her was when she went to church.

It's Sunday morning in Rocky River. The parking lot is packed, as always. The atmosphere, as Kathy enters the church, eases her spirit. It's expansive, calm, rational, a haven of genuinely friendly collective purpose. The minister speaks about the myth of the Fisher King, retelling one of many variations on the myth of the Holy Grail.

A knight named Parsifal wanders over the wasted, dying king-dom until he finds a castle, where the Fisher King is wounded and ailing. The king has every possession and form of bounty he desires. He possesses the Holy Grail, the cup used to collect Christ's blood as he was crucified. The king is using this magical chalice to conjure all his material comforts and pleasures, and yet his life has no order, no lasting meaning. He exploits the Grail to grow wealthy and soft, when he could meditate upon it as an icon, an inspiration to become a just ruler. Though he has comforts and satisfactions, his life is without joy. He is sick with despair, and his illness infects the land around him. The king's contagion lays waste to the entire nation. As a visitor, a spectator, Parsifal watches but does nothing to ease the king's pain. He asks no questions. He shows no concern. He's fascinated by the Grail and its magical power to create this world of prosperity. He has entered into a mirage of abundance, but he doesn't realize it provides only a passing shelter from the surrounding wasteland. Parsifal makes no attempt to inquire about the king's disease, shows no compassion for the king. He goes to bed, and when he awakes in the morning, the castle is gone. The Grail has disappeared, and so has every-thing else.

After this strange visit to the Fisher King, Parsifal rides into the countryside, searching for the Grail. He cannot find it, and as he searches he forgets the king's suffering. Slowly he forgets the riddle of the Grail. He gains fame as a knight, jousting and killing, conquering others in games and wars, abandoning his quest. As he becomes more successful, his life begins to mean less and less to him. Parsifal doesn't realize his night at the castle was a challenge to solve the puzzle of the king's sickness. The king grew sick because he lived at the bidding of his own appetites rather than a higher form of love. Parsifal and the king can attain wholeness only by placing themselves in the service of a greater good than the mere satisfaction of their own immediate impulses. Parsifal himself is to learn that, rather than fighting battles and winning them for his own glory, he has to defeat himself, not others, by allowing his life to be ruled by a different sort of force. Parsifal needs to ask others, "What is your sorrow?" and care passionately about the answer. Had he asked the king that question, his quest for the Grail would never have begun; he would have possessed the Grail from the start, the wasteland would have become a garden, a thriving nation, and the king himself would have been healed through Parsifal's compassion.

The minister asks his congregation: Do you serve your own selfish needs, your own immediate desires, or do you have a higher calling? Do you serve yourself or do you serve a higher power? His sermon offers more than just a commentary on the myth. Hidden in its message can be heard a larger indictment of the state of modern life:

Look at what drives you. What forces you to do the things you do every day? You are Parsifal. You are searching for some sort of meaningful prosperity and abundance, of the sort that seemed to be provided by the Grail. You, along with every other human being alive, engage yourself in a quest for acquisition or achievement or sensation or simply physical comfort, just as Parsifal chases the Grail. Why? Why isn't what you have, what you are right now, enough?

You live, usefully and purposefully, in a state of continuous discontent. That pinprick of dis-ease drives you to new heights. The whole corporate organism survives by twisting this thorn, by thrusting itself outward—like the imperialism of a world power— always expanding, always growing, always acquiring. Like an empire, a corporation obeys the same rule: grow or wither. There is no equilibrium, no harmony, no rest. Your stock never stays level for long; it is always rising or falling. Every individual in the corporation lives by the same law. Either you rise or you fall. If you want to survive, you need to grow, to move up, to feel the prick of that thorn wherever you are, whatever you are doing, right now.

And for what? So that you win a few crucial battles in order to become a major accounts rep rather than a marketing rep. To become a sales manager rather than a major accounts rep. To be crowned district manager after paying your dues as a sales manager. And then—glorious coronation!—to become a vice president! And once you reach that height, you take on a previously unimaginable burden of responsibilities and assume all the postures of servitude required of corporate officers. Many of you can't wait for that loftiest state of discontent.

In reality, all of this dis-ease serves not you but the host organism: the corporation, the economy, the nation, the currency itself. Keep people wanting more, keep them spending, and all will be well, all will be abundant, all will prosper. Keep them wanting to move up in status and you won't have to pay them too much—once they reach the salary limit at one level, make them want to move up or move out, and get somebody else into that spot at half the salary. Keep the customer wanting a newer automobile, a better home, a more efficient copier, and you can keep the money circulating from one account into another, and that's what makes the world prosper. Just keep the money moving from one account to another, the lifeblood flowing through one limb of the organism on its way to another. That's what drives everybody toward a more prestigious, slightly more luxurious state of discontent, where everyone sets off to work every morning like a knight on the way to his next battle, his next joust—where everyone lives to win the game or the war.

Is there no way out? What of those people who've flown from the corporate labyrinth? What about the ones who escape? What about those who work out of their homes, who start their own businesses, buy a franchise, or become independent contractors for the corporations they once served as employees? That's where the world is going, isn't it? Into service? Into independent contracting? Into free agency? To each his own little personal kingdom. Yet the independent ones feel the thorn of discontent too, maybe even more profoundly than the ones who stay within the corporate fold. They are no more free than the corporate shock troops in their cubicles and offices. They escape nothing, and those of you who stay in the corporations know it. It seems even safer to fight the battles you face there than to ride off into unfamiliar lands and fight unknown enemies.

You will accept the servitude of almost any competitive quest in the hope of material prosperity because through abundance you hope to taste the freedom and well-being you imagine the wealthy enjoy. But does anyone *want* absolute freedom? Do the winners of the lottery quit their jobs? Do they welcome a life of idle pleasure? Do the wealthiest people play golf all day, every day? No matter how much abundance people taste, they always want more, don't they? Even the king is sick with desire. Even the richest crave another win, another billion, a bigger yacht. Discontent becomes an inescapable drive. It becomes a life force with no ultimate end, a hunger no nourishment can satisfy, a submissive craving for achievement.

The American dream isn't a dream of independence. It's a dream of ever-greater abundance won through ceaseless, invigorating conflict. The dream of abundance is what drives your quest. The chance to taste abundance, to wrest it from a reluctant or hostile world—to find that golden chalice and bring it home and place it on the kitchen table and watch it conjure your drafty old house into a castle filled with riches. Yet—and here's the catch—no matter how abundant your life becomes, it doesn't soothe the discontent, because you've come to need that discontent to stay alive, to keep growing, pushing toward a bigger win, a feeling of greater fulfillment. The discontent, by now, is what makes you feel alive and effective—not the sensible state of moderate abundance that results from it. That's the king's disease, in the myth of Parsifal, his dis-ease. He's ill with desire, with want. And so is Parsifal—seeking greater glory with each battle he fights, hoping for a bigger and more remarkable win, because he's forgotten he needs to solve the puzzle of what he witnessed in the king's castle. His quest for the Grail becomes a quest for his own personal glory—he forgets what it's supposed to mean.

Yet is this the way things need to be? What of Parsifal's unspoken question? What of this compassion that's supposed to heal the king and do everything the Grail itself only appeared to do? Is there no way to forget your quest for a moment and simply ask this question of other people, even in the context of your work or your marriage: What is your sorrow? What do you need? Where does it hurt? How can I serve you? And if you did ask it, what would happen? You might need to relinquish your whole concept of success as victory in battle, triumph in the joust, and your concept of happiness as a state of ever-greater victory. You might have to face the reality of human life as a community of people who, if they hope to live in true prosperity, show as much love for one another, including their opponents in the game, as they do for themselves. It's a vision of life and economy as genuine satisfaction and flow and service, rather than discontent and battle and one-sided victory. It's a vision of life as a state of rough harmony rather than war. You don't live to conquer. You live to care.


When Kathy returned home, the sermon stayed with her, and yet it faded too. Wasn't that the way of all ideals, all visions of truth? The power of words gets diffused in the world, and a preacher's values dissipate in the unruly day, and still they have a muted and subliminal impact on things. What could have been a better commentary on her life and her husband's life than this interpretation of an ancient myth?

It sounded so simple. Just ask a single question every day, like a ceaseless prayer: *What is your sorrow?* Don't put it into words. Put it into action. Put it into the game. Ask it silently of every person you meet, and see how things start to fall into place. What if Fred were to do exactly that with his customers? Wasn't that supposed to be the way things worked? Wasn't that where his business was taking itself in its quality program—toward the universal articulation of that question on every sales call? But was it possible to keep asking it, with genuine care for the customer's answer, and survive from year to year? How could you uphold this ideal and still make a pragmatic compromise with the nature of the world, and when would your behavior become hypocrisy? If someone talked about quality and then engaged in high-pressure sales and trickery to get a deal, did that mean he was a liar, or did it simply mean he did the best he could, as long as he could, and then did what he needed to do to survive? Was the preacher really preaching or was he just selling people a pleasant dream in order to get a higher denomination in the collection plate after all those pious words? Was it a little of both? Life was so much more complicated and messy than the myth, once you walked outside and started living it. Or was it?

Was she capable of asking that question—*What is your sorrow?*—of her own husband when he came home at night, especially as he was so eager to tell her exactly the nature of his pain when he walked through the garage door into the laundry room, not even giving her time to ask how he felt before he started to tell her? And then, when he began to speak, she never knew what to trust, what to discard, in all these impassioned words he floated her way. It *was* hard to ask that question and mean it.

In this old myth you had a choice between a quest and a question. Either you rode forth into the world in order to triumph over others for your own glory as you searched for this magic cup of abundance, or you asked other people a compassionate question and did what was necessary to help them—and found everything you needed in life followed from this act of compassionate intelligence. Fred was certainly someone obsessed with his own quest, though much of his success depended on his ability to show genuine interest in the feelings of other people. Kathy's life worked both ways too. She had her own quests, in her inventions and her ambitions to become a teacher or a volunteer in the inner city, and yet in her deepest ambition lay this impulse to ask that ultimate question of other people, trying to recognize the face of the Fisher King in the eyes of the children she met as a teacher or volunteer.

Fred would keep searching for one sort of grail or another, even if he left Xerox—he would keep riding forth into the wilderness of greater Cleveland, fighting his battles and struggling to win against all those opponents he liked to bemoan when he got home. Kathy, though, wanted to live in honor of something beyond the tunnel vision of someone on a quest. If life was a struggle between the quest and the question, she knew where her sympathies led her. She understood the nature of that question better than she understood what drove a person to embark on another search-and-destroy mission every day. She didn't want to keep living her life within the limits set by her husband's compulsions. Fred couldn't prevent her from living her own life, no matter what he said or did, no matter how much he claimed he needed her income to change his own life. Teaching seemed the best and most honorable way of serving others—a compromise between the jackpot possibilities of an invention and the moneyless altruism of inner-city volunteering. A life halfway between the quest and the question, the way most human lives were lived.

Her calls and interviews with the schools in the district yielded several substitute-teaching possibilities, but it wasn't easy getting Fred to understand what the prospect meant to her. She was scheduled to teach two days at a nearby private school. Fred—and this was no surprise to her—was less than enthusiastic. It seemed bogus to him. It wasn't part of the public school system, so the job seemed to lead nowhere. He said repeatedly he wanted her to work, but when an income seemed to be dawning for her, he found fault with it. He was afraid of losing her, little by little, even as he urged her to go forth into the world—the way a parent fears the loss of a child on the verge of college. Fred wanted to know who would watch the dog all day. The dog didn't need to be watched. What if she were working full time? That's what he wanted, wasn't it? Then what would they do with the dog? Was this a real job? It wasn't in Avon Lake.

When the call comes for her first teaching job, at Lake Ridge Academy, she's filled with a mixture of dread and excitement. The night before the day she's scheduled to teach, she sits at the kitchen table, planning what she'll do about breakfast, rehearsing all the things she needs to cover before she leaves the house the next morning. In the bedroom, she selects what to wear and sets the alarm clock even earlier than Fred's normal waking time. She wants everything to be predetermined with no room for needless improvisation in the morning, because she doesn't expect to have much time before class to plan her day once she arrives. She wants to get there at least half an hour early, get prepared and be familiar with the room and the curriculum. It's been a long time since she last taught, and though it's only a class of kindergartners, she wants to do a good job.

Then in the morning, to her surprise, Fred gets up and helps her. He stays home later than usual to help get the children off to school while Kathy gets ready. When it comes down to the crucial moment, Fred doesn't fail her. He helps her, the way he helped her do things twenty years ago. He shows her how much he cares. When they quit talking and start living their lives, everything falls into place. For an hour her husband is exactly the way she wants him to be: He's working to make her happy, sacrificing his own time, putting her own needs above his. He loves her. And then they go their separate ways for the day. Maybe, despite his fears that she wants to escape her marriage, he is coming to realize she doesn't want to escape—she wants to delve more deeply into her own life, to find refuge not outside herself but within her own talents and beliefs, in her own imagination and intelligence and heart. She doesn't want to play some game to win. She wants to grow as a human being. She wants to take her life not to a higher level but rather to a more meaningful depth—and maybe Fred is beginning to understand this path doesn't lead permanently away from him.

5.

IN THE LOUNGE at the Beachwood Marriott, a man is stepping into a glass cage on the raised flooring toward the back of the bar. This smiling man, dressed in a business suit, has been chosen from the audience. He's being shut into his cage by a disk jockey mouthing something about a game in which the man will be trying to catch money. The man wears pin-striped slacks, a white shirt, dark braces, and a colorful necktie. He looks exactly like someone who works for Xerox, or for any other large American corporation. He smiles sheepishly at the people he left behind at his table.

Once the man is shut into this large waterless aquarium, a blower sweeps gusts of air around him, ruffling his hair over his temples. Next, a bushel of money flutters into the enclosure, and the ones and fives and tens swirl furiously in a green tempest around his arms and legs. He thrashes within his cage. For half a minute, a minute, two minutes, the man swims and flails and grasps at the loose money twirling around him.

He's a puppet. Everyone's a puppet in this little Beachwood Marriott vision of life. Everyone is lured and hamstrung and mocked by money. The customer is the salesman's puppet. The salesman is his sales manager's puppet. The sales manager is his district manager's puppet. The district manager is his vice president's puppet. (Nobody could tell Fred that Frank Pacetta was some kind of maverick. He was doing exactly what the corporation wanted him to do, whether he knew it or not. He was selling more and more copiers every year, even as he pretended to be a rebel.) And the VP? He's hanging by a thread to the finger of some executive who's on a first-name basis with the president. The president himself does his little dance for the sake of Wall Street. And Wall Street obeys the bestial roar of the trading floor itself. Money, the impersonal god of currency itself, reigns over it all. Who isn't a puppet when money dictates the terms of the game? Who doesn't live in a glass cage?

Fred's seen this game before. Someday, if he's invited into the cage, he'll do a better job. He will wear his jacket and open it wide, scooping the currency under his arms. He'll sweep a few stray bills off the floor around his feet. He'll pick them from the air with both hands and stuff them into his pockets. But he knows that no matter what he does, the money he claims will never equal the money that gets away. It's a delicious, infuriating, desperate game because so much free money escapes, so much cash he'll never even touch, let alone catch and spend. The dart and twist of money, as it eddies and drifts and pirouettes, makes Fred yearn to enter this glass box, despite himself—and it makes him want to escape it, too. He can't help it. He wants to grab all the loose money and *then* get out. The point is to escape, but not too soon.

Then what happens, if he does escape? Someday Fred might be solvent, but he will never be rich, no more than this man in the cage, no more than most people who work in the district and find themselves thrilled to get a gratuitous hundred dollars at one of Pacetta's motivational gatherings. Only a week ago Fred had to force himself to keep walking when he spotted twenty pennies—twenty of them!—scattered carelessly in the parking lot at one of the companies he visited. It wasn't the sum that excited him. It was the twenty chances for good luck, spread out at his feet. Twenty chances to make a fortunate change.

So what will happen to him? If he has no realistic prospect of making a change in his life that might make him rich—if he doesn't even want to move up in the corporate hierarchy and become district manager somewhere—then what in the world is he going to do with his life if he does what he loves to do and keeps selling? Everyone in the district, at this time of the year, begins to worry about the future. The guessing game begins in the summer. Who's moving up? Who's moving out? Who's digging in? What territory will you get? What assignment will she get? When will it be announced? What do you need to do to get the accounts you want next year? It intensifies each month until job changes are announced by the end of October, but this year a freeze is ordered on almost all moves and promotions for the coming year. Results are hard enough to achieve this year, and Xerox management doesn't want anyone distracted by the behind-closed-doors machinations that usually began to ferment about this time of year.

Bruno was talking as if he knew where he'd be going in the coming year, and Fred was sure of Bruno's promotion. He'd heard speculation as to where Pat Elizondo might go—Atlanta or Columbus or San Diego—if Pacetta didn't leave. But it looked to Fred as if Pacetta was already planning to be out of Cleveland in January. It was clear Pacetta wanted to move on. Where would Fred go if Pacetta left? Who would go to bat for him?

Fred and Pacetta had conversations about what spot he might move into at the end of the year, and Pacetta assured him he would create a job suitable for Fred if nothing opened up, but Fred suspected his boss didn't have that power, no matter how loyal he felt. When he faced the truth, he realized Pacetta made no commitments to him of the sort he seemed to have made to Bruno and Pat Elizondo. And even if Pacetta stayed, how far could Fred trust him? His boss told him again and again he'd find a place for him in the coming year, and he trusted Pacetta's friendship. Yet he still didn't know if that friendship would ever translate into direct action. He still didn't know when, if ever, Pacetta was being genuine and when he was bullshitting him—he wasn't sure Pacetta was *ever* sincere.

Besides, Pacetta seemed to be running out of energy. He didn't seem to believe in *himself* as much as in earlier years. Life in the district was losing some of its emotional fuel because Pacetta's act was beginning to seem more and more transparently phony. Every day Fred discerned new signs of Frank's weariness. The district celebrations seemed even more perfunctory to him now, as if

Frank couldn't quite believe in his own routine anymore. Everyone arrived and drank and played along, but without a sense of abandonment.

Frank goes into one of his game-show routines at the latest recognition meeting, held in a Polish hall, which looked about as underfunded as a typical Veterans of Foreign Wars local. (Apparently, Pacetta was spending less money. That was a sure sign a few cylinders were starting to misfire in Pacetta's engine. How could he make money if he didn't spend money? Was he listening to corporate at last? Was he beginning to obey?)

Someone shouts: "It's time for Monty!"

Slowly the crowd begins to chant: "Monty! Monty! Monty!"

Pacetta puts on a plaid jacket and becomes Monty Hall. It's time to play *Let's Make a Deal.* He calls into the crowd: "Anybody—I've got five dollars for anyone who has a fifty-cent coin. I'll give you five dollars for it. Michelle, I'll give you ten dollars for what's in box number two."

Pacetta points to a numbered, wrapped gift box on the stage.

"No," she says.

"Twenty."

She thinks about it and then shakes her head.

*She'll take the box!*

"Give me a planner with five appointments in it. I'll pay fifty bucks for a Day Timer with five appointments."

Now the game ends on a weird note. Pacetta comes forward and with a straight face says: "Now everybody follow me around to the bar. There's a big vat of Kool-Aid, and I want you all to take a drink from it." Only the older people understand his reference to the followers of Jim Jones in Jonestown, who drank poison when their cult leader ordered them to do it. Pacetta thinks these people will do anything he asks them to do, simply because he asks them to do it. It's as if he's saying: *If I tell you to kill yourselves, you'll kill yourselves. That's how much power I have over you.* Even in this expression of contempt for his people, even when he's telling them how little respect he has for their independence, how he'll stop at nothing to squeeze yet another ounce of work out of them, he does it to their faces, as if he's picking a fight, challenging them to take a swing at him. When Fred hears this remark, though, he knows what to make of it. Pacetta's telling everybody it's the end. He'll be gone by this time next year. And an hour later, when he tries to form the Huddle again, half the people don't even bother to raise their arms to touch Pacetta's erect fist.

*Why are we doing this, gang? That's right. Because we have to.* Their work was an obligation now. How could this be? It used to be an act of adolescent rebellion. It used to be as romantic and thrilling as a Butch Cassidy train heist. What was happening? Where was the feeling? Where was the emotion Fred used to taste when he joined these gatherings? A salesman needed those feelings to keep going.

A salesman survives on feelings. If you stop to think about what you're doing, you're dead. The point is to keep *feeling* something, anything, if only to keep a constant turbulence flowing past your heart, the way a shark draws salt water through itself to stay alive. You feel your way forward. Emotions are the sea you breathe. Feeling becomes something to be used, something to be charted and tamed. It keeps you moving. It sells the product.

Feeling *is* the product. You know that to buy is both to surrender emotion and surrender *to* it. People don't buy things; they buy feelings. You know the need for a desktop copier works on the heart and cortex the way any desire works: gratify any craving, satisfy any need, no matter how pale and thin and cost-efficient, and you get a little quiver of response. You aren't a merchant as much as a manipulator of desire. (One manager's wife told him: You aren't a liar. You're a professional manipulator. And I'll never forget it.) You breathe an atmosphere, you swim in a medium, constituted of desire, the way an early Greek philosopher imagined himself at home in a universe of fire. I want; therefore I am.

You sell this Ferrari, you sell its allure. You sell this house, you sell an entire life, an entire world of feeling within its walls. You sell this copier, and you sell a particular feeling of satisfaction. The purchase of one thing is an attempt to buy all things, to obtain a momentary sensation of pleasure, affection, and warmth. A buyer wants more than a copier, a hamburger, a heavy-metal CD, a fifteenth-century manuscript, a Matisse interior, a cruise on the Côte d'Azur—he wants the feeling of wholeness these things restore within him. You know life is a quest for this feeling, a taste of how a life of absolute abundance might feel. If you could peel away the husk from the ten thousand things people seek, you would unveil this yearning for emotional equilibrium, this shy hunger for the humblest of all sensations, a sensation of well-being. Make a customer feel good, and he'll hand you unmarked bills in a paper bag. *And you say you need fifty copies per minute in a walk-up environment with two-sided capabilities and the opportunity to . . .* Bullshit. In every conversation, subliminally or covertly, you are really saying what the paramour says to his mark: *What is your pleasure? Your desire? Your sorrow? I can provide it. Satisfy it. Soothe it. Forget about the box. It's me you're buying. Surrender to me, and I will make you happy in a way the others can't.* You know how to make the emotional link. And these hints, these dizzy promises, give life to more than commerce and love—they quicken all human transactions, all human relationships.

Once, Pacetta was the engine of the entire district's emotion. Was he running out of fuel and fire? Apparently so. The games, the free money—it wasn't as much fun anymore. It was getting old. The job was becoming an obligation rather than a joy. People were breaking the code. They had figured out how it worked. After a while, people caught on to the old-school selling techniques. After three or four years, customers got wise, and so did employees. They saw through the bullshit. The quality approach wasn't simply the right way to do things, it was the only way that worked, once you ran out of tricks and artificial emotional stimulants. You had to give your customers and your employees something of real value—not just a rush, a kick—to get them to do what needed to be done. Too many people were watching now, in your company and in your customer's company.

It was coming to an end. Frank was ready to leave Cleveland, and so were some of the others. Everyone was pushing for a change. Everyone, that is, except Fred. If he stayed at Xerox, would he be able to enter this new world of selling, using the quality model? As a sales manager, would he be able to devote himself completely to that change? Weren't the pressures for short-term results too great? Under pressure, wouldn't he always need to fall back on old, familiar selling techniques?

With each passing week, as Fred's year approached its inevitable climax, he itched to know what kind of upheaval to expect in the district. At meetings after Halloween, he entered the conference room with a sense that it was time for Pacetta to offer all of them an update on his own future. When was somebody going to make a firm commitment?

"Where has the year gone?" one of the managers asked. "I closed my eyes in February, and I wake up now and it's November." Another manager was describing how, the night before, she doused the lights and hid from the children at her door: "Ding. Ding. Dingdongdingdongdingdongdingdong. They never give up."

Did anyone get their names? Maybe the district should hire them.

Pat looked across the table and said, "You should be happy. In Gary, they shot bullets through your windows if you ran out of candy. They would come in and find you in your closet. Good thing you don't live in Gary."

"Frankie was Superman," Pacetta said. "All the parents sit out front. Boring as shit, but it's a nice atmosphere. Listen, I think our performance in October was very poor. I'm very disappointed. I don't think we can do twelve million. There are a lot of people sitting around the office. A lot of people not grinding it out. Those of you who think we're grinding, think again. We're just working the big deals. We're slipping. This is not like us at all."

At these meetings, one after another, each manager stood and offered his or her outlook for November, and everyone applauded. When it was Fred's turn, he described some of his deals in progress and said, "I'm going to continue to take the attitude of getting new names. We need new prospects. That's what will get us through."

"The next two weeks are the whole ball game," Pacetta said. "People who had zero orders this month should get a letter of reprimand."

Fred bristled: "I think that's totally, totally demotivating."

Pacetta begged to differ. Fred's reps weren't going to quit if they got a letter. Fred said nothing. Frank looked around the room, gathering his thoughts.

"As of now, I'm the DM here," he said. "Pat is a DM candidate. If I fall off the chair or they promote me, she'll get the job here. Otherwise she's up next for a DM spot elsewhere."

"Let's just hope something happens to the DM in Atlanta," Pat said.

Fred was morose. This mood wasn't his vigorous, professional state of discontent. This uneasiness felt more like an inflamed tooth. The reality of Pat Elizondo's inevitable promotion became inescapable. Frank wanted everyone to know the line of succession—he wanted to give everyone fair warning. Fred caught Rob in the hallway. Pacetta was leaving. He was sure of it. In his office, Fred looked up the phone number for a stock brokerage downtown and wrote the number on a sheet of paper. But he didn't dial it.

He called his reps into the office, one by one, and forced them to commit to an outlook for November. Between meetings he glanced at the phone number on his pad, without calling it. He leafed through his yellow message notes and returned a few of those calls, glancing at the phone number. Why not draw a line vertically down the center of the page and do a Ben Franklin, as he called it, on the question of becoming a stockbroker? In the left column, you list the pros. In the right column, you list the cons. The pros: more freedom, better money, more prestige. The cons: no experience, might not pass the test, might lose money the first year. This sort of thing worked with customers—as long as you weren't too candid about the cons. Would it work with him? He glanced once more at the phone number. It was time to quit fooling around.

"Mark! It's Fred Thomas. Remember me? How are you?"

"Fine. What's up?"

"I'm very interested in getting into your business. I've always wondered, could I get that test without actually tying myself to a company?"

"I could probably help you find out about the test. As far as I know, though, you have to be in the business to take it. You have to have a sponsor."

"You guys ought to hire me—"

"We should," Mark said. "You're absolutely right."

One salesman talking to another salesman—it was amusing how they could blow smoke at each other and see right through it and keep talking through all the fumes.

"I've always wanted to do it. Years ago, I signed a hell of a contract with another brokerage. Five years ago. People at Xerox worked on me, though. They talked me out of it. But, Mark, I had a hell of an offer."

"Who were they?"

"Kidder, Peabody. Back in Toledo."

"Oh, that's right. I think you told me," he said. "What were you going to be doing, retail or industrial?"

"Retail."

"That's where the real selling happens," Mark said.

"Retail is tougher. Yeah. It's hard for me because I've been here twenty years. So that's the only way you can take it? You get sponsored?"

Fred was beginning to understand that the only way to qualify as a broker was to make the leap and get hired provisionally while studying for the test—which meant there would be no safety net. If he quit, became a broker, and didn't pass the test, then he would be out of work and unable to return to Xerox. Unemployment frightened him more than anything else. He'd never been a star in the classroom, only on the ball field. He wasn't good with rote memorization. He didn't have a good vocabulary. He didn't like to compete with people who were, as he put it, book smart. The idea of a stockbroker exam in one of those sticky little windowless classrooms where you filled in tiny boxes with a dull number two pencil—he shivered.

"Yeah, that's the only way. You have to work for a firm. It's very tough. The test. It's hard. It isn't for everybody. You should talk to somebody about the business first."

"Like who?" he asked.

He gave Fred the name of a friend who lived on the next block.

"I've got two brother-in-laws who are doing it too. I like dealing with big accounts here."

"Would you want to do something else in the brokerage business?"

"No. I want to sell stock. See, they gave me a hell of a salary to leave Xerox, Mark. Five years ago, anyway."

"You should pursue them again."

Fred liked to flirt with a new career this way. The nice thing about flirting was you weren't actually *doing* anything. You could talk about getting hired without actually quitting your job. You could fantasize without being unfaithful. The idea of making a career change seemed so inevitable sometimes, and yet so forbidding, considering how vested he was at Xerox. But now, as he listened to Mark's voice, he knew what he was getting. Ignored is what he was getting. Mark wasn't playing along. He was telling Fred not to waste time. He was saying Fred Thomas didn't have a prayer of finding a job at *his* brokerage. He was telling Fred to forget it—to go knocking on somebody else's door. It was a relief, in a way. Fred knew a man who left Xerox to work at this fellow's brokerage and he failed. He didn't pass the exam. He quit his job at Xerox and then lost his brokerage job.

"Okay. Well, thanks, Mark. Maybe I'll give you another call."

"Any time, Fred."


The irony was, Fred didn't want to escape. He didn't want to go anywhere. But he felt he had no choice. He didn't want to leave Cleveland and put his family through that sort of wrenching change if he could avoid it. So if he stayed in Cleveland, he'd probably need to leave Xerox eventually. He had no desire to follow Pacetta as district manager, and there were few jobs in the district where he felt he'd learn anything new—except possibly as a national account manager.

NAM (rhymes with Spam) was a prestigious title within the

sales organization. A NAM was considered a sort of supersalesman who had a consulting relationship with a small, select number of large accounts. The NAM assigned to an account played the role of adviser and coordinator of all business Xerox did with that account, in all the cities where Xerox sells copiers to one of its facilities, without having any direct line of authority over the other Xerox sales people. By becoming a NAM, Fred could move out of management and back into full-time selling and yet still be moving up in status. As a NAM, he could stay in Cleveland, because, though NAMs were based in certain districts, they didn't actually work for specific district managers. They answered to sales headquarters in Rochester, where the staff guided their relationship with accounts spread out across the United States and the world.

The NAMs were able to sell according to the new model, the quality model, without the short-term stress faced by most sales managers. In other words, NAMs weren't nearly as concerned with thirty-day budgets or half-year goals or even annual plans. They cultivated permanent relationships with the company's blue-chip customers, helping them create long-term strategies for handling documents more productively. By becoming a NAM, Fred could move completely into the new school of selling, the quality model, without the kind of year-end pressures that usually forced him to fall back on his old-school selling tricks. If the world of sales was moving away from the mercurial power of emotions into a realm of compassionate intelligence, then this sort of migration, from the old school to the new, would make sense for Fred.

Yet, as wonderful as it seemed, there was little hope of making that kind of move in Cleveland. The district had its full share of NAMs already—two of them—and neither of them appeared to have any inclination to move into a new job.

6.

A u t u m n   w a s   e e r i e  in Ohio, a perpetual twilight. Hazy clouds obscured the skyline every day, floating low past the new Society Bank building, hiding and then revealing the tower with its pale ziggurat at the top. That jagged white peak, so much brighter than the bulk of the gray building, shimmered during the day and gleamed like travertine at night, illuminated by flood-lights. Mounted high above the steel mills and the flaming plumes of afterburners, translucent and alive, it looked like a snow-capped Mount Fuji beyond the reach of the city, serene above the turmoil of the Flats, the stadium and the banks, the barbershops and the bars, the airport and the lake.

This image of serenity seemed to have no place in Fred's city, let alone his life, as the year built toward a finish. He lived at a much lower altitude. His team wasn't trailing as badly as the whole district, but he needed to close another big order. He felt jumpy, impatient, restless. He spent every day quizzing his reps on how things were going, trying to spot the deal that might bring him another closing call, another moment of satisfaction—something to keep him going, something to give him hope. This was one of the most agonizing parts of the year. It was too early for the big deals to start popping, too late in the year to allow for any sense of comfortable distance from December's deadlines. He had to wait, uncertain, for everything to happen, and he found little he could do to help his reps move business forward. It was torture.

The quality methods could take him only so far, and then he began to run out of time. As the year drew to a close, slowly he began to rely more and more on his old-school sales techniques. He needed to sell a 5100 to Evan at Citadel. Evan didn't actually *need* the machine. He wanted it. Even so, Crawford stood in the way. Fred knew what he had to do. He needed to drive a wedge between Diane and Libby. They were as close as ever. Their friendship had gone too far. Diane had lost control of it. It wasn't just a business friendship. It was real, and it was hurting his score for the year. Diane couldn't close the Citadel deal because Libby didn't want it to happen. There was no excuse for it. Diane needed to risk the friendship for the sake of the partnership.

Fred knew Diane had talent. She didn't need to get this close to her customers. Fred recognized her type. Diane loathed the idea of prostituting herself for an order. She felt if she pushed Libby on Citadel, then it would reveal the price tag behind her friendship. It would be a betrayal of trust. Fred felt no squeamishness about this. Salesmanship was salesmanship. The friendship only made it easier to do the business. It was always a backseat brand of friendship. Forget that, and soon the customer would climb up into the driver's seat.

Fred decided to visit Evan at Citadel. Fred wrote out, on the back of an envelope, all the points Evan needed to justify the purchase. Then he handed the envelope to Evan and told him to review the selling points. In Fred's opinion, Evan loved the machine the way a child loves a new video game on the market. Evan met him in the lobby. Fred placed the order form on the table between them, without talking about it, and then he made conversation about the box. Evan picked up the order form without any prompting. Should Fred get back to him Monday? Evan didn't commit himself one way or the other.

Afterward Fred told Diane he wasn't sure Evan really needed the machine. It didn't matter to Evan, so why should it matter to them? He wanted the machine. Yes, well, Libby didn't want him to have it. Libby called Diane and told her to put the order on hold. He told Diane to pay attention to this. Look at what Libby was doing! When something came close to Libby, she turned it into business. Where was the friendship now? Libby stuffed Diane.

Why couldn't Diane stuff Libby? Why couldn't Diane play this game to win? This deal might cost Diane her trip to Palm Springs. Did she want that? Fred knew where Diane stood, year to date. She was just short of making trip. If she lost California, it would be her own fault, not his.

Diane said she was getting tired of Libby. Fred lit up at the sound of those words. Progress! They should have shipped that machine to Citadel and let the war start! Diane returned from her next call at Crawford and reported Libby was angry with Fred. She said he was pushing the Citadel deal, when she'd been clear about her feelings.

"She's setting you up. We don't have any really strong reasons why Evan needs the machine. That's the problem. You need to *sell* it." Libby didn't *need* it. They had to make her *want* it.

Suddenly Fred felt a wave of elation. His face, pliant as putty under the force of his shifting emotions, puckered itself into a cunning smile, eyebrows floating. He loved a deal when it reached this point, when he had to fight for it. This was more than taking orders, this was selling—and he wanted Diane to love it too.

"This is great. This is what I've been saying. *You* need to sell it."

"She's not really mad. She's mad at you, and not at me."

"That's great." That's what he wanted. Fred as bad cop, Diane as good cop.

"I think this worked well."

"Now this is what you do," Fred said, getting ready to do one of his role-playing solo performances. "Now you say, *I told Fred and . . . How do we want to handle this?* You say, *he started to get huffy and puffy. We talked it out. You've got to give me an opportunity here. I've kept Fred out of it. I told him it's my account.* That's the approach you use, Diane." She needed to pressure Libby by making her think Fred was pressuring Diane.

"I'm starting on my diet for the swimsuit at Palm Springs," she said.

"Now take your shrewdness to her."

"You got me back on track, Fred. I was falling off the edge," Diane said, animated, delighted. "I wasn't sure we were doing the right things. I thought we were being snakes. Now I at least feel better about being a snake."

Diane could feel as good as she liked, but there was no way they would get the Citadel order by the end of the year. If ever. Fred was convinced of it. He needed good news, as soon as possible. He scanned his list of deals, wondering if he might have better luck with Bruno and the deal at Bedford Telecommunications. After Bruno called on Callahan again, he told Fred what happened.

Callahan was taking an item from his walls or his desk every day or so and packing it away in a box, still hinting about his departure from Bedford, without having made the commitment to leave. Could they get the order in December? No. Even if he didn't get an invoice until the following year? Callahan told him no. He told Bruno it was going to be a tight year coming up. Bruno ought to spread out the wealth. Bruno wore his game face during this conversation. Nick kept giving him looks, wondering if maybe Bruno might show the least sign of sympathy for Nick's impending banishment from Bedford. The man hadn't left yet, had he? There was no proof he'd be leaving. Why should Bruno feel sympathy? Bruno was playing this mind game because he had no way of knowing whether or not Callahan was playing one too. Much of the effort that went into a deal for some reps was spent in trying to spot where they were being tricked. Where was the customer telling the truth, and where was he bluffing? Bruno didn't want to get fooled.

So Fred resigned himself to a December conclusion for Bedford and with a mounting sense of uneasiness searched the bullpen for Nancy. There seemed to be no excuse for the delay on Akron Automotive. If all these quality procedures were so effective, why didn't they have the order? Jay Cook told her he wanted the machine. Why wasn't the deal finished?

Nancy was failing in ways she hadn't thought possible, and there didn't seem to be anything Fred could do for her. She had more reasons to give up hope than all his other reps put together. She tried to stay busy, mostly to keep her mind off her personal life. Her husband, Gary, had lost his job as a chemical engineer at M. K. Ferguson. He was home every day circling want ads, watching television. Gary was one of the recession's casualties. She wanted Gary to be *her* emotional support through the trials of her new assignment and their new marriage. Now Gary would be expecting Nancy to be the emotional rock. At her most recent review with Fred, she told him, "Fire me. Fire me. I don't know what else to do. I don't care. Ruin my life. It's already falling apart as it is."

"Nancy, nobody here wants you to leave," Fred told her.

Pacetta kept telling her she was doing a wonderful job, and she *was*, in a sense—she was creating relationships at accounts where Xerox hadn't been able to get secretaries to take a message in the past. But she knew she wasn't going to make her plan for the year, let alone get to Palm Springs. The Akron Automotive order and one other huge order would be enough to push her above the hundred percent mark for the year—though nothing would be enough to get her into President's Club. Her accounts hated Xerox; they didn't hate *her*. But it was impossible not to feel despised when day after day she faced rejection and month after month she came up dry.

It felt as if she'd been sentenced to this job as punishment for some crime. When she sat at her desk in the bullpen, she would look at the telephone and know that nobody would be calling her with a surprise order for ten machines—the kind of call Diane and Bruno and Larry could expect a few times during the year. Everything required effort. And even when she applied as much force as she could to the course of events, still nothing happened in her favor.

Even so, she kept getting up in the morning, luring Gary out of bed, coming in to work, calling on her list of prospects. They ignored her. They refused to return her phone calls. She went on one call with Fred to a medical center downtown, and the customer invited Fred into his office, asking Nancy to stay in the waiting room while he and Fred discussed business. It was like the times she'd called various other customers who made it clear they didn't want to buy from a woman. She couldn't entertain them the way a man could. They couldn't tell the same jokes with her. She wouldn't understand a man's world. She remembered the phone call from one of her customers. They had a flood down in their copier room. If she wanted his business, she should bring a mop. Then they'd talk. She hung up in a rage. Probably she should have done it. It would have been a genuine, original act of salesmanship. It would have shamed him and put him in debt to her. It would have weakened his position. She probably passed up a rare chance to make a breakthrough, but somehow, in her desperate mood, it would have seemed like the final humiliation, even if it turned her year around.

Near the end of an especially trying afternoon Fred asked Nancy about Akron Automotive as he passed her in the hall. Did she get the proposal to them? Yes. Great, so they could go down and pay a visit? She wasn't ready.

Where was she making an impact? Did she open up Akron

Automotive? He did. Crockett Lang? They gave her Crockett Lang. She wasn't taking a leadership role. They gave nonuser accounts to reps who'd been successful, like her. But what had she done? It was tough, he knew, but why could he go see these people and she couldn't? What did she do? Where were the activities? What was she doing Tuesday? What was she doing Wednesday? What was she doing Thursday? What was she doing Friday?

On her calls, Nancy wondered if Gary was at a job interview, but she didn't call home to check on him. She didn't want to bother him. He played Nintendo video games when he wasn't checking the want ads—he said he was paralyzed with anger over the loss of his job. She told him to channel his anger into the job search. So it disturbed her to hear the bleeps and bells and electronic melodies of Super Mario when she got home in the evening. Those ringing gold coins Mario collected wouldn't buy her a new scarf at the Liz Claiborne shop in Tower City.

He told her that if it were her, she'd feel the same way. But it wasn't personal, she said. It was the economy. He said it *was* personal. It was his career. She reminded him that when he got out of college, people were begging him to work for them. When *she* got out of college, nobody was hiring. She thought her world was coming to an end because Red Lobster didn't want her as a manager. After she got to Xerox she felt like calling that guy and saying, *Okay, pal, let's compare our W-2s at the end of the year.* Gary said he didn't think that would happen to him.

Maybe he would get a job soon. Maybe their combined income would top a hundred thirty thousand, the way she hoped it would, soon. But until then, maybe she had to hide the Nintendo cartridge. Already she was parking her white Toyota in the garage at home so Gary would have to pull in behind her with his truck in the evening, trapping her car. That way she had an excuse to insist he get out of bed to move the truck in the morning. She didn't know how to drive a stick—at least that's what she told him. It was her way of forcing him out of bed. She hated to drive in to work at seven, knowing he was still sleeping. It was enough to ruin her day.

Despite all her problems, when Fred met with her he showed no mercy. She was talking about her future the way Fred often talked about his, with great uncertainty. He didn't care about *her* future—he didn't have time for that. He wanted to know what was happening right now. She was in a philosophical mood, wondering about the years to come. What were they going to do with their lives? Neither of them was trained in how to sell computer systems, which was the direction the company was headed. They needed to know digital the way Larry knew it, didn't they? But this wasn't one of those idle moments when Fred found himself plagued by such concerns.

He brought things back to the current week. Why not concentrate on selling the current product line, rather than worry about what they might have to sell after the turn of the century? She told him she knew how to sell. Maybe so, but he didn't like the way she did it. She wasn't in front of the customer enough. She told him she didn't like the way he managed her. He told her to knock on doors. (Did he think Akron Automotive would want her knocking on doors of end users in that building? She could just go wandering around?) She told him maybe she ought to just quit and be a housewife.

"I don't mean to burst your bubble," he said.

"Why are you so down?" she asked him.

"I'm tired of this. What's wrong? You got a cold?"

"I've been sick for three weeks. Where have you been?" she said.

.  .  .

One day passed, and then another, and another. All she could do now was wait to hear from Cook. Finally the phone rang. She suspected how it would turn out. She had just as much instinct and intuition as the rest of them—at a certain point in a deal, you know what's going to happen. Larry Tyler liked to think of it as a moment of eye contact where the customer's eyes meet the rep's eyes and the customer blinks first—that's when the deal is really closed, long before the signature. That's when the customer surrenders. Yet in a deal like this one, it was much harder to locate that crucial moment. Nancy needed this deal—not to get her to Palm Springs; at this point, she needed it simply to keep her self-respect.

Cook told her he was ready to sign. It was always like a phenomenal golf shot when the customer said *yes*. No matter how good you got at your craft, no matter how much you felt you could take credit for closing the deal, it felt as much like a gift as an accomplishment. When a six-iron shot sailed up into the sky and landed a foot from the hole, it was more than just an exercise of skill. It was magic. The gods breathed on that ball when it was airborne. And they breathed on a deal like this one too. She was thrilled. It felt the way selling felt in the earlier years, before she'd taken on this territory filled with enemies. Yet she suspected this would be the peak of her sobering year. Nothing else like this would happen from now through December. It was enough to get her through. She could still do it. She hadn't lost the touch. It wasn't just *her*—it was the territory that was making her life so miserable. That was easy to forget.

It put her only two thirds of the way toward her own plan, yet it gave Fred exactly the sort of encouragement he needed. Briefly, he was happy. But not *too* happy. There was too much left to do. As it turned out, his team topped a hundred percent of its budget for October. He left a group message to each of them on voice mail. He told them it was twelve-fifteen in the morning, and he had energy. He was raring to go. He was looking forward to a great December and end of the year. He wanted them all to know he was really proud to have Team One working for him. When Larry picked up his phone the next morning and listened to Fred's message, he shook his head and peeked around his partition at Nancy and asked what Fred had been drinking.

Fred was feeling cocky, despite himself. He refinanced his mortgage, and he handled the bank's representative as if the man were selling him a used car. The discussions on the refinancing lasted for days, ending finally in an arduous, point-by-point questioning of every clause in the contract, the two of them sitting in Fred's own living room. Afterward the bank rep looked like a man who'd been mugged. Fred kept pushing for a better rate, a better deal, and the bank officer kept telling him he was offering the best possible deal already. He kept turning his palms toward the ceiling, his arms outspread: What did Fred want? He was giving him everything he could. After the agreement was signed, as the man was on his way out, he asked Kathy how long she'd been married to this unusual creature.

Eighteen years, she told him. He felt for her. He told her he'd say a little prayer. She told him he wouldn't be the first one. He laughed. So that was how she did it. After he was gone, she turned to Fred and said that guy was a completely broken man. Fred grinned. Mission accomplished. They got a good deal. That's what counted. Fred knew all this confidence, all this satisfaction, was as fleeting as everything else in the life of sales. It was no guarantee.

His team was on the verge of topping its annual goal, and there was too much left to do. Making plan didn't count. You had to go well beyond it to be a success, no matter what the cost.


7.


AS DECEMBER APPROACHED, everything started to fall apart. Fred had been hoping to get some no answers, just to hear an answer, any answer—just to know where he stood—and now his reps began to hear the word *no* from their customers in a chorus. Hearing that word wasn't as much of a relief as Fred had hoped. Larry was stuck. Bruno lost a big order at one of his insurance companies. Nancy was getting nowhere with her non-users. What about you, Nancy? She told him the only thing she could do was put a gun to her head and say *Buy this.*

At one of the last big staff meetings of the year, everyone assembled in a dismal mood. Everyone was behind. Rob Onorato entered the room carrying a large blue-suited troll doll, the Wish-nick. Everyone looked at Fred and smiled. Rob placed the Wish-nick on the conference table and smiled at Fred. Rob had received the doll a month earlier, as punishment for his poor performance. Throughout the year, the Wishnick was adorned with little gestures of affection from the managers who got it. One manager tied a twine noose around the doll's neck. Onorato himself took a long letter opener and shoved the knife through the middle of the Wishnick's head. Everyone knew who would get the Wishnick in November. Everyone leered at Fred. Rob ordered the Wishnick: *Begone!* He told everyone he'd tried to amputate the doll's finger. Everyone looked at Fred. All year, he had missed getting the

Wishnick. Now, at last, it was his turn. As everyone chanted "Fred, Fred, Fred, Fred," Rob shoved the doll across the table, and Fred accepted it with his head bowed.

After the meeting Fred put the Wishnick on his desk beside his phone, where he would see it every day. He decided to make a call at one of Larry's accounts, hoping for a miracle. He met with an old friend at a company where Fred hoped Larry might have a slim chance of selling a DocuTech. While Fred wasn't counting on it, that deal alone would have put him over the top, making up for the deals falling apart around him, with plenty of cushion to spare. It was strictly an emergency measure. Larry had worked on it for months, but the company appeared to be in the process of selling itself to a larger corporation in Europe. Everyone was living in a state of suspense. It was a dead deal.

Fred returned to the office nervous and depressed. Little by little, his hopes were eroding. He needed every order—even the smallest. Bruno took a brief vacation and went hunting. Larry was unreachable. Diane stayed home sick after a trip to the dentist. Fred was astounded. "I had a filling! I had a filling! It's getting out of hand. You don't go home with a filling." Rob, passing by Fred's office, didn't bother to come in, but glancing through the door, he said as he walked away, "Don't chew on your fingers, Fred."

Fred pushed Nancy to let him ride with her, and they visited a couple of her prospects. It looked bad everywhere. After they got back to the office, Fred called one of the customers they'd seen and asked her, point-blank: *So what did you think?* I don't think we're ready. *What did you think of us?* We didn't like you, tell you the truth.

Fred couldn't help but laugh after he hung up, but the woman meant what she said. He felt she expressed something maybe all his customers felt. Maybe none of them liked him. Maybe he should become a parking attendant somewhere, or deliver mail, as his mother suggested once. It was steady. It was safe, except for the Dobermans. No sales quotas to meet. As it stood, he seemed to be losing the popularity contest. That wasn't all. He was losing Palm Springs. He was losing the whole game.

When you fail in sales, it's more than disappointment. You feel the tingling at the root of your spine you might have felt at the age of five, losing sight of your parents wandering through a foreign wood. You feel as if you're standing alone at the senior prom. As if you've been left off the list of people invited to the dinner party. Failure confirms your deepest suspicions that you're the most boring, least intelligent, most forgettable, or most laughed-at member of your graduating class. People don't buy from reps they don't like. A salesman needs nothing less than to be loved by everyone, so he's haunted by the specter of failure as a personal rejection, a sort of unrequited love. Failure makes you feel like a fool.

In a moment of desperation, like a prisoner trying to escape in the last few weeks of a twenty-year bid at Attica, he called one of Kathy's brothers, who'd gone into the securities business, and he asked about the exam a person needed to take to become certified as a stockbroker. Was it square roots and things like that? It was a pointless phone call. There was nothing to do but bear down and grind out the last few orders of the year. Fred felt as empty as he'd ever felt in his career. He had no rhythm with his team.

He wandered into Frank Pacetta's office, looking for energy, hungry for something that might spark the feeling he needed to keep making calls, to keep pushing. Everything had been going so well. What was wrong? He didn't want to believe his entire year could collapse in these final few weeks. Pacetta looked as crisp as ever, but Fred could see the anxiety in his eyes, the rash forming under one eye.

"You're battin' two-sixty, and you just can't do it, Fred," Frank said, trying to provoke him into anger.

"It's not over," Fred said, listlessly.

"It's over."

"We'll survive."

"We need a three-run homer."

"I gotta keep grinding, Frank. I'm not giving up," Fred said. "I'm not giving you lip service, either."

"I couldn't be any more exhausted and sick," Frank said.

"You look pretty good."

"Thank you. Freddie, for the first time in years, you're not going to do it."

Fred began to feel the urge to defend himself, and along with it, a surge of confidence. Pacetta had no right to predict Fred's doom. That was Fred's own privilege—he loved to predict his own demise, and he didn't want anyone else doing it for him.

He said, "I think there's something going to happen."

"Freddie, you got to step up to it. Block, tackle, execute. Block, tackle, execute," Frank said, and then yawned. "We're going to set every record, and I'm going to ride away into the sunset. I am outta here."

Suddenly Pacetta was a dynamo again. He sprang out of his chair, came around his desk, and got Fred into a half nelson, trying to wrestle him to the floor. Rob Onorato walked through the door, laughing, and Pacetta released Fred.

"I don't know about that tie. It's got too much going on," Pacetta said, and then clapped his hands together loudly, grabbed Rob around the neck, and started wrestling *him* to the ground. For a moment, it looked as if Fred and Rob might get a tag team thing going between them. Rob, laughing and grinning, struggled free.

Pacetta belched loudly enough for everyone in the bullpen to hear and returned to his seat.

"I had three major calls," Rob said.

"That takes a lot out of you. Fred, you used to invigorate me. I haven't seen it this year." He shook his fist to demonstrate. Fred once used to come running into Pacetta's office—during their first year in Cleveland together—shaking his fist in the air in triumph. Not anymore.

"Because they're—"

"You'll cruise into another President's Club while I stand here with my dick in my hand," Pacetta said, and then pointed toward Fred's chest and said, "Ninety thousand," and then pointed toward Rob's chest and said, "Eighty thousand," the implication being they were earning that kind of money every year while doing nothing but sitting in Frank's office talking all day. "Come on, guys. Let's all sit down. What you wanna talk about? Sports?"

Fred left Pacetta's office in a completely new mood. Laughing and wrestling and getting angry—he was sailing on a trade wind, as he always did leaving Pacetta's office. He became a cheerleader again with his reps.

"Larry, I don't want you to lie down on me."

"Fred. My buddy! How could you ever say that?"

He told Larry they should call on a customer. Fine. Larry didn't think it would do any good. They drove downtown to an account where Larry was trying to close a deal for a 5100. Fred felt maybe he could talk the customer into it. Larry said it would never happen. Fred wanted to find out.

*This is rock and roll. This is fun. I've got a goal, I'm going to make it. I'm still not giving up. I'm getting to the point where I'm fed up with everybody. I think people are giving me a lot of nice talk, and that's about it. I'm getting tired of it. Hey, we're running out of time. It'll be Friday soon. MondayTuesdayWednesdayThursdayFriday. That's the way it works. Poof, it's gone. Let's go get an order.*

Downtown, they met with Larry's customer in a conference room with the sort of contemporary decor that might be characterized as early Unidentified Flying Object. It looked like the dining-room scene from *Beetlejuice*. Art deco lamps, green shades like rings around Saturn, two small lamps hanging over the table like long fangs with black megaphone shapes stuck onto the ends.

Their customer, Hugh, had curly black hair that looked as if it had no organic link to the man's forehead, a strange countenance, with averted blue eyes, a long, sleek jawline, and a diffident manner, finicky, as if he were coiled up inside, waiting to strike, listening, but hardly making eye contact. He looked as if he wanted to step outside and fire some heat-seeking missiles down the hall, just to break some kind of inner tension no one else could possibly understand. He was wearing a white shirt, a dotted blue tie.

"Friday? Ha, ha, ha ha. Friday? This Friday? No way. No possible way I could do—"

"Now that we've gotten the humor out of the way," Larry interjected. "The rationale behind this last-minute offer is we want to reach our target this year for installed revenue. If not this Friday, then—"

"We're closed the following week."

"The thing is, if I understand it correctly, is that you would save thirty thousand the first year because there's no invoice."

" 'Cause, I mean, you're getting the savings up front, which is big dollars, big dollars," Fred said.

Hugh didn't look at Fred. He stared at the proposal in his hand. He issued a long sigh.

"I need justification for doing anything right now. Doing it by

Friday looks absurd. You spell it out for me," Hugh said, leaning his elbow on the table. "Exactly. Again, slowly. What am I getting by replacing the Kodak machine?"

"We were asked to look at replacing it," Fred said.

"Yes. It's a five-year-old machine."

"You must have problems with it. We're offering you the most advanced two-sided copier on the market. You're looking at getting something different. You have a need for everything it offers. We're not just selling sizzle."

"We can use these things. But they aren't enough to justify the machine."

"When you make a change, it will cost you more money. Here we're not charging you for that first year. You could run the wheels off this thing."

They could run this thing into the ground the first year and save big, big money on copies. What did Hugh want? He could save enough by loading it with work that first year—the money he saved on that work alone would more than make up for what it would cost him later on.

"Right now, we're moving faster than I wanna go. I'm not prepared to move this fast. Larry has been terrific, though."

On the way back to the office, Fred knew this was another dead deal. No miracle deal would save him this year. He would have to grind out the last few reasonable orders with his reps and see if they added up. Fred wouldn't devote another ounce of energy to this one. December was upon him, and he could count his hopes on the fingers of one hand: Bedford Telecommunications, Citadel, and Wellco. Nothing else was worth the effort of a wish.

# THE GRAIL

*1.*

THERE WAS NO time left for dreaming. Faced with the inescapable truth, people reacted in different ways. They redoubled their efforts or lost heart or threatened to quit or grew superstitious. One manager piled souvenir balls on a horseshoe, building a charmed pyramid of Titleists on the iron crescent. A younger rep, after dressing every morning, stood at his bureau and fished his three lucky pennies from an ashtray and dropped them into his pocket, carrying them on every call. Diane Burley wore her closing flats, with their broken hearts and lightning bolts, hoping they might let her walk on water at Crawford Manufacturing. The entire district seemed to have become a single organism, plugged into a single grid of shorted-out nerves. If you pricked a rep on Pat's team with an acupuncture needle, someone on Fred's team might feel better.

Fred looked around in amused wonder. What a genius was Pacetta that he could turn a sales district into a hospital ward! In comparison with all these other people, Fred was in comparatively good health, both mental and physical. It didn't make sense. After all, they were selling copiers. They weren't doing bypass surgery. They weren't refinancing an economy based on the ruble. They were refinancing machines that wedded paper to certain intelligible configurations of black dust. Why should six reps suffer from colitis in the effort to sell one more box? Why should Pacetta himself check his thermostat every hour, adjusting it up and then down, approximating the perfect temperature, turning his office into an oven, afraid too cool a temperature would trigger another case of shingles, like the one he'd developed during his first year in Cleveland, when the painful rash covered large tracts of his body, giving him a passing resemblance to the Creature from the Black Lagoon? Why did one rep's eczema get worse in reaction to these seasonal tensions? Was human skin especially vulnerable to the rigors of a difficult sales call? Did other kinds of effort tattoo the labor force this way?

One rep, in a spasm of anger, threw her frozen Thanksgiving turkey down a flight of stairs at her husband, missing the spouse but breaking both the turkey's legs. Several reps took Dramamine to deaden the nausea they felt on their most crucial sales calls. Rob Onorato, whenever he looked at himself in the mirror in the morning, tried to spot another pimple, what he liked to call either a pressure pimple or a nerve zit. In the office, he liked to worry about his complexion, his circulation, his sleep. He claimed he was getting morning nosebleeds from the tension of waiting on his Goodyear deal, the multimillion-dollar sale he needed to make the trip to Palm Springs. They all boasted about what they needed to suffer for Pacetta's sake. A pimple took on all the bogus grandeur of a shrapnel wound. Everyone wanted to win a Purple

Heart. *I just closed a huge deal, boys. Hyooge! Call me an ambulance! I haven't slept in three days! I'm fading fast! Tell my mother I love her and, here, send my dogtags home to my sweetheart, along with this order for three color machines!* People vied with each other to have the most amazing symptoms. Everyone wanted to suffer more than everyone else. One rep claimed that by dint of spending so many sleepless nights before her television she could rattle off the entire Nickelodeon schedule of sitcom reruns, the whole Nick at Night Television Heritage Preservation Lineup. Every Sunday night one of the youngest female reps walked into her closet and planted a pair of aspirin in every pocket of every suit she intended to wear the following week, as a precaution against evening headaches and morning hangovers.

December's tension infected everyone. One rep was as worried about his future as Fred. When his Christmas tree fell over, he left it lying on the floor and wouldn't touch it for a day. The next day he went outside, found his chainsaw, yanked it until it growled, and carried it into the dining room. Smoke and sawdust and the deafening scream of the engine filled the room. A lumberjack had been set loose in their dining room. After cutting an inch off the bottom of the trunk so it would lie flat in the stand, he carried the saw back outside and then cleaned up his mess.

Nancy Woodard was having strange dreams at night. In one dream she stood outside a banquet in the cold. Through the windows she could see the President's Club winners laughing, drinking, feasting. One of them came outside and proffered a drink. But she said no. She wouldn't be allowed to celebrate with them. She hadn't made trip. She was required to sit outside in the snow. One Sunday, during mass at St. Mary's Catholic Church, she stood and walked out. She started weeping, not discreetly, but with big tears trailing mascara. Every day she told her husband: "Why don't we both do something. I'll quit my job, and we'll buy a farm. I'll run a little gift shop somewhere." Gary said, "Fine with me." But neither of them bought the farm. Her life would return to normal when her territory changed. Until then, she needed to keep reminding herself that years like this one were the sort of thing that refined a sales rep into something exceptional. You had to lose in order to know the meaning of a win—even if the possibility of winning seemed so far away as to be nothing but an illusion. In this game, as in all the others, learning how to endure the losses was sometimes more important than knowing how to celebrate the wins. If anything, this year Nancy was learning far more than she ever wanted to know about a life in sales.

Pacetta was proud of all the walking wounded in his ward. He was grateful, pleased. They played hurt. What more could a coach require of his players or a commander in chief of his troops? These people were so devoted to their jobs, some of them threw up on sales calls just from worrying! Wasn't that something! Was there ever a team this devoted to their mission? Ah, the glamorous world of sales—and please remember to stick close to a toilet when it comes time to ask the customer a direct question.

Some of them had reason to feel nauseated. The district appeared to be in trouble. Millions of dollars were still unsigned for the printing systems team. No one expected the printing systems business to pop any earlier than December. Those customers knew how to stall. They had, as Pacetta put it, broken the code. The shrewdest customer knew he could get a better deal the longer he waited to sign. Stall a rep until the end of the financial quarter and the rep would be more desperate. Stall until year's end and the district would give you the lowest possible price. Whether or not it was true, the printing systems customers believed it, and they acted on it. So Fred knew the millions Pacetta still needed to write before the end of the month would probably come from the printing systems team. Pacetta didn't appear to be taking it for granted. He was moving constantly, sticking his head into doorways and asking for a number, showing a personal interest in everyone on the district team. He went on calls daily. Like Fred, he was constantly in front of customers, managers, and reps, constantly selling. He embodied the virtues listed on the signs he hung on doors so people couldn't walk through the office without seeing the words twenty times every day: PERSISTENCE, CONFIDENCE, HARD WORK, PERSISTENCE, CONFIDENCE, HARD WORK, PERSISTENCE, CONFIDENCE, HARD WORK.

In response to all the year-end anxiety Fred doesn't become ill. He resolves to do with even more intensity what he's been doing all year. He shuts his door, for privacy, and composes himself. He places his hands together in mock piety, palm to palm, in front of his chest, like a child kneeling beside his bed. He chuckles and smiles the smile he uses with his best customers, as if this might help, just a bit, so that just this once he might be able to put one over on God: He had been as good as he could be this year. He had a tear in his eye when his son played tennis. He went to ice-skating every Wednesday night with his daughter. He hadn't done anything fun. He hadn't gotten into any trouble. He'd been an ordinary boring husband all year. Then he claps his hands together loudly. *Let's take the hill!*

Out in the halls, he becomes the Fly again, buzzing from one cubicle to the next. He alights on Nancy in the hall: "What about copiers at Crockett Lang?"

"Fred, don't ask," she says, and keeps walking.

He turns around, like a traffic cop doing a U-turn before flashing his lights, and he catches up with her in three strides.

"I *will* ask. I *will* ask."

Yet nothing. No response. She walks away from him. When he

finds Larry Tyler in the hall, he calls him into his office and closes the door. It will be one of those meetings the reps call Assuming the Position. It's always the same plea: Just cut the bullshit, Larry. What's going to close?

Larry's face reddens, his gestures grow quick and precise. He slashes deals off the list with a yellow marker and then, when yellow doesn't look bleak enough, he uses a black marker. *Larry's snapping,* Fred thinks. *It's about time.* At last Larry is in the grip of something larger than himself. It's called I'm Not Going to Palm Springs, No Matter What I Do Now.

"I'm tired of all this shit about not doing anything!" he shouts, slashing another deal off the list. Fred smiles. Self-satisfaction glows in his face: *Yes, Larry has snapped. Now we can get to the truth.* "That's gone. Dead. That's dead. Dead! Why leave it on the books, huh? I found out today. This one's dead. I was processing the order, and it's dead. You won't get spit out of that one. But look at this. It's not like nothing happened."

"That one? Dead?" Fred says, all softness and sympathy. The Mystery Man has snapped. And the mystery, as it turns out, isn't so deep after all. A lot of dead deals. The truth has finally emerged. Fred would have preferred to keep dreaming. "Hmph. We'll call upstairs. They'll take it off the books."

Larry won't make trip, and neither will Fred if he doesn't find some way to push some crucial large orders this month. As always, his reps are bringing in orders, yet it never seems to be enough. It never *feels* sufficient. It doesn't help to play manager and grill people about where they stand. Fred wants to do it himself. Now he faces the crisis he's craved all year. Now is the time to scheme. Now is the time to get back in front of a customer.

· · ·

All year long, Fred had struggled to land an order that kept getting smaller and smaller at Smith Brewer, one of the largest law firms in the world, with headquarters in Cleveland. The odds were against it. But he'd lost so much ground there, he felt backed into a corner. When he was in this emergency state of mind he found himself able to do things he might not have the energy to do at any other time of year. When the whole game seemed lost, when he had nothing left to lose, he could rise to a higher level, he could surprise even himself. He needed just one win to get himself started—one successful home run to turn his mood around and get the chain reaction going, sparking the emotional momentum he needed to save his last few necessary orders.

This particular deal, for a big duplicator, had begun almost a year earlier and had built slowly to a crucial lunch in the spring, when he almost got his customer's signature for five of these same machines. The problem was, this woman invited an older manager to the lunch. The manager cast a chill over everything. She wanted to look strong in front of the older manager, to prove she wasn't swayed by Fred. So the deal dragged for months, and now his main contact, a young man named Bob Robinson, is stalling an order for only one duplicator. The deal has dwindled to this single order. The flame's almost dead. Fred knows he'll get nothing from Smith Brewer if he doesn't act immediately.

So he plans to meet Rob Onorato and Tommy Bill for lunch downtown and then pay an unannounced call on Bob Robinson at Smith Brewer. He intends to get the man's signature. Time has run out. He's tired of waiting. For months they've kept him waiting, disappointed, feeling like a footnote to their lives—he'll get the order as an act of revenge for his customer's weakness. If Robinson doesn't have the courage to make a decision and buy what he wants to buy, then Fred will force the order to happen. He will joke and cajole and press his customer into submission. He feels he's prepared to stretch out on the floor of the lobby and refuse to be carried away until he gets a signature. After what they've put him through this year—and he knows all he needs to do is get Robinson into a conference room and close the door. In a room, face-to-face, Robinson will be too embarrassed to say no after six months of waffling. He will shame the man into signing without having to say a word, if only he can get him alone.

He feels the stirring of a confidence he's felt only rarely this year. A warmth kindling behind his ribs, a feeling of craving and delight. It's the way he feels when he scores a nearly perfect game of golf, everything working together, everything happening of its own accord, the ball melting into the clouds and materializing in the blue and landing softly on the green. It's as if something else commanded him, enabling him to command his life. It's like peeling ripe segments of a nectarine off its crimson pit, the fruit just falling away from the seed, seeming to fall into his palm. He lives to feel that tingling in his muscles and joints and fingertips. The world feels exactly the way it feels when it seems merely an extension of his body as he walks down the eighteenth fairway, part of his heart, his mind, his will. He doesn't even call Smith Brewer to make an appointment. He intends to show up without notice and seize the order—it will be such an unpredictable thing to do, it might just work.

"No more phone calls. I go right from the restaurant to Smith Brewer. No more calls. I eat lunch, and then I go shoot up Smith Brewer. These guys are jerks. A goddamn copy machine. That's all it is! This is fun."

No matter what he's doing, Fred's thinking about all the other deals he needs. He's always peeking over the partitions, peering into Larry Tyler's empty cubicle. His voice rises into a whispered falsetto, the sort of singsong, dreamy voice Ophelia might have used before she fell into the water: "Larry's here. That's his coat. But he's hiding. Larry's here, everybody. The fly boy. I like Larry. Son of a bitch. The Mystery Man. Larry doesn't want to do his outlook with me. I can read Larry's mind. He's hiding. I'll find him, though." At this time of year Larry has only one comment about Fred: "He's going ballistic."

When Fred arrives at the restaurant, he hangs his coat on the rack, quarreling with Rob Onorato about who will pay for lunch. The table of strangers seated near the coatrack falls silent, listening curiously to the exchange between Fred and Rob. Rob hangs up his coat and walks away, and yet Fred keeps talking to him, from a distance of thirty feet, over the heads of these eavesdropping strangers.

"I am not going to pay," Fred says.

"Yeah, you are," Rob says, sitting down already.

"No, I'm not."

"Yeah, you are."

"No, I'm not."

"Yes, Fred, you are," Rob says.

"No, I'm not."

During lunch Fred thinks about Smith Brewer. If he sells one machine, he'll be happy. If he sells two, he'll be ecstatic. Lately Fred is thinking about more than machines. More than ever, he wonders about his marriage. He sells himself to everybody else all day long, the way he'll sell himself at Smith Brewer today. But not to his wife. She gets lost in this process, this focus. He tells people he'll wake up some day and realize he's succeeded at work but screwed up at home. His mother talked to Kathy's mother one weekend. Afterward she asked him, did he realize how he'd treated his wife all these years?

When they pay for the lunch—each paying for his own food—Fred walks to the Smith Brewer building. When he rises to the proper floor and gets off the elevator, the lobby's opulence startles him, though he's seen it many times. It's long and wide, with glossy surfaces that give the impression of marble and hardwood, and hazy abstract paintings almost as large as the walls themselves. Everything seems sophisticated and costly, even the half-light throughout the lobby, the flow of air through light and shadow, the muffled sound of ringing telephones in other rooms. He introduces himself to the receptionist and takes a seat. An hour later he's still waiting for Robinson to emerge from one of the doors.

*Why am I doing this to myself? Because I have hopes of making you-know-what. Gee, is it tomorrow yet?*

When Bob Robinson finally appears, he's disengaging himself with some discomfort from the group of customers he's been hosting. He's young, with a head of brown hair, a dark flannel suit, loafers with tassels, a symmetrical and friendly face. But when he turns and sees Fred, his friendliness seems strained and false.

"What are you doing here?" he asks with a lifeless smile.

"I was downtown," Fred says.

"I see."

"Well? Are we doing business?"

There's a long pause. Bob has nowhere to turn. He owes Fred this order, after all this time. In this pause Fred feels everything ride on Bob Robinson's response. If the man says yes, then Fred will have a chance to get his signature today—but it won't be simple. A *yes* improves the odds. Without the signature, Robinson can always back out. And if he says no, the order will never happen. He knows Robinson's pregnant wife is scheduled for the hospital tomorrow, to have labor induced, and Robinson will be away from his office for two weeks after his wife gives birth. In that period of time the momentum on this deal will be lost, and Kodak will have a chance to demonstrate a competitive machine. If he lets Robinson slip away now, Fred will lose this order. The law firm will back out of the deal if they see the Kodak machine—the competition is that intense.

"I'm going to sign for one machine," he says.

Fred can hardly believe it. "Thank you, Bob. Thank you." But these words mean almost nothing in this situation. Now the selling begins, and it has nothing to do with words. Fred produces the order form. At the sight of it, Bob's face turns ashen. Fred knows the look. It's the look that comes over most faces when the moment arrives for an irreversible commitment. They've come to the altar. Now's the time for vows. It's a look of fear, excitement, and bewilderment.

During the next five minutes the sale becomes physical. Slowly, Fred backs Bob across the lobby, edging him closer to the conference room behind them, the way one person pushes another person across a room at a cocktail party simply by shifting his foothold bit by bit, shrinking the comfort zone, forcing the conversational partner to keep retreating to restore his airspace. In this way Fred nudges Bob toward the conference room, where they can consummate the deal in privacy. They just need Bob's signature. He knows Bob has another pressing appointment. This will only take a couple minutes. It's better if they can get it today. They want to make sure everything is in order.

These words mean nothing. They fill the dead air as the real selling continues in the movement of legs and feet. Slowly, imperceptibly, as Fred advances on his customer and Robinson shrinks from his advances, they shuffle their way to the door. The nearer they get to the conference room, the more their backward shuffle becomes an outright walk, with Fred leading the way. With every step forward, he's closing a miniature sale. It's almost entirely physical, an act of will and emotion. By the time they reach the conference room, Fred has closed Robinson twenty times already, each step bringing Robinson closer to a complete surrender.

Finally they arrive at the room. Fred notices how Bob parts his hair in the middle, with the hair blown back. He has a rosy Irish complexion, and though he isn't overweight, his face still looks babyish, unmarked. He's a man who will look youthful even in his forties. This does not endear him to Fred. They close the door behind them and sit at the conference table, Bob in his chair, the order form on the table, and the pen placed atop the order form. Fred does everything with an air of inevitability and assurance. In the way he moves through the room, he shows Robinson that neither of them has any choice but to sign without delay or forsake the deal altogether. Fred raises the wager in this game by staking everything on that one act of commitment now—not the following day or week or month or year.

They really need to get this order to Chicago, to get Bob the equipment. They know his wife is going to have that baby tomorrow. That's why they've got to sign this order today. There's no reason to delay.

And then, as if through an act of supreme confidence, Fred backs away. He stands and moves back to the wall, leaving Robinson to gaze at the form and the pen. Robinson hesitates, looking at the papers. After he has agreed to the deal, to refuse to sign these papers now would make Robinson look like a fool. He is boxed into the deal. There is no escape. Fred's greatest accomplishment was simply to back Robinson across the lobby and into this room. In these four walls, he believes he has no choice but to surrender.

But he thought they were talking about five months on this part of the—No, six months. Case closed. Your signature, Bob.

There's nothing more to discuss. It would appear that Robinson has no choice but to surrender completely. Bob places his name at the bottom of the document. But the order isn't finished. Another form, underneath, awaits his signature. This is the most precarious moment of the call, yet Fred acts as if it were the most routine.

Larry Tyler would love this move. He loves to make the under-stated, casual gesture when the most crucial moment arrives—acting as if he were absorbed by other, more important things. When he arrives at that moment, he acts as if it were the most boring, most matter-of-fact stage of the sale. Fred stands and moves to a corner of the office, picking up the telephone and punching the number to review his voice-mail messages back at the office. He turns his back to Robinson. Bob Robinson might object to some clause in these forms as an excuse not to sign them. If he does, the deal will dissolve. If he signs, Fred will have his order and will be near enough to Palm Springs to smell the desert air. If Fred shows any fear, any hesitation, at this moment, Robin-son might feel as if he's being fooled into doing something that isn't in his best interest.

Fred glories in the tension of this moment. As he stands there, slightly behind Bob, he starts making goofy clown-like faces. He makes faces to the air, to the Neil Welliver and Alex Katz artwork on the walls, to the empty hallways outside. Fred makes faces at his own demons, in the shape of this intransigent customer sitting at this expensive table.

This is the sort of showdown Fred loves. He leans against the flocked wallpaper, and as he watches Bob, he realizes all the year's calls and luncheons, and demonstrations and proposals often come down to nothing more than a moment of physical presence—as if he and Bob were facing each other across a line of scrimmage. As Fred watches, Bob signs the second form as well, almost without comment, and the deal is done.

It seemed so easy, once it was finished. It felt as if he'd been paid to do nothing but lunch people, talk to them, flatter them, entertain them, show them how to do something that made good business sense and then ask them for a little reciprocation. Where was the work, where the effort, in all this? But five hours earlier, before the signature, his job felt as if it weighed three tons and he'd been carrying it for days on his back. The nectar of selling nestled in this supreme moment of relief—the feelings of weightlessness after the signature happened, the balloon ride, the brief certainty of one's own omnipotence, the inflated sense of painlessness. Selling was narcotic. Fred loved it more than anything. He would die without it.

Back in his own office, Fred recounted his win for Rob Onorato, who wandered into Fred's presence after almost everyone else in the district had gone home that night. There was no way to tell whether or not Bob Robinson had read and understood what he was signing in that conference room, but Fred portrayed the sale to Rob as an act of pure sleight-of-hand salesmanship. As Fred pictured it for Rob, the Smith Brewer customer didn't understand his company would need to pay a separate invoice for what it owed on the Kodak machine. Xerox would cut a check for what the customer owed on the competitive machine, and the customer would use that money to pay off the balance on the old machine. If the sales rep didn't fully explain how Xerox would later bill the customer for this same amount separately, a customer could believe he wouldn't be invoiced for it. Fred believed his customer didn't mind paying the Kodak balance, as long as he didn't get a separate invoice for it. All customers were required to sign a form at the close of the deal proving that they understood how this arrangement worked.

Rob didn't act as if he put much credence into Fred's vainglorious moment. A lot of self-serving boasting was done in this office. Some of it was based on fact, and some of it wasn't. Without much enthusiasm, Rob told Fred he'd done a nice job.

In his delight, Fred went through the files outside Pacetta's office, looking to see how many tickets to Cavaliers games remained. He didn't find the one his son most wanted to see—when the Cavs played the Bulls—but he did come up with two tickets to the home game against Atlanta. He called Christopher at home and told him he had the tickets, but without telling him he hadn't paid for them. The tickets were free, but Christopher didn't need to know that.

"It's going to be one of your birthday presents," he said. "A big game, buddy."

Christopher was surprised and impressed. Everyone was happy —Christopher, Bob Robinson, and Fred. For a few hours, maybe even a few days, everything would be right in the world. Everyone had gotten a good deal.

At the end of the year, as everyone tried to please Frank Pacetta, a deal perfectly executed on the Leadership Through Quality principles—building a sense of partnership with the customer, showing the customer how to improve the way he did his own business—might end with a minor twist that was pure gamesmanship, the feint just before the slam-dunk. The only difference between selling and basketball, though, was that the customer didn't know until much later that Xerox had scored those points. The other team didn't know it lost the scrimmage until long after it was over, if ever.

Fred could have quit now and considered himself successful— more successful than most. But he'd been trained to see President's Club as a personal standard, not a rare award granted on the few years everything happened perfectly. He felt the pressure to go beyond what might normally be expected, the pride in making President's Club every year for a decade, the need to keep proving himself, distinguishing himself, in the hope someone upstairs might notice and bestow the raise or promotion that would change his life for the better. Most of all, he needed to keep going because Pacetta needed Fred's results to make his own target. What Fred did at the end of the year, he did to please his boss. As one rep put it: "Nothing can be beneath you at the end of the year. It will prevent you from doing what you need to do."

At Wellco, Fred worked out a way of inducing his customer to sign for the equipment by baking into the price the cost of more than a hundred thousand dollars' worth of supplies, and then offering these supplies at no charge. Wellco would never pay a separate invoice for those supplies, but only because it would pay for them in the price of the copiers themselves. Getting this deal was the only way he could make up for *all* the deals he'd lost in November and earlier in the year.

There was no need to tell Al Brook how much less those machines would cost without the supply costs factored into them. If Brook agreed to the copier price—which paid for both the lease and the supplies—then he would be agreeing to the deal itself, even without knowing exactly what he was paying for. Fred wouldn't explain it unless he was asked. This was especially daring because Wellco had become disenchanted with Xerox six years earlier, as Fred understood it, because they'd been told they wouldn't have to pay for supplies and then had ended up paying for them. In those days, apparently, it hadn't been so easy to add the supply costs to the monthly fee. For five years after that disaster, Fred was told, Wellco would have nothing to do with Xerox.

This sort of tactic with financing had become commonplace on large orders. Some Xerox reps told the customer everything about the deal's financing. This was a disadvantage, because many competitors disclosed almost nothing in *their* proposals. Others narrowed the financial information in a proposal, with an emphasis on one number—the monthly fee for a leased copier.

Unless a customer asked for the deal's total cost and an itemized breakdown of what that price included, there was no way the customer could know—at the proposal stage—exactly what he was paying for. This sort of flexibility, on the part of the seller, is a common element of old-school salesmanship. When someone buys a car and the dealer throws in a car stereo at the last minute "for free," the smart buyer knows the cost for that option has been factored into the car's price somewhere already.

Now, if you're a Xerox rep, you can easily slip extra charges into the deal. If you spread payments out over longer and longer periods, the total cost rises while the initial monthly fee stays comfortably low. You can bake things into the deal, raising the deal's total price, without calling attention to it—even though the customer could have gotten a lower monthly fee without those things baked in. You don't need to list the deal's total cost in the proposal—and if the customer doesn't ask, it becomes irrelevant. Nor are you ever obligated to tell the customer he can get a lower price than he's getting on the machine itself.

This situation creates fertile ground for churning, and in this situation the term takes on its full meaning. It's a term borrowed from stock transactions where brokers trade stock within a portfolio simply to earn commissions on needless transactions. To churn equipment, you go back to loyal customers and ask them to replace their current Xerox equipment with new Xerox equipment before the lease on the old equipment is paid off. You entice customers with lower monthly fees during the first year of the new lease. The customer might get an unusually low monthly payment during the new contract's first year, then the price leaps next year. In the third year, or sooner, you show up again—years ahead of the second lease's expiration—and do the same thing again. In effect, you build a greater total debt for the customer, while the customer keeps delaying the payments deeper into the future, spreading the debt—now for more than one machine—over three years and then five and then seven.

Often, when your customer leases a new machine, he believes he's being forgiven for what's owed on the previous machine. This never happens. You bake the debt on the old machine into the cost of the new machine, adding that balance into the total cost. Some customers know how this works and don't mind. It's a temporarily easy way to postpone the payments. But many customers have no idea what's happening. They don't bother to ask about details on the financing. Many of these details will be spelled out, in the proverbial small type, in the final contract—but by that time it's usually too late to back out without looking foolish.

Most reps justify churning in two ways. First, the customer's buying a monthly payment schedule, not a total debt. If the customer can accept the monthly payments, it doesn't matter how those payments add up. It doesn't matter that the customer will be paying for the new machine *and* the old machine at the same time. Second, if the customer doesn't ask key questions, then the rep is in no way obligated to ask those questions on the customer's behalf. The less information you present, the less chance for "muddying the water."

Besides, on this level, buyers go to school for negotiating skills, and they're as professional and skilled as good salesmen. They're trained to be opponents. In basketball, nobody frowns when Michael Jordan fakes a pass before he flies over the paint and slams the ball through the net. In football, nobody yells foul when Jim Kelly fakes a handoff to one of his running backs before he makes the pass. In poker, a good bluffer is honored as a master of the game. The curve ball, the faked handoff, the bluffing wager—the hustle's just as much a part of selling, and when buyers attend seminars on how to negotiate and play this same game, the sleight of hand is what makes the sale a delight, a victory. There's only one catch—this view of sales makes the customer your opponent, not your partner. It's the very antithesis of the new school, the quality approach. It's exactly the kind of approach a team of Assassins, as Pacetta would have it, could use without a qualm.

Many reps felt these financing techniques were perfectly justifiable. If a customer agreed to a monthly fee schedule over the course of the leasing agreement, then it didn't matter exactly what charges were factored into that fee schedule. The customer found it acceptable—that was all that mattered. Other reps felt ashamed of telling the customer he was getting a great deal when, often, he was paying top dollar for the machines he wanted to lease. Customers had no way of knowing how low a rep could go in his pricing of the machines, and a rep could tell a customer the price was rock-bottom when in fact it was near the top of the sale range. In Fred's view, though, there was nothing wrong with asking Al Brook to pay a premium price for the machines to make up for the credit he was giving him on the supplies, even if the customer didn't know he was paying top dollar for the machine to compensate for the supply credit—it was all a matter of semantics. Nothing was free. It merely looked and sounded free. If Brook found the cost of the machines acceptable, it didn't matter if Fred was making up—in the high price of the machine itself—for what the company lost by not charging Brook for the supplies. It was the way everyone did business—when something was free in sales, it was only cosmetically free.

On the day of the Wellco call, Al Brook and Sue Kelly looked pleased to see Fred. It was no wonder, considering what Fred was offering him.

"This is pretty amazing," Fred said, handing over the proposal. They were giving Brook a credit memo for a hundred and thirty thousand dollars. He could use that memo toward the cost of all his supplies for the next thirty-six months.

"Totally free supplies?" Sue asked.

"That's right," Fred said.

They sat on the same side of the table in a small, unadorned conference room, the sort of cell where the bulk of American business was conducted every day. So much of Fred's life had been spent in these rooms, with their generic artwork and swivel seating and long, burnished tables. Grandfatherly and midwestern, with his wavy gray hair and his glittering narrow eyes, Brook was a relief to see, smiling at Fred across the table. Fred struck him as a man who understood how sales came down to one thing, as he put it, holding out his open, empty palm: Sales was pressing the flesh. The act of trust, of partnership, of friendly congress. Fred knew how to press the flesh, how to merge himself quickly and painlessly into a customer's heart. Fred had offered Brook and his organization the Xerox wisdom about Total Quality Management. Fred could read gratitude in the man's face. He'd made Al Brook a courier of information important to his own company. Now he owed Fred.

When Fred passed the written proposal across the table to Brook, he knew how little the proposal told his customer. It offered only the most essential information. It spelled out nothing about how he was paying a higher monthly fee for the machine in exchange for getting the free supplies. The toughest customers would ask for more information and would keep asking until they got it. Those were the customers who stalled a deal until the last possible day, grinding it down to the lowest possible price. But most customers wanted to preserve their friendly relationship with the salesman. They dickered, they asked questions, but within limits. They allowed a rep and his manager to make the trip to Palm Springs. They valued the relationship as much as they valued the particulars of a given deal. Al Brook was one of those customers.

"Sounds good. What we'd like to do is sort through this," Brook said. "It's only a matter of months since you got through the door. The purchasing department would have shot me. But it's the quality connection that did it."

"Is this something we can get this month?"

"It could happen."

He liked Al, and Al liked him. He could make the man laugh. That was why he was giving Fred this order. Fred hoped it would work. He had to maintain his confidence. He didn't have any choice. He needed Wellco, and his time was running out.

## 2.

IT WASN'T GOING to happen for Larry Tyler, and he knew it. He would make his budget, but he wouldn't exceed it enough to make trip. He felt like a man wandering through a desert, pushing his feet through the rippling sand. Every day he was in the office by seven-thirty, making phone calls, driving out to visit his best customers, still struggling for two or three small orders. He had almost nothing left to draw upon. Everyone felt this way in December. One of the reps from the other teams put it nicely, when her manager hammered her for more orders: *What do you want me to do? Take my clothes off and lie across the guy's desk? My customers are putting them into their basements at home! My territory is dry! I'm not going to stand on my head and spit jelly beans.*

In the second week of December, Larry got into his car and drove east to Mentor, a quiet town on Lake Erie, to close a deal on a personal copier with a friend of one of his customers at Avery Dennison. It was a long drive. So much mileage, and so little money. A less diligent rep would have found excuses not to make the drive, but Larry needed every penny he could get in compensation.

The man, John O'Neill, had retired from the company and wanted a copier for the business he ran out of his home, where he managed his family's inheritance. Larry was making this call as a favor to the people he knew at Avery, people who controlled the purse strings for much larger deals. Yet he wanted the deal for himself too, no matter how small. He was eager to write business—any business. This sale wouldn't get him anywhere near Palm Springs. Yet it was a chance to sell. He would keep fighting, even when he knew the battle was lost. He wasn't about to pass up an order.

In the ditches and furrowed mud of Mentor, the snow was deep and dirty, like marzipan glazed with ash. Years ago, all the snow in this region looked rusted, with a coat of oxidized orange grit from the steel mills. Some things in life *did* get better. Larry's grandchildren were better-looking than he was. He was more successful than his father. Cleveland's snow wasn't coated with grit the color of chili powder anymore. And yet there would always be bad years, years when he felt obliged to call on lonely lakeside cottages. This was such an odd call, though—it had been years since Larry knocked on someone's front door. The little sign said: THE CITY OF MENTOR ON THE LAKE WELCOMES YOU. In the window at Burger King: TWO BURGERS TWO FRIES TWO BUCKS. The bungalows along Lake Erie looked somnolent and cramped, with scrubby lawns and discarded toys in backyards. The lake looked opaque and rumpled under a tin sky.

Larry parked in the drive. Behind John O'Neill's bungalow he saw a breakwater, a little bar of breached sand covered with rushes and brackish muck, and a power-boat launch farther down the shore. O'Neill answered the door in jeans and a black designer sweater. Polite and serious, he looked a little younger than Larry. He led Larry through the house to a study in the back, with a broad view of the lake. The house seemed at the edge of some ocean, with nothing but gray wind-pummeled water stretching to the horizon. Larry started his pitch for the midsize copier he planned to sell O'Neill, bringing out his brochures. His voice carried the pleasant, fluent warmth of mastery. With a big enough copier, he could make some money on this sale. Not much, but *some*—more than he deserved—if he made the right moves. One glance at O'Neill told him he could sell this man anything. Then the phone rang.

"Is she breathing?" O'Neill asked. "Damn it. I'll be right over."

He hung up, and the muscles in his face slackened. O'Neill looked forlorn. He looked too young to seem so weary of things.

"My mom has lung cancer," he said. "She lives two doors down. She's having a coughing attack. I'll have to cut this short. Do you mind? I'm really sorry. I'll go on down and come back. We may have to reschedule this. I'll be right back."

He didn't know Larry, and Larry didn't know him. It was absurd to be talking about one's personal life with a stranger, but sales required fleeting, instant intimacy of the kind nurtured by neighboring seats on a long jet flight. He rushed out, and Larry waited. He noticed two toothbrushes resting beside the blotter on the desk (where did *they* come from?), and then he glanced at the walls. O'Neill had sundials on a shelf, a few books, and an acoustic guitar leaning in the corner, with a numbered list of songs taped to the side: "St. Louis Blues," "Shine on, Harvest Moon," "East of the Sun." In the newspaper stand, a small box of incense. On the chair, a corduroy jacket and a tweed jacket. O'Neill's inner life seemed to be exposed everywhere, unprotected. Leaning against the wall near the guitar was a sword: ornate, antique; it looked as if someone had pulled it from a stone somewhere, long ago, and it had been handed down from one generation to the next so many times, that no one recalled its origin.

Larry wanted to sell O'Neill a 5018, but it was becoming apparent O'Neill didn't need it. This was not a high-tech office. He had no computer on the desk, no answering machine attached to the phone. On the bulletin board he'd posted Polaroid photographs of the nondescript real estate he bought. Next door the man's mother was dying, and yet he was muddling through. There was no way to separate the man from his work, no way to make it simply a matter of some corporation's money. This money wasn't an impersonal column of numbers shifted from one place to another on a spreadsheet. This money was different. It would come out of a bereft man's pocket. Within a few minutes, O'Neill returned. He appeared distracted and rushed.

"Let me fill out the paperwork," he said. "I've got to go back. She's hysterical."

"Well," Larry started, flustered, ready to resume his pitch but at a loss, now that O'Neill looked ready to sign an order form. This customer didn't know what he was buying, and already he wanted to order. Larry wanted to be done with it. Here, sitting before Larry Tyler, was probably one of the easiest marks, one of the weakest customers, ever encountered in the history of office equipment sales. Larry could make more money than he'd anticipated, if he had the stomach.

"All these machines, you'll be paying more, but there's a reason," he said.

If he wanted to, Larry could sell this man a bigger copier than he needed, using a lease, apportioning the payments in such a way that O'Neill wouldn't know the difference.

"I do real estate, see. Stocks and bonds. All the stuff I've got here I'll have to put on a computer. I figure I need a copier too."

Yes, Larry understood. He ruled out the 5018. It was too big. Why was he ruling it out? O'Neill hadn't objected to it. Was he losing his nerve already in this sales call? He could still push for the 5014, though. There was a little money left for him in that deal.

"What we're looking at for you is a small desktop model. The 5014 is different from the 5012. It does reduction and enlargement," Larry said. It was absurd to be selling anything to this man, wasn't it? Selling a copier in these circumstances? Everyone in sales talked about how wonderful they were at establishing a personal relationship with their customers. What, in a circumstance such as this, would qualify as a personal relationship? Why not just bag the sale and talk for fifteen minutes about what this man's mother had been like when she was younger? Was it completely human, pushing copiers in this situation, prattling copy from a brochure? He could have been asking normal, human questions.

"Mm-kay," O'Neill said.

"If you have to do heavier copying, you can do it with this better model," Larry said. It was best to finish up and leave. Larry would sell him the 5014, even if it was more than O'Neill needed. Make it quick and painless. Get it done and get out.

It was clear what machine O'Neill needed. It was the smallest copier Larry was prepared to sell him. The cheapest model. But O'Neill could be swayed to buy anything in his present state of mind. Larry faced a decision. He could still make money on this, if he wanted to. He could do the valiant thing for his district and give this man more than he needed. He could do it for Fred and Frank and the corporation and Wall Street and the shareholders. Or he could do what was best for his customer.

"Okay, so where do I sign?" O'Neill asked. "I've got to give you some money and sign."

"Whoa. I didn't know if you wanted to lease it or not."

"No. I want to buy it," O'Neill said, lighting a cigarette. He took a deep drag. "And I'll need a receipt."

Fine, he would give him the better copier. O'Neill wasn't objecting.

"Today's the sixth, right?" Larry asked, filling out the order.

"Listen, do people do reduction and enlargement a lot in my kind of business?" O'Neill asked, puffing.

All Larry had to do was say yes. He could lead John O'Neill anywhere. But, instead, O'Neill was leading *him* toward the smallest machine.

"No. You don't really need that feature," Larry said, halting in the paperwork. He was no Assassin. It was going to be the smallest machine—the machine that really suited O'Neill's needs. He was going to make almost no money on this deal. It was unavoidable. Did it matter? Either way, he wasn't going to Palm Springs.

"So we have to change the paperwork, huh? If I could think of a reason to use it, I probably would. So what is that? The 5012 I'm getting now?" O'Neill asked.

"Yes, sir," Larry said, smiling at last, starting new paperwork. He was going to give the man only what he needed and nothing more—no manipulation, no baked-in payments, no churning of old equipment, no pressure, no smiling mockery of the buyer, no craving to make trip. John O'Neill was going to get exactly what he wanted and needed. He, the customer, was going to be served in the best way possible. The phone rang again.

"Hello. Okay. Is she calmed down? I know you can't answer me. Let me see if I can put it in words you can say yes or no to. When she was throwing up, was that blood or was that Darvocet? Mm-hmm. The fellow here is going to leave, and I'll be right over," he said, and hung up. He dragged on his cigarette. "And I'm smoking. She's dying of lung cancer, and I'm smoking."

Larry scribbled frantically. He wanted to leave. He handed the forms to O'Neill. "Would you mind using the ballpoint? This is a felt tip."

As he was shown to the door, Larry said, "I wish I could have come at a better time."

"So do I," the man said. "This is the worst time of my life, actually."

If this were the way every sale happened, most major corporations would go out of business. Even Larry knew Xerox wouldn't last long if every buyer could turn a salesman into a sort of nursemaid to every buyer's feelings and needs. Where did the rep's need for an income, and the company's requirement for a profit, come into balance with the customer's desire for the right product? Could a company make a profit without sometimes pushing beyond the limits of human decency, without forcing things to happen that might not always be in the best interest of every human being who bought the product? Did a customer really need to break a salesman's heart to get an intelligent sale? In order to get a good deal, was a customer well advised to have a close member of the family on her deathbed in the cottage next door on the day a Xerox rep walked through the front door? Usually, all it took was an effort to slow down the sale and ask a few extra questions—and yet how seldom a customer thought to pose the most obvious queries about a deal, as O'Neill did, despite all the distractions.

As Larry climbed into his car, he watched John O'Neill trudge through the snow in his salt-stained cordovan loafers, hunched forward. He looked as if he'd made this trek, this pilgrimage from one house to another, a thousand times. He looked like a boy walking home from school late in winter, heading for light in a kitchen window. The man's entire life seemed to weight his steps through the snow—childhood, adulthood, middle age, and what lay beyond. He looked as lonely as Larry felt. Larry wished he could have done more for the man. Silently, Larry had asked the essential human question: *What is your sorrow?* And he'd done what little he could to make the man's life a little easier. It was its own reward.

At best, a salesman was supposed to do what Larry had done—grasp the core of another person's humanity and then serve it. A salesman *could* make a living by serving other people with compassion and intelligence and genuine friendship. At the moment, though, it just didn't seem to be the sort of approach that got a rep to Palm Springs—nor the kind of approach that would enable a company like Xerox to survive.

3.

IN THE EVENINGS, it wasn't unusual for Fred to run five miles and then wolf a nervous, eccentric dinner—a bowl of cereal, a large bag of peanut M & M's, and twenty chicken wings. At home Fred was more agitated than he'd been all year. He was certain Pacetta would be leaving Cleveland. He was certain he would never make President's Club. Once again he was telling Kathy he knew he would die before the end of the year, smiling while he predicted his own death, as if it would be an amusing apotheosis of his devotion and self-sacrifice, the final and unimpeachable exhibit of his worth as a worker. No mere disease, no mere Purple Heart—no, death was the Medal of Honor itself.

"I mean, there's twelve days left! Twelve good working days, I mean. I'm starting to get antsy. I'm wishing things to happen!" he said.

Was this doom and gloom again? Kathy was running water in the sink, and Fred was sitting at the kitchen table. Behind him, small bulbs recessed into the ceiling cast their glow on portions of wall and appliance. The entire room was reflected in the microwave's black door. From upstairs, Kylene shrieked, "Turn off the water!" The loss of water pressure upstairs was scalding her in the shower.

"Diane has had three straight horrible months, when you take Citadel out," he said. And who knew if they would get Citadel?

Kathy shook her car keys and grabbed her purse. Fred looked up from the table.

"Where you going?"

"Store," she said.

"Grocery store or store store?"

"Just odds and ends."

"You coming back?" he asked and smiled.

"No. I'm leaving you."

"You got the VCRs?" he asked.

Kathy knew what Fred meant. Instead of "videotapes," he said "VCRs." Instead of "Heimlich maneuver," he said "Hinelick remover." Instead of "*The Pelican Brief*," he liked to say "*The Pelican's Nest*." In conversation with Fred, Kathy's brain worked like one of those boxes that unscramble cable signals.

"Oh, yeah," she said.

"See how I remember everything?" he asked.

"You're amazing, Fred."

"I am. I'm incredible."

After she left, he coiled spaghetti on his fork, eating rapidly, filling his cheeks with food, squirreling nourishment. Then he got another serving, and then another. As he ate, he was absorbed by his thoughts. *Bruno creates the need for a new machine. Nancy does not create the need.* He watched Christopher go down to the basement, to work on his train set. He followed his son downstairs. (Did anyone notice how much of himself he devoted to his children? On Monday, basketball practice with Christopher. On Tuesday, the father-daughter Brownie dance with Kara. On Wednesday, skating with Kylene. On Thursday, basketball practice again with Christopher. The other night, he'd been down in the basement showing Kylene how to serve a volleyball.)

Christopher was dressed in one of his Michael Jordan shirts and unlaced basketball shoes. Fred was still wearing his shirt and slacks from work. The track segments weren't linked together firmly enough, and he helped squeeze them together. The basement was where Christopher used his imagination, where he dreamed of things other than sports. After Fred tightened the wires, the train lurched and toured its track, grinding and clicking along. Like that train, Fred circled the basement.

"Hey, Chris. This is where the pool table will go. We'll have weights over there. The wet bar goes here, and you can watch television in this area and from over there when you're doing weights."

"You just dream," Christopher said, grinning, happy to hear his father's quiet optimism. It wasn't a typical mood for Fred.

Fred went back upstairs, and the phone rang. It was Larry Tyler.

"Super job, Larry. Hey, even though I give you problems, I know what you're doing. Between you and me, I don't think it can be pulled off this year. One order isn't going to make or break you." Larry did a decent job, even though he wasn't making trip.

They discussed other deals that would never close before the end of the year, and then Fred hung up. He thought about what Larry had told him: *Oh, and by the way, Fred, I called. They're going to turn over all their machines in October next year. Fine, Larry. Next year.*

*October. Great. Thanks, Larry. How about this year? How did we get out of this year already?*

Everything was uncertain now. Even Frank Pacetta had disappeared. Fred wondered what his boss was *really* doing in New York City. At the peak of the sales year, Pacetta left them all to fight their last battles on their own. When was he coming back? Nobody knew for sure. Oh, there was an official explanation for the week-long absence—Pacetta's father was in the hospital after a heart attack, and the dutiful son flew home to Brooklyn to be with him and to help his housebound mother get through the ordeal. There were, however, other explanations. Few people in the district believed Pacetta was ever on the level. There was always a second or third or fourth level of meaning. He was probably flying to Washington or Georgia or Texas for a job interview.

One day, Fred discovered that two other managers had been given conference phones. One of them taunted Fred about it. Why didn't the major accounts sales manager get a conference phone? Was there a message waiting for him in that little slight? He didn't care. What would he do with it? But in December everything took on a charged signficance, thanks to Pacetta. He wanted to create conflict everywhere. He loved conflict. Before he left for New York, Pacetta stuck his head into Pat Elizondo's office and said something to make her angry, and then, to make her laugh, he sighed: "Now I've got to go piss off Rob." Everything fueled the year-end paranoia. Everything became an omen, down to the rationing of conference phones. Fred asked Rob what he planned to do with a conference phone. *That's a little petty of you, Fred.* No, it isn't. What are you going to do with it? *You're being petty, Fred.* Pacetta was probably smirking. He might be orchestrating the whole thing to make Fred insecure enough to push his hardest in December.

Kathy arrived a few minutes after Fred hung up. When she came back into the kitchen from the garage, Fred felt cold air sweep his ankles. Shopping of any sort could chill the room, especially in December. It was the second week of December, and no one had shopped for the children. Fred expected Kathy to do it, and she expected him to do it. It wasn't getting done. Kathy went on strike, in essence, because no matter what she bought, Fred criticized her choice of gifts. How much did it cost? Did the kids really need it? Did she charge it or pay cash? He would tell her he was going to take it back the next day. So instead of putting herself into position to be criticized, she refused to shop.

Fred glances at Kathy, after she puts away the groceries. She stands beside the butcher-block counter in the center of the kitchen, highlights in her blond hair, her mouth set in a familiar line. She looks beautiful, even at this hour, after a long day.

"I know what they want, Kathy," he says, lowering his voice. "They like going to the mall and picking out something."

"Fred, Christmas is supposed to be a surprise. This is what I mean. The whole meaning of Christmas goes out the window."

What did Fred buy for himself at noon? What were the clothes he brought home today? Sweater and slacks, from the Liz Claiborne outlet downtown—he liked Claiborne clothes for men. Kathy said that was just the sort of thing she meant. He went in and picked it out and just bought it. She'd love to do that. She'd love to buy right off the mannequin. Instead, she sifted through racks, looking for sales, discounts. She searched for labels.

"I have no desire to go to Christmas parties," Fred says.

"Why?"

"I have no desire to go. None. I buy clothes so I have something to wear during the holidays. That's all," he says.

She returns to the subject of who will be doing the Christmas shopping for the children.

"Do you realize, when all the Christmas shopping was done in September and not one word was spoken except that I paid full price—"

"Kathy, there's no game plan," Fred says.

"It's got to get done, with or without a game plan. If I don't do it this year, you'll do it. That's the way I look at it," she says.

"No, I can't do it. That's like Diane Burley—if she doesn't make President's Club, it's her fault, not mine. How bad do you want it? How bad do you want to raise the level of your game? Whether you like it or not."

Upstairs, Christopher yells down at them. Their voices carry throughout the house now. But he isn't telling them to quiet down. He wants the television turned off in the family room. It's been on since dinner, tuned to CNN. Fred gets up from the table, turns off the television, and returns to the kitchen.

"You don't realize," he says, lowering his voice again. "It's going to get done. Why put yourself under stress and pressure by postponing it?"

"In all the years we've been married, I've tried every possible game plan, and—"

"You are stressing out," he says.

"But I'm not worried about it."

"*I'm* not worried about it," he says.

"Why are you bringing it up every half hour?" she asks.

"You can't get yourself physically started. That's your problem. You're mentally drained. I don't care if I make trip."

"Can I get that in writing?" Kathy asks.

"You don't understand. My expectation level is high. I'm at the stage of my life where—I don't like it, but I'll get over it. If I don't go. As you get older, things change. I'm not going to—if I'm going to jump through hoops, I'll go through them myself," Fred says, his voice much quieter, more thoughtful.

"When I go to get the things the kids say they want, you tell me how stupid they are."

"I think I can satisfy them better. Chris needs a real basketball. An outside basketball. He'd love to have an alarm clock for his room. You just want to get a bike for each of them and then a computer," he says, keeping his voice lowered, glancing toward the open door in the dining room. "Kara doesn't need a bike."

"Is that what you're suggesting?"

"I really don't want to go to Christmas parties. I just want to stay home and watch *King of Kings*. Who's that blue-eyed actor who's in it? I was trying to remember today. You know, I've got twenty years left on this round ball, and I truly care about my kids and about you—"

"You care about me?" she asks, with mock surprise.

"If somebody in my family is threatened, I have to get up and go ward it off. That's my life. That's work. Aside from that, it's over, my life is over."

"I don't know where you get the energy," she says, softening.

"Paul MacKinnon brought it up today. He said, *Fred, you've got to decide. In five years, you'll need a high income.* It's true. You should get a full-time job, Kathy."

"Did he tell you something you didn't know?" she asks, annoyed that he listened to Frank's right-hand man on the subject of their future when he won't listen to her.

"He told me I've got to make a decision. If I end up as a sales rep, that isn't high income. Not with Xerox."

"As if you don't know that."

Fred bristles at her tone. Rather than defend his own suggestion about her career, he defends Paul MacKinnon's honor. Fred jumps up from the table and pinches Kathy's checkbook from her purse.

He was into her checkbook earlier, spying on expenditures, and suddenly he's in a rage again, looking at it.

"Paul is a tremendous human being. Paul doesn't cash twenty dollars here, thirty dollars there, ten dollars over there."

"Oh, here we go—" Kathy says.

"Kathy, you cashed ten yesterday, and what's this for? Withdrawal, withdrawal, withdrawal. Ten, fifteen, twenty. Day after day. These aren't bills."

"There've been no groceries in the house. I get those amounts because I know you'd scream if you saw a withdrawal for a hundred."

"None of those are bills. It's just cash, cash, cash, cash, cash. Where are the bills? We are living way above the income I bring home. The charge cards get bigger, bigger, bigger, bigger. We have no money left to apply to the plastic. What do I spend? I don't belong to a club. I don't belong to a golf league or a bowling league. I don't belong to anything. There's no system. There's no budget."

"Oh, but for certain things the money just comes out of the sky," she says, her voice high again. "When you want that basketball court, the money's there. When you want landscaping, boom, it's—"

"That's not an analogy. That's planned. I plan it."

"What about money for necessities: food, clothing. You plan the basketball court, but you yell when I withdraw twenty for—"

"But you don't manage your money. I manage my money."

"Either you have it or you don't," she says. "Planning doesn't have anything to do with it."

"What about a game plan? When the relatives ask what to buy for school, what do you do? You should tell them what clothes the kids need. That's a game plan."

Kathy isn't sure she understands this. They should spend what they want, when they want, and then—as part of the game plan—ask other family members to pay for the necessities? They're spending too much, period. Isn't that the problem?

"When you're spending two thousand over what you earn, how can you have a budget?" she asks.

"We'd have to make six or seven thousand more per year to break even," Fred says. "My problem is, why do this when I'm this old. You don't understand the anxiety."

"What's the point?"

"Someone help me do it *my* way. If the risk factor isn't as great, then I'd make a change. If John left the company, there isn't the risk factor. His wife works."

"Then why doesn't he do it?"

Fred doesn't see any point to this conversation, because Kathy has brought up a significant point of comparison between Fred and his brother—she believes neither of them would leave Xerox even if he had a financial cushion, as John does with his wife's income—so Fred switches directions.

"I'm tired. Too bad! That's just the way it is! I would probably leave if Frank left. Tommy Bill's got a Visa bill that would choke a horse. This job? It's easy. That's why I stay."

Kathy shakes her head, gazing down at the table. All this anxiety, but the job is easy? It doesn't make sense. It doesn't add up. Nothing comes out balanced in the end. Kathy believes Xerox has brought wonderful things into her family's life, a sense of financial security, a pride in working for a well-known and well-respected company with the finest products in the market. It has given them a reasonable level of middle-class prosperity and a secure future. Yet the company has tinkered with her husband's soul. It has turned him into something other than the man she married. She feels the company, over the years, has tried to adopt him into its own household, its own family, like a cult. It has taught him to motivate himself with a discontent that never seems to die.

When does this emotion push a man too far and become destructive? When does an artist's creative outrage become a force that turns him into an alcoholic suicide? When does a coach push his players so hard they begin to risk their lives with steroids? When does the corporate executive begin to corrupt the lives of his subordinates in his endless craving for short-term profits and personal advancement and another hundred thousand in salary? When does that life-giving craving for success become an addictive venom, and how do you withdraw from it? A person can indulge in regulated doses of his own darkest emotions in order to attain a greater wholeness and rise to new heights. Up to a point, certain passions, such as this energic discontent—in moderation—become essential to achievement. When do you cross the line? When do you pull back and realize you've surrendered to the darker side of this energy you ride in your best and worst moments? When does the force that drives you to the top begin to push you over the edge?

"You just want to put the screws to me, Fred," Kathy says. "That's all this is. You want me to squirm. Why's there all this tension, all this commotion all the time? It never ends."

"Kathy—go get it done. That's what I'm saying. There's no aggressiveness. There's plodding. I'd be pounding on doors. You can't get hired now—"

"Then what are we talking about?" she asks.

"You're stuck. The aggressiveness should have been earlier. To be honest, I'd rather have you home. Is there any aggressiveness for August of next year? That's what I'm asking. Keep the paychecks. Keep whatever you make teaching. I don't want to see it," he says.

"Tell me how to get a job."

"I told you how to sell Herbalife."

"Oh, that's a whole 'nother story."

"Here's what bothers me," he says, and for a moment it sounds as if something new will be conveyed across the table. "You know who's the loser tonight? It's eleven-thirty. You can leisurely wake up tomorrow morning. I can't. I'm glad you didn't work when the kids were young. You did a tremendous job. I liked it—I wanted you home for the kids. Whenever I'm with anybody, I say the wife should be at home."

Does Fred have any idea how much he contradicts himself? Kathy doesn't think he ever listens to himself speak.

He tells her he used to do more. He used to be a whirling dervish. He gave his reps letters of warning, letters of concern, letters of corrective action. The files were fat with them. He doesn't have that enthusiasm anymore. He doesn't enjoy playing mind games with them anymore. He doesn't enjoy beating on people. A few weeks earlier, Frank told him to put a letter of reprimand in the files for anybody who was below plan. He refused to do it. His reps were working as hard as they could. It wasn't right. He was tired of it.

"Physically, you can't take this anymore," Kathy says.

"I agree."

"But—"

"I don't have time."

"But—"

"Kathy—"

"Why can't you come home on time?" she asks.

Kathy didn't want to make it sound like she was making demands. She simply figured, after so many years with the company, he deserved the power to set reasonable hours for himself.

"I still have to make money."

"But this has been going on for years and years. And then you're never to bed before midnight," she says.

"You've had a better-than-normal lifestyle."

"Materially or in quality?" she asks.

"Imagine what you would be like if you were still living in Plot Number One."

"I liked that small house in the neighborhood. You wouldn't come home to it. You couldn't stand it. I didn't want a bigger house. I wanted you to come home. I've never been one to want for things."

"Kathy Kathy Kathy! If I made twenty-five thousand—"

"If you were this way, personally, no, I wouldn't like it. But if you were a calm, peaceful person—" She chokes on the word. "You know it's gotten to the point where it's a relief when you're not here."

Kathy's face turns red. The tears form in her eyes but don't drop onto her cheeks.

"It's a relief," she says. "What do I care if you don't come home on time? I used to care. It used to bother me that you could go wherever you wanted, whenever you wanted. Now I don't."

At times like this, Fred retreats into the past. *I think I can remember that time I lost my wedding ring in a beer can. I think it was a beer can. I think I remember the ding as it hit the bottom. I need my rest. I've got to get some sleep.*

Fred shuffled off to the bedroom, now that it was almost midnight. He will rise at five. Kathy moved into the family room and sat on the couch, listening to Fred thrash about in the bedroom, getting ready for bed. He closed the bedroom door behind him, but after five minutes, the door opened.

"Kathy? Have you vacuumed lately?" he asked.

As he said this, two balled-up socks flew down the hallway and landed, bouncing, on the family room floor. The flying ball of sock looked strangely hirsute. The fabric, while it was on Fred's foot, picked up a thick coat of dog hair as Fred walked through the house. It had been a while since she vacuumed. She started laughing, quietly, to herself. She could hear Fred chuckling to himself in the bedroom. Even as they laughed together, in their separate rooms, she knew she would wait until Fred fell asleep to venture into the bedroom. Once again the evening ended in laughter, but it was a mutually solitary laughter.

Laddie, the source of all the dog hair, slept through the entire fight, stretched out all evening on the family room floor. Their dog, like their children, was completely habituated to the sounds of argument. Only when the bedroom door closed and the house grew silent, with Kathy sitting and waiting in the family room by herself, did Laddie lift his head and look around. The silence, rather than the noise, woke him. In December only the novelty of peace stirred him.

### 4.

HE NEEDED CRAWFORD Manufacturing. The Citadel order could wait no longer—Libby was hoping it would turn to dust and blow away, and if she stalled it long enough, that's exactly what would happen. Finally one afternoon Diane came into Fred's office and told him Libby had come up with ten machines that needed to be replaced. This wasn't something Diane expected to happen. The value of the machines would come close to the value of the big centralized unit they wanted to sell Citadel. She gave

Fred a knowing look. See? Libby came through for them. Even though they weren't getting Citadel.

After Diane left, Fred shut his door and wrung his hands with delight, like a miser, grinning. In its own way, this was success. They pushed for six months to get the Citadel order, and now Libby gave them this package deal as a substitute. He got the extra compensation of this equally large order, instead of Citadel. It was a guilt order. Libby felt she owed it to them. The friendship *and* the pressure paid off.

Yet Fred wasn't going to let Diane off. He recognized the order for what it was—a consolation, a way for Libby to maintain her control over the relationship. Even if its value *was* equivalent to the Citadel order, he wanted the money his way, not hers. It was a matter of salesmanship, a matter of principle. He wanted to be the one in control.

So that's how it worked? You felt bad about the friendship, so you gave ten orders to cheer up your friend?

Was he complaining about the orders?

No. But he wanted Diane to stay in control. He nagged her until she made one final attempt to lure Libby into the Citadel deal. She stayed up past midnight several nights in a row, rewriting the proposal, creating a deal, with Fred's help, to keep payments low the first year. In other words, she did everything she could imagine to get Libby to succumb. This was risky. They might look ungrateful. They might imperil both the order for ten machines and the Citadel deal. Yet it was a chance he wanted to take.

When Diane came into Fred's office, she looked fresh in her tweed suit, her brilliant lipstick, her hair pulled back from her face. She wore a houndstooth jacket patterned in red and blue and gold, with a navy wool skirt, gold jewelry, and a blue bow on the toe of each shoe, a bow tied in a pattern that vaguely resembled the

Crawford Manufacturing insignia. Her skin looked flawless. She was as beautiful as ever, though she'd been working until midnight on the new proposal.

"Hey, how about we—"

"Good morning, Fred," she said.

"—go on this call and—"

"Good morning, Fred. How are you?" she asked.

"I'm fine. How about—"

"It's a wonderful day, isn't it, Fred? You know, with those ten orders she's giving me, I think I made club. I was mad about Citadel, but then I figured my comp. It's almost two hundred thousand toward my budget."

He'd talked to Libby on the phone. She said she hoped they didn't take up a lot of her time. Fred studied Diane's face. Success was dawning on her—he could see it in the relaxed contours, the delight around her eyes. She was certain she would be getting the ten orders. She was envisioning date palms and heat waves on the California desert. The Citadel order didn't matter to her. She had the substitute orders to make up for the loss. Yet Fred wanted the Citadel order too, for himself, as insurance against future disappointments.

"I am not going to get intimidated by her," he said. "She should be able to tell us yes or no today. That's the attitude you have to take. If she says, *I'll let you know,* you say—"

"I'm tired, Fred," Diane said.

"So am I."

"I don't know why I'm tired. I do my step aerobics. I like it, but maybe it doesn't like me. I'll get a little pain sometimes. It worries me."

"This is the week!" Fred shouted.

"Oh, Lord. You know what I need? I need my life to be spared one more day."

"This is fun! This is when it gets fun!" he said.

When they got to Libby's office, she looked composed but remote. She was in one of her moods. On occasion, in reaction to some offending remark, Libby could seem to go into a trance. She became unresponsive, as cool as a stranger. This morning she was polite and responsive, but completely unemotional. She was punching numbers on her calculator—listening, but calculating. She wore a black dress, with elegant gold beads around her neck. She looked as unapproachable as a duchess or a schoolmarm.

"We're doing budgets," Libby said. "This copier budget is going to kill you next year."

"We have a way to save you sixteen thousand dollars the first year. Seriously," Fred said.

"Just give me the proposal," she said. "Don't read it to me."

Diane took the Citadel proposal from her briefcase. Fred opened his mouth wide, giving her a look of astonishment and terror, then winking at her. He was clowning the way he clowned at Smith Brewer, making faces behind his customer's back—not mocking his customer so much as mugging like a gargoyle to ward off his fears. Diane frowned at him, wanting him to behave. It was Fred's oh-my-God face, his silent scream, his mouth sphinctered into a puncture of shock, and she didn't need to see it at this point. She didn't need his antics now, not at this crucial moment. *But you do need these antics, Diane,* he would have told her, *because you need to rise above all this and show them you don't give a damn. You need to pretend you fear nothing, because otherwise you'll never sell a single copier. They're like a schoolroom full of kids. As soon as they spot fear, you're sunk.*

"Kathy is starting to substitute," Fred said, to Diane's relief.

"I'm so glad for her, so she can have freedom from *you*," Libby said, smiling. "Now, please run through your proposal quickly."

"But it's exciting," Diane said. "It really is. We'll never be able to offer this again. The big benefit is the impact on next year's budget."

"This is a unique end-of-the-year Northeast Ohio offer that Frank has approved. It's right on the border of being unprofitable for us."

Libby made a face to show she didn't believe it.

"Is it possible for him to get any more excited?" Diane asked, glancing at Libby.

"You know, Diane, you two should go to a commercial now," Libby said.

"I'm excited too," Diane said.

As they explained how the Citadel deal would keep the payments affordably low the first year, and then carry the premium into the second and third years' payments, Libby bounced the tip of her pen against her desktop, staring at the pen.

"You're excited. Which is great," she said. "I suppose there's some hope here."

"Our goal is to try to have the machine by December," Fred said. "If you want to talk to Frank—"

"No, I'm not concerned where you get these discounts from."

By now, Diane had produced the order forms for the ten machines meant to be a substitute for the Citadel order. It was clear to Fred they had violated that unspoken understanding by bringing up Citadel again—and now they magnified the offense by closing the package of orders immediately after talking about Citadel. In Libby's view, they acknowledged the gift and then kept asking for more. Even so, she got out her pen and began to sign her name. As she proceeded, they kept the conversation away from the orders, pretending nothing was happening here, the way a nurse makes idle talk as she draws blood. When Libby handed the orders back to Diane, Fred smiled and thanked Libby. As Libby walked them out of the building, she pointed to a new Canon color copier they were trying out. Fred smiled. The mind games never ended. When they reached the lobby, Fred offered his hand to Libby, but she wouldn't take it.

"I'm not going to shake your hand, Fred," she said. "You should kiss mine."

As they drove back to the district, Fred understood what Libby meant. He smiled with respect. This woman would never surrender. The ten orders were a gift. Fred owed her the kiss, and she owed Fred nothing, not even a handshake. It was her way of telling him they wouldn't get the Citadel deal. Instead, she'd given them the ten orders. She won, and they won. It was a draw. A stalemate. It didn't satisfy him, but it gave him what he needed from Crawford Manufacturing. Now, if Wellco held up, all he had left to close was Bedford Telecommunications.

Nothing is certain. Nothing is decided. At one point, it looks as if even Pat Elizondo will leave the district. The tension and uncertainty are especially hard on her. Fred notices signs of her uneasiness. She's frustrated. She's been designated as ready for a promotion since June, and yet nothing is happening. She keeps getting annoyed with Pacetta. She snapped at him in the hall: *There's something about people who philosophize through rock lyrics. It's limited.* Pacetta said people all his life had been telling him he was limited— his teachers, his father. He was the first to admit his limitations: So he was limited. So what? He was going to ask his father to send him his lousy report cards from school, and he was going to blow them up and hang them on the wall. He was a kind, loving family man, and he hadn't been drunk in four years. Well, he hadn't been drunk at a company function in four years. Except for Firestone. And that time . . . Anyway, he hadn't been drunk. He had no watering holes. He couldn't be cleaner. Did it kill him? Absolutely.

Yet Pacetta seems to be in top form, ready to push the district over the top. He writes warm memos to people, congratulating them on the good work being done. Pat notices her husband, John, has gotten no credit for certain deals he was instrumental in closing. She gets angrier when she talks with Bruno on the way out of the building, and he hints what kind of promotion he expects to get the following year. Though she might replace Pacetta, she isn't being included in certain discussions about who would be working for her, and in what capacity. Bruno might get promoted, and she knows nothing about it. She tells Pacetta she's upset, but she doesn't say why.

She tells her husband: She doesn't know if she can deal with Frankisms anymore. He asked her recently what was up—what was wrong? She told him not to ask. If you are single or gay or if you play in the school band in high school, forget it. The way Pacetta operates, some people are part of the in-crowd and some aren't. If you aren't, forget it. Nobody recognizes John for the work he's done. He's qualified for President's Club, but she doesn't hear any congratulations, does she? Pacetta's the best DM she's ever worked for, but she can't operate like that.

Finally, one evening, she confronts Pacetta in his office. John waits for her at home. They live in Cleveland Heights, a neighborhood lined with huge old mansions big enough to house several families each. Their home has more than forty-five hundred square feet, with a large third floor. Gleaming hardwood floors are covered with plush Chinese sculptured carpets in pale green and salmon. White sofas in the living room and dining room make it clear this is a household without crayons and sip-top cups and prohibited grape drinks. Costly lithographs of urban park scenes from Chicago and Paris and Manhattan hang in the living room, dining room, halls, bathrooms, and bedrooms.

The bookshelves are unusual for the home of a district employee because they are actually stuffed with books: *A Thousand Days, How to Win Friends and Influence People, To Kill a Mockingbird, The Sun Also Rises, Bob Knight: His Own Man, Sophie's Choice, Summer Crossing, Portnoy's Complaint, The Last Days of Patton, The Sand Pebbles, The Catcher in the Rye, Mistral's Daughter, Managing for Results, All the President's Men, The Baby Trap: The Value of a Childless Marriage* (with key passages highlighted in pink), *The Changing World of the Executive, Dr. Kookie, You're Right!,* and *Little Women.*

When she comes in, Pat takes off her coat, gets a soft drink from the refrigerator, and sits in the corner of the living room, deflated. In the next hour, she recounts, as best as she can, the nature of her talk with Pacetta. He was polite, concerned, persuading her to stay in his office whenever she rose to leave during their talk.

She told him people loved what he'd done with the Cleveland district, how he'd turned it around. But things were happening that she didn't agree with. She enjoyed and wanted to work for him because he was enthusiastic, he cared, and he had more marketing knowledge than any district manager she knew. Yet it was hypocritical of him to talk about employee satisfaction and customer satisfaction. Some of his managers did an atrocious job. As a matter of course they took their people, used them, and gave no thought to their future. Who was worrying about someone like Fred Thomas? Who was making sure he went to Leesburg, Virginia, where he could be trained in digital systems, getting better prepared for a future with the company?

Frank disagreed, but he allowed her to continue. She told him, as long as the managers got results, he didn't care how they got them. Some of their managers, who were doing well—their ratings for customer satisfaction were unacceptably low. If Fred had satisfaction ratings as bad as some of the others, Frank would have whipped him. But he didn't flay the others. Why? Because he knew Fred would stay, no matter what, and the others would leave. He needed all of them to make his annual nut.

She focused on the way people were treated in the district, yet behind her disgruntlement over these internal issues lay a greater discontent. All her animosity about the way customers were pressured into thinking they were getting bargains when they weren't—in other words, all the most troubling dimensions of selling itself—fueled her talk with Pacetta. She hated some of the most fundamental techniques used in old-school selling, which came into play especially at the end of the year, when there was no other way to make it over the top.

Again, Frank nodded patiently and allowed her to continue. When he had a personal bias against someone, she told him, he was standoffish. He wasn't fair. She'd seen it with a couple reps, but when he treated her husband the same way, it was more than she could tolerate.

She told Pacetta she would take a leave of absence or quit before she stayed under the present conditions. And then he said the key thing. He told her to call him after her first or second or third year as a district manager. Tell him if she thought Frank Pacetta did a good job. Then they could talk about these issues. It was hard to argue with that. She told him he'd made her so sick about this, she didn't want to be a district manager anymore. Because if they did it her way, they might go out of business.

Frank told her she had a good point. She could do all the right things, but if she didn't bring home the bottom line, what good was it? What made her think Frank didn't want to do it her way? Why did she assume he didn't want to be a blameless human being? She could do her own thing, and it would take them three years to get rid of her. She wouldn't even know it was coming. She could try it. But he warned her not to expect results. He'd seen people do it the way she said it ought to be done, the quality way through and through, and they went down the toilet, and nobody pulled them out.

"What training do we have for district managers?" Frank asked her. He urged her to stick around and stay on track—to be there when he left, because no one else was as qualified to take over the district. He wanted her to take over. He convinced her to stay, waiting for him to leave so she could take over and give her own methods a try.

When John looks at Pat, he's amused by this woman: One day she will say she needs to do something meaningful with her life, needs to leave Cleveland and fly to South Central Los Angeles and feed the homeless. The next day she frets because she doesn't have a mink coat for a winter party. And when Pat looks at John, she sees a man who's so compulsively honest that when they returned from Toronto a month earlier, he told the customs officer they had nothing to declare except ten bottles of liquor they bought. The officer gave John a look that said, as she put it later: *Please pull over to that spot where we send morons to pay duty on bottles they could have gotten away with not mentioning at the gate.* Maybe what she hated about selling was simply built into the system, or into human nature itself. Maybe there were limits to how honorably one human being could treat another when everyone played to win.

As all of these doubts hang in the air around him, Fred enters the hardest time of the year. He hates to wait. He has no patience. If he could fill his day with face time, time in front of a customer, time on the road, he would be a blissful individual. He wants action, wants to push things to a crisis. He doesn't want to wait for the phone to ring. And yet the bulk of a life in sales is built of waiting, the way a tree's built mostly of air. And if he ever rises higher in management, even more of his life will be confined to those hours of patient watchfulness inside an office, a building, a conference room. People compare sales to a chess game—because of the strategy, the tactics, the checks and stalemates—and yet it resembles chess mostly because both games are filled with so much dead air, with too much thought and too little burning of calories.

At the end of the year, when you wait for the final word on a crucial deal, you lose all confidence in yourself for hours at a time. You sit at your desk and question everything you've ever done in life. It isn't the sort of doubt that confines itself to the deal in question. It's a categorical doubt, a metaphysical doubt, as a German thinker once defined it, a doubt that calls into question you, the questioner, along with your entire universe. You wonder about the way your face looks at nine in the morning over a cup of coffee. You wonder if there's something deeply flawed in your dry cleaner's use of sizing. You wonder if anyone ever laughs at one of your jokes with more than a polite enthusiasm. Does anyone of the opposite sex really find you attractive? Was that night with her at *Put-in-Bay* just an act of pity? What was it she said the next morning? What in the world will you be doing in ten years? Twenty years? Where is God when you need Him most? For that matter, where was He earlier in the year? You look around you and count the number of faces of people older than fifty. Is this career just some kind of dead end? The phone rings. It's your customer. He says yes. Suddenly you are superhuman again. You forget every question that crossed your mind over the previous half hour at your desk, where you sat shaking a little plastic ball that played a recording of a madman's belly laugh while you worried about the ozone layer or your loss of hair or various matters connected to your relationship with your mother early in your life.

Yet even as he waited on some deals, Fred found ways to act on others. He didn't wait for the phone to ring. He called on Al Brook one day to clear up finer points on the pricing of the machines. They spent a couple hours going over the numbers and then he returned to the office. And then he waited for another summons, and that's when the self-doubts hit the hardest. Maybe someone would look so closely at the deal it would become obvious how the supply costs were baked into the total price. These people were comfortable with the monthly payments—they agreed to the fee; what difference did it make if the fee could have been lower if the supply costs had not been baked into the deal? Finally Brook called, and Fred drove downtown to see him.

"Let's give you some news that's not so good," Brook said. "Would you believe Pitney-Bowes is going to offer a counter-proposal? I don't see how they can be too competitive."

"The offer on the table is a tremendous offer. For the first seven months you have no charge."

"But we'll pick it up in later years, right?" Brook asked.

Fred nodded. This felt like a tightrope walk. They were talking about an action that allowed Wellco to escape the fee on this machine for seven months—and Brook showed he obviously understood the way it worked. You get free use of the machine now, but you pay for it later. That was exactly how it worked—you took away the payments early in the deal, and then you charged the customer later on. If Brook really understood this now, he didn't seem concerned. Fred sighed with relief. Brook wasn't outraged. He didn't pursue it. He didn't ask about the supply costs. There was no telling whether or not he understood the financing. There was no telling how he would react to that knowledge, either. Now there was Pitney-Bowes to worry about, though. Fred would see if there was anything else he could do, with Pitney-Bowes trying to get creative.

"The thing we gotta have is the signed contract by the end of December," Brook said.

"It's mind-boggling. We'll have to sit in our office and write out each of those hundred orders individually," Fred said. He had an idea. What if they applied a forty-thousand credit in addition to what he'd offered before? It would come out of his team's compensation, but he could afford it. When Pitney-Bowes came back with an offer, he wanted Brook to count the forty thousand.

Now he waited. Fred knew Pitney-Bowes could undercut Xerox and save Brook even more money. Xerox sold some of the most expensive equipment on the market. There was no way, even with the financing, to make the deal cheaper than the competition's. The only hope was that Brook would feel the friendship mattered more than the money—and that he owed Xerox for all the effort it put into training him and his people in the quality program.

A few days later Fred could think of nothing but the Wellco deal. How was it going? Why hadn't they heard from Brook yet? This much time—it had to be bad. The man was afraid to call and tell Fred it was over. Without Wellco, the year was finished. No amount of incremental business would make up for it. Then the phone rang.

It was Sue Kelly, from Wellco. There was nothing in her voice to indicate what she'd decided. Pitney-Bowes had indeed undercut the Xerox offer. Fred slumped into his chair. The deal had to be dead. But no. Wellco wasn't going to decide on the basis of price. Money wasn't the only issue. They were going to go with Xerox. They considered what Xerox stood for—quality and partnership. They recognized how much time and money Xerox put into the quality training, the flights and the seminars, and they knew Xerox had turned an important corner. As he heard all this, with the phone still at his ear, Fred jumped from his chair and stood at attention in front of his desk and clicked his heels together. It was all coming together now.

"You know what I want to do?" he said. "I want to put the phone down and jump for joy."

Larry Tyler happened to be sitting in a chair beside Fred's desk at the time. He started to mock Fred's enthusiasm. As Fred spoke, Larry pretended to be using a shovel to dig into a pile of manure. He stood on his chair and pulled both legs of his slacks up to his knees, showing his white shins, and he dug more deeply into the imaginary compost around his feet. Larry was still working on setting up business for the following year, cheerful and indefatigable, coming in early every day and going home late. He was still an enigma to Fred, doing his pantomime by Fred's desk, as if he felt no anxieties for himself, as if he'd found an escape from the circus—the anxiety, the winning and losing—without actually leaving it. He wouldn't make President's Club, and yet he was happy, productive, calm, amused at Fred's fawning rejoinders.

"I want to thank you and get together with you. Can you sign tomorrow?" Fred asked.

He rushed into Frank Pacetta's office and, on hearing the news, Frank stood and came around his desk. They did a high five, and Frank got Fred into an affectionate headlock and started to wrestle him to the floor, grinning all the time. Fred felt like a fool when Pacetta did these things, but it got his heart pumping.

"Come on. Let's go at it. Come on, you son of a bitch. Freddie! That's more than a half million in revenue for the company!" he said, and did a soft head butt, bumping his invisible football helmet against Fred's. "That's where quality really worked. It got us in the door and got us the order! That's a big win, Freddie. A hundred sold machines. Congratulations."

That evening, Fred was quietly happy at home. He wasn't in Palm Springs yet, though. Wellco made up for all the deals that fell apart during the year. Bedford Telecommunications would put him past the finish line. He had no choice but to make it happen. It was all he had left. It was all or nothing now. In the end, for Fred, it came down to one last popularity contest.

5.

IT WAS TIME to close Nick Callahan. Fred had to do for Callahan what he'd done for Al Brook. It had nothing to do with the machine, or the money, or any other details of the deal. It had to do with the feeling one human being could give to another. To get the order he would need to make Callahan feel like a player again, give him a feeling of power and significance. If he wanted to get this final, crucial deal at Bedford Telecommunications, he had to lunch Nick Callahan, buy him drinks, beg for the order. Tom Haywood gave him that advice early in December. They were standing in the hall outside Fred's office, under the Exit sign.

"He doesn't give a shit," Haywood said. "Beg him. Take him to lunch and thank him for fifteen years of business. Lie across the table and say, *It doesn't make any sense, but I need the business for my bonus.* Beg him. He respects honesty. He despises being manipulated."

Haywood was as modest and straightforward as Pacetta was proud and theatrical. As he stood in the hallway that day, Fred admired the way Haywood kept the district's service organization operating with no fanfare, no arrogance, enjoying none of the parochial acclaim and spectacle Pacetta engineered for himself every time he got up in front of a group. He was giving Fred some free advice, asking nothing in return. He had a stern face, a poker face, a high forehead that disclosed nothing. He was a decent man, a good friend, a great golfer.

"He's not real fond of Bedford," Haywood said. "He might want to stick it to them." In other words, Nick Callahan might sign the order just to spite Bedford. Fred loved the sound of that—the secret victory, carried out under the watchful gaze of the oppressors higher up in the company.

Fred asked Bruno to set up lunch with Nick Callahan. If not lunch, could he see them somewhere else? Was Bruno going to call Callahan today? Was he going to ask Callahan the direct question? Callahan wouldn't even see them for lunch last year. He was making them beg. He was taking it right to the end. He had few pleasures left in life.

Bruno called and got a date. Meanwhile, Bruno had his own concerns, and this deal was not at the top of his list of anxieties. He and Fred met with Frank to discuss Bruno's future. In this meeting, Frank told Bruno to pursue the high-volume-specialist spot. Being an HV specialist was the best thing for him. They were sitting at the round conference table in Frank's corner office, surrounded by large windows that gave onto a view of Independence with its lush hills, its Uncle Sam fireplugs, its little grave-yard on Rockside Drive. The sky was pale with haze, and the sun hung low on the horizon, shining through bare birches and cotton-woods. Frank was wearing the pants of his usual double-breasted suit—he'd hung the jacket behind his door. He wore his favorite braces and one of his loud and fashionable ties; his striped shirt was so starched every wrinkle seemed ineradicably pressed into the fabric. When he leaned forward to emphasize an idea, his shirt crumpled into a labyrinth of ledges and folds.

He was at his most genuine during meetings like this one—attentive, candid, open, and friendly. His voice dropped into a normal conversational range, as if he were letting his guard down for once, giving up the stage presence. Fred liked him most this way, when he was talking with one of his loyal followers, like Fred or Bruno or Rob. But still, under the casual honesty of the conversation, Fred knew Pacetta had his agenda. This too was an act. In his own way he was going to dictate what Bruno would be doing next year. How Bruno felt about it didn't really figure in the transaction.

"You can learn from it, Bruno. Learn and make some cash," he said, leaning back in his chair.

"I need to make money," Bruno said.

The sun broke from behind a bank of low clouds, and the afternoon light shot through the windows. The light turned Frank's ears a bright orange, shining through them from behind. It looked as if somebody had pulled a switch and lit up Frank's head from inside. He often had that look, even without the backlighting. Bruno was suggesting he wanted to manage a team, in a position similar to Fred's. In Frank's view, Bruno wasn't ready.

"I love you dearly, and you're a tremendously talented kid and you've grown, but there's some things you can't participate in," Frank said.

"I'm concerned about my pocketbook," Bruno said. He was wearing his new Hugo Boss suit, baggy in the shoulders and legs, and he looked as if he could have concealed a private arsenal under all the fabric. When he wore his long, flowing black raincoat on top of this same suit, Bruno had the look Pacetta loved—a cross between a spy and a caped Sicilian avenger. Nothing could have been in greater contrast to Bruno's actual temperament; he was so open and warm he was probably the least-threatening rep on the entire Cleveland team. Unlike Ron Nelson and Rob Onorato, Bruno shunned the high-pressure selling, was rarely pushy. He knew how to bake things quietly into a new lease payment, but in his relationships with customers and other reps he was like Pat Elizondo—he drew things out of people by being solicitous, thorough, persistent, and seductive, not by getting tough. Ergo, in Pacetta's view, Bruno wasn't quite ready to manage a team.

"Let me tell you, you don't have to be an HV to become a sales manager here. You can stay right where you are. If you're comfortable, you can make good money and get into the program to become a sales manager."

"I think you're in a win-win situation," Fred said, finally speaking up.

"What happens if you're not here next year, Frank?" Bruno asked. "I may be on the path, but I may be cut off, too, if you leave."

"You're set, Bruno," Frank said. "Besides, my replacement is pretty high on you. She thinks more of you than I do."

"But your replacement may go somewhere else. I guess my concern is, somebody else comes in new—let's say Pat gets a spot in Columbus and you leave in three months. Let's face it, we all have our allegiances—"

"This this this and this—in all honesty, I may be here longer than you," Frank said.

Fred broke in, grinning: "Hell, I might die."

Bruno paid no attention. The prospect of Fred's death didn't seem to concern Bruno. This did not surprise Fred. Whenever he thought of his own death, he imagined a small, discreet memorial service for himself, with a mixture of tears and sighs of relief all around.

"You and your wife have to decide," Frank said. "Go for it. Get some balls! You could carry the water bucket or be on the team."

After Bruno left Frank's office, Fred looked at Pacetta and said, "You're right. Bruno's scared."

What will Fred do, though? When will Frank take this sort of direct and paternal initiative with Fred? Fred wonders if anyone has anything in mind for him, after his twenty years of working for this company. Does anyone know he exists? Yet these anxieties can't get much of a foothold in his mind and heart on days like this, at the end of the year, when they ought to be spurring him to lobby on his own behalf for a new position within the company before the new year begins. Instead, he does what Pacetta wants him to do—he devotes himself completely to the attainment of just enough business to get himself to Palm Springs and help his boss make his own target. The short-term anxieties always edge out the long-term ones. If Pacetta doesn't have something lined up for Fred next year, well, that's just too bad. He'll be the major accounts sales manager yet again. Things could be worse. He could be a parking attendant somewhere. (Then again, maybe that would be better—he doesn't know for sure.) He knows he's being used. And though part of him resents it, another part of him welcomes it because it's putting money into *his* pocket too.


So, on the way to Johnny's Grill, where they were meeting Nick Callahan for lunch, Fred knew Bruno's greatest anxieties weren't centered on this particular deal, even though Fred's trip to Palm Springs seemed to pivot on it. Fred would be the point man on this call, and Bruno would back him up. Bruno wore the Hugo Boss suit again, with his Italian loafers, the Varese shoes he bought in Toronto on a trip with his wife to see *Phantom of the Opera*.

"He wants you to take the HV slot," Fred said. "I think you should step up to it."

"I also want the teams that I want."

"You don't get to dictate that. He's got to make sure other people are happy too. That's the piece of management you don't understand yet. Why don't I give all my best accounts to my best rep, Bruno Biasiotta? The rest of them could starve. If I took that attitude—"

"Yeah, yeah, yeah," Bruno said.

Fred started to tell the story of the last ten minutes of a high school championship game back in his baseball days. Bruno was studying his fingernails, and the winter view. They were driving through one of the most hostile parts of town, with its abandoned storefronts, its chain-link fences with razor wire, its prowling unemployed, and its vertiginous shadows. This plush little bar and grill, situated in such a downtrodden part of town, seemed luxurious when you walked toward the entrance after activating three sets of car alarms in the parking lot across the street. Walking into that bar was like entering a love scene from *Doctor Zhivago*, with its opulent warmth and fragrance, the romance of it intensified by a cold backdrop that made it seem twice as inviting as it would have seemed in Trinidad or Monaco.

"I guess you had to be there, huh Fred?" Bruno was commenting on Fred's baseball story. "What did you weightlift in those days?"

"I'll weightlift *you*, buddy. I've got my gym clothes. You wanna play racketball tonight? I'll whip you and go straight to basketball. I'll whip you."

"I want to play for a hundred bucks," Bruno said.

"I dread this lunch, don't you?" Fred asked. "Once they say no, they never change their fucking minds. Does he know I'm coming with you?"

"No."

"Oh, oh, oh, oh. No? I think next year's it. It's all over this year. I can't put up with this bullshit anymore," Fred said.

Once you were inside, Johnny's looked, as always, like the private haunt of low-profile Ohio mobsters who wanted to go legitimate and trade their image up to something more pedigreed.

In one room the walls were still painted with murals that looked like the lush work of a drugged-out Rousseau. On the floor of the small main dining room, the leopard-skin carpet seemed hip and ironic, as if it had been salvaged from inside Pee-Wee Herman's demolished playhouse or the set of a music video by the B-52's. Jazz played softly overhead. Nick Callahan waited for them at a banquette table near the back. He was dressed in his usual gray suit and slightly wrinkled shirt, the look of a man who'd grown beyond any concern for the semiotics of appearance.

"What's the news?" Bruno asked, a polite query about whether or not Nick Callahan was leaving Bedford Telecommunications.

"No news is good news," Callahan said. "But I can't believe I'll be here January first."

"You've got, what, twenty-seven years?" Fred asked.

"Uh-huh," Callahan said, and they ordered drinks.

"What are you going to do?"

"Go to Florida, become a beach bum for a while. I'm sure I'll change careers. I don't know what it will be," he said. "If something happens this week, I may change my mind."

Fred was touched by this admission. Every time Bruno called on him, Callahan was still cleaning out his office, acting as if he were threatening to leave. It was like Gerry Faust's confession to Pat Elizondo at Firestone that he would return to Notre Dame if they asked him to coach again. In a love affair, one side always loved more than the other, and that was always the sad part.

The drinks arrived, and they ordered salad. When the salad came, the dressing was tangy and bitter and vaguely unfamiliar. Fred found that when he swallowed a mouthful of greens, it was hard to breathe through the fumes they left in his nose. Maybe it had nothing to do with the salad, though. He wondered about his heart, about his state of mind, about how nervous he was, facing Nick Callahan, who had nothing to gain or lose in this deal. (On the other hand, Nick was on his second Bloody Mary, and that was good. This deal would require more of those before the coffee and cognac.) As Fred gasped, he knew he'd be feeling better if Nick Callahan were the breathless one.

"Wow! This salad dressing!" Fred said. "What's going to get this economy going? Putting a cap on credit-card spending isn't going to do it."

"Me, I'm going to have more money to spend soon," Callahan said, in a stab at gallows humor at his early-retirement package.

"What scares me about leaving Xerox is the retirement plan, profit-sharing, whatever you want to call it. Can something happen that will screw with all those years you've stayed with a company?" Fred said.

Fred and Bruno were sitting against the wall on the plush banquette, and for the first time Fred noticed their seats were lower than Nick's. He looked down at them from a higher chair on the other side of the cramped table. Fred didn't like that. As a rule, in a selling situation, it didn't hurt to be higher than the customer, standing taller beside him, sitting a little above him, shoving your smile into his comfort zone. But in this case it was probably better this way—Nick was in control here, and why pretend otherwise?

They ordered, and the meals arrived promptly—fettuccini with chicken and shrimp, orange roughy, veal scallopini. It was delicious, as always, and the drinks were starting to buzz in everyone's head. The lilting jazz overhead, the elegant colors, the winter light in the windows—everything turned pleasant and congenial. Soon it would be time to talk business, but not quite yet.

"I'm going to like retirement," Callahan said. "I won't have any obnoxious salespeople after me."

"We're here to make sure you spend your money well. That's all," Fred said. "I'd love to be on your side of the desk—"

"I haven't slept more than an hour and a half this week. Do you know what I'm going through? Should I do this or that? I write the pros and cons on a sheet of paper—"

Fred could have interjected *We call that a Ben Franklin, Nick. I do it all the time.*

"—and it doesn't matter. You can see when the people in my situation at Bedford have made a decision. Whether it's to stay or go. It doesn't matter. You can see the relief. It's right in their face. With my luck, in the past five years I've fucked up every personal decision, so I figure I'll decide and then I'll do just the opposite. When I got divorced, instead of thinking with my head, I thought with my heart. If I had the money she's sitting on out there—"

At one moment it sounded as if Callahan wanted to leave Bedford, and at the next turn it sounded as if they were forcing him out. Sometimes it was hard to tell the difference. Callahan's hair looked especially gray. In his pin-striped suit, his polyester shirt, he looked somehow vulnerable, as if these clothes would soon become useless to him. A certain cool thread of obsolescence seemed woven already into the fabric of everything he wore. When he paused to think about what he was saying, he sucked air gently through his teeth, the way the Japanese did to express disapproval. In Japan, no words were needed to say no, just that little sound of air vented through a couple teeth. *Tsst, tsst.* Fred shivered.

"If you're no longer climbing the corporate ladder, they can't understand it," he said.

"Exactly!" Fred said. He knew what Nick meant. He wasn't a climber either, and he felt just as disregarded most of the time.

"I wanted to move up so bad in this company, it cost me my family. Then my boss says, *You've got a bad attitude.* So I do my job, and then I'm gone. The problem is, companies don't understand somebody sitting there, liking what they're doing."

"Tom Grohl? Our finance guy? He loves what he's doing," Fred said. Grohl was smooth, urbane, easy. He was doing a tremendous job. He had found what appeared to be a patch of shade, outside most of the turmoil, where he could stay until he retired. He would come into Fred's office and keep Fred updated about the progress of his nephew's career, the drummer for Nirvana—instantly famous, emerging out of the Seattle fog. The kid was twenty-two, and Grohl said the band grossed four million since September. He was considered the hottest dummer in contemporary music. He toured Europe. He appeared on *Saturday Night Live.* The kid had it made. And so did Grohl—he'd found his own nirvana. Some people were living their dreams, even at Xerox. It could be done.

"They're probably looking to get rid of you, Fred, because you're dead weight," Callahan said.

They ordered black sambuca and espresso.

"In the old days I was young and cocky," Callahan said. "I had a family. I wanted to hit the third level. But all the promotions started going to minorities. White males sat there—nothing ever happened. A lot of others like me, they're bitter. They've seen others get promoted. They see women get promoted. The trend was to go to the East Coast and get your ticket punched. Then divestiture happened! I never got promoted. I lost my family."

"It happens to us," Bruno said.

"It happens to everybody," he said.

The espresso arrived in diminutive black cups with a slice of lemon peel, clumps of brown and white sugar, and a cookie. The sambuca arrived with it, coffee beans resting in the bottom of the glasses. Traditionally, a certain number of beans meant you were fingered for execution by the Mob. They all joked about it and looked to see how many beans they got. No one had four beans. There were no assassins involved in this meal, though you'd never have been able to guess it from Nick Callahan's mood.

"Four beans is death," Callahan said.

"What's no beans?" Fred asked. "Uh-oh, I got no beans."

Callahan poured his black sambuca into the espresso. The anisette liqueur gave the coffee a flavor of licorice. The white linen tablecloth was covered with a sheet of paper, cut slightly smaller than the dimensions of the tabletop. As Callahan poured his drink into the espresso, it splattered a fine spray of gray and sepia droplets across the paper around his cup. It looked as if a heavily lubricated machine had been fired upon.

"Espresso is good, but it's so heavy," Callahan said.

"At your age, you're so well-rounded, it amazes me," Fred said.

They asked the waiter for the exact name on the bottle of sambuca. He went to the bar and fetched it. It was called Opal Nera. Nick said he thought it was really Opal Negra, but that they had changed the spelling *for obvious reasons.* Gingerly, Fred steered the conversation in a new direction.

"You want to stay in Cleveland?" Fred asked.

"I'm not opposed to leaving. I'll probably leave. I'm dating a gal here. She's upset, but she won't say it. That I might be leaving." Nick gazed at his empty glass and added in a weary voice, "I get tired of counting the beans."

It struck Fred as a motto for his life the past year. He was tired of worrying about whether or not he was in the good graces of Xerox, tired of worrying about getting four beans in his glass—tired of worrying about how his year had built to the crisis of this single, ephemeral sales call over lunch. He was tired, too, of counting beans every night in his wife's checkbook. He told Nick about the first time he got a kiss on his forehead from Frank Pacetta. He wondered at the time if it was supposed to be a kiss of death. Finally, by mentioning Pacetta, he opened the door for them to discuss the deal.

"This is Christmas," Nick said. "Don't bring up business—"

The waiter, standing nearby, overheard the remark and smiled.

"Bruno's got a new wrinkle for you," Fred said.

"I'm a short-timer. I can't handle any more wrinkles—"

"Haywood's behind us on this," he said, bringing up the name of the Xerox partner Nick Callahan liked. The name of Pacetta angered him, as always. "Obviously, this has to do with the 5090—"

The waiter leaned toward their table, exchanged a smile with Nick Callahan, and said, "Gentlemen, you've heard of no-smoking sections? This is a no-business section."

They smiled politely and proceeded, as the waiter walked away.

"Really, on a serious note—Bruno knows what he's going to talk about—"

"What're you going to talk about?" Nick asked, annoyed.

"It's interesting," Fred said, and then backed off. "How many years you have? Twenty-seven? If I had twenty-seven, and my kids were gone, I would love to have somebody come back and give me a retirement package."

He'd looked into early retirement himself. He had the papers in his briefcase for a while. Maybe not now, but in five years? Fred would be ready. He was backing off, cowering. The harder he pushed, the closer he would get to hearing a yes or a no, and that was the most fearful moment for a salesman. If a customer was going to say no, you had to hear it, but no one *wanted* to hear it. So he quit pushing for a few minutes. Yet he had to keep the conversation on track. He had to get it back to the deal at hand. Bruno gave Fred a concerned look. Neither of them wanted to hear what Callahan was going to say.

"I'm forty-seven. I'm not retiring. I'm changing careers," Callahan said.

Fred was surprised. He'd figured Callahan for older than forty-seven. He looked older. This *was* a tough time for him. Callahan was in total control now. He was drawing it out, loving to see the two of them squirm, the way most customers loved to see a salesman squirm. The jazz in the background became more discernible, as if someone had nudged up the volume. The sales call got completely off-track. Callahan could see what was going on, how fearful Fred was becoming. This was the fateful moment when lesser salesmen backed off and postponed the question until the next call, and then the next, and the next, until the year was gone and another failing year was under way. A closer didn't postpone anything—he kept pushing until he heard the word *no* as early as possible and then attacked that refusal as if it were a knotted rope, working on it, loosening it until the rope swung free. Nick could see how courage had failed both Fred and Bruno, how they'd lost that hunger needed to loosen the knot of his unspoken *no*. So, as an act of kindness, Nick Callahan didn't bother to say it. But he did this in such a subtle way, Fred and Bruno almost missed it.

"So do your business," Callahan said. "You're not giving any damn machine to me until January."

"You're helping us. You are," Fred said.

It was time for Bruno to speak his part.

"What we did, we sat down—we're counting on you to give us this business. We need it both personally and for the district this year. How can we get from point A to point B? The way we can do it is for us to pick up the tab for two months on the machine," he said.

"Think about it," Fred said. "Pretty nice."

"You don't get a bill until February next year. Exactly same price as I faxed you. We need your help to get out alive this year. We appreciate what you're doing."

"Why?" he asked. "Why do you appreciate it? You won't even be on the account next year."

"Hey, you guys won't see the bill until March or April," Bruno added.

By now, looking at Callahan, Fred knew Callahan had given them the order. He'd committed himself to the order already simply by saying he didn't want it *until January*. In other words, he wanted it. The only issue he wanted to pursue was when he'd get the machine installed. He'd shown his cards, and now all Fred had to do was play out the hand without seeming to take the order for granted. Sometimes all you needed to do to sell a machine was be smart enough to realize when the customer placed his order. He was thrilled, but he kept his excitement to himself. A fish was never caught until it was on ice. There were still problems that could, in the course of fifteen minutes, cause Nick Callahan to change his mind. They might not get the machine installed in time for Pacetta to get credit for the order toward his own bonus. His money depended on installation of the equipment, and that was what Callahan wanted to deny them. He hated Pacetta, and that was the last thing Fred wanted to pursue. That kind of animosity could kill a deal.

"When do you want it installed?" Nick asked.

"First day of the month—"

"No."

"Hear us out—" Fred said.

"No."

"Just hear me ou—"

"No. No way. Not going to do it. Deliver it somewhere else, some warehouse, and hold it. Deliver it to your own office. Watch my lips. You haven't even got the order yet, guys. Can you deliver it to Haywood's garage? What's he got? That 280Z in there?" he asked.

"Yeah. A 280Z."

"I'll tell you something right now, guys. I haven't made up my mind on the order," he said. "Why the hell should I care about you guys?"

Fred took a deep breath.

"We're begging. We're down on our knees. You've shot straight with us," he said.

"You want a straight shot? I'll give you a straight shot," Callahan said. "This pisses me off. This two months you want to give me? You could have offered this six weeks ago. That's what I mean. This really pisses me off. I don't like pushy salesmen. And I don't like your boss. Period. He's the biggest pimp I've ever met."

"We've had this discussion," Bruno said.

Fred wondered about Callahan's grudge against Pacetta, but he knew it would be unproductive to pursue it in this context. There wasn't enough time left in the man's career—let alone in the lunch hour—to change his mind about Pacetta's character or make up for whatever damage was done this time. It was better not to know, not to discuss it. Just work around and beyond it. Sometimes you had to move on to something more productive as quickly as possible.

"I do not like to be pushed," Callahan said.

"I used to toot my horn. But not now. We are not handling this account the way it should be handled. You have put a lot of money into Xerox people," Fred said.

The sound of jazz picked up, a piano and bass and a pair of brushes caressing the skin of a snare drum. Fred looked around quickly, and he realized it was almost two-thirty. The restaurant was empty, except for their table. Other people had gone back to work, but he doubted anyone was working as hard as he and Bruno, still finishing their lunch. His shirt was damp under the arms. His legs ached, as if he'd been running a marathon.

"We're losing six hundred people from headquarters. There's X amount of machines coming out. We've had the edict to reduce copiers. They'll drive them out. Royals, Konicas, Laniers. Every market in the world. My replacement is going to have no choice but to deal on price. Five bucks a month will mean something. That's why your boss hasn't been in the account. He's the biggest pimp in the world. He walks in, and I throw him out the door," Callahan said.

By refusing to install a machine until the following year, Callahan was, figuratively, throwing Pacetta out the door, even as he remained comparatively civil toward Fred and Bruno.

"You know who's going to be here next year," Fred said. "Haywood, Bruno, and I will be here. Pacetta will be gone."

"My personal feelings are my personal feelings. The two times I met the man, he lied to me. They were out-and-out lies."

"If you do this, you do it for me and Bruno," Fred said.

"You said about pushy. Hopefully, this year, you haven't been pushed," Bruno said. He prided himself on his ability to get orders without forcing them. He was troubled by the implications of what Callahan said.

"I'm going to tell you right now. You'll get the order—"

Fred wanted to run outside and do a few laps around the restaurant, if not around the block with its razor wire and raucous graffiti. This was the moment he'd waited for all year. The word *January* was one thing, if you knew how to interpret it, but now Nick Callahan finally spoke the words that counted. This was selling. And they hadn't said a word about the features of the product. This was what he loved, one man pitted against another, a contest, with a score. And it had nothing to do with the product itself.

"—but I won't tell you when you'll get it. You'll get it on my last day. I don't want to see a bill before next year. I don't want to see the machine until next year."

"But the only way it can help us—" Fred said, still pushing for installation, for Pacetta's sake.

"Put it in your garage. Make it look like we took it and install it next to Haywood's sports car. Then in January and February—you have it in your garage, see—you work it."

"Maybe we can install it in January. Now stay with me—"

"Not unless something changes in the next few days," Callahan said.

"There's more important decisions on your mind. I know. It's tough for us to ask."

"If I'd had three more sales calls from you guys, I'd have given this order to Kodak, just to be a pain in the ass," Callahan said.

"You've had an impact over the years. You've been very important to us. We know. We know. The tough decision is on your part."

"Back in October, if you'd dropped it then—you'd have had it in November. I don't like salesmen. Leave it alone, guys. The best thing ever happened to you guys was me. Xerox will give my replacement some numbnuts who doesn't know his ass from a hole in the ground. You've been screwing me with a smile for the last twenty years. You've never been hurting because of us."

"If I'd taken that attitude, I wouldn't be sitting here," Bruno said. He was still hurt that Callahan felt he'd been a nuisance. "You're different. Most of my customers are different. I don't fuck with them. If I'd have fucked with my customers, they would have had my balls."

"We didn't realize you—" Fred started.

"Every time you called, I put it on the back burner for another week. You do it internally any way you want to do it. I'm not going to budge."

Bruno was signing the check while Callahan aired his old grievances. They had the order. It was pointless to defend their approach. It would only muddy the water.

"So what you're saying is, I have to write this order up—" Callahan asked.

Bruno started to speak, but Fred touched his leg under the table and whispered: "Listen." Nick had decided to order the machine, and now he was asking how to do it. The fish was reeling himself in—this was not to be messed with. They worked out the details, up to a point, letting Callahan take the lead.

"Can we have proof you want us to ship it?" Fred asked.

"You sign it. NC are my initials. Forge my initials."

"You wouldn't want us to do that."

"Take it and hide it from us, then," Callahan said.

He was being stubborn and senseless now. They had gotten as far as they could get. They would work out a way to get the machine listed as an installation on the books. They had the order. That's what counted. If Fred could make Pacetta happy with an install, fine. If not, then there was nothing he could do about it. He would get his money for the order whether or not it got installed. There was only so much he could do for Pacetta without risking his job.

"Just pray I don't decide to stay at Bedford in the next four days," Callahan said.

"Stay. It would be great."

"You think you've had problems in life—"

"Life's a war," Fred said.

"Haywood and I used to go out and get drunk all afternoon. Next morning, I woke up at four-thirty and I was in my office at six. Now I drag my ass in there at eight. That's why I'm leaving," Callahan said.

Bruno was writing ideas on the paper tablecloth as Callahan talked, using the waiter's pen. Now he tore his corner of the paper off, folded it, and slipped it into his pocket. They moved to the bar, where they stayed for another hour, talking about what Callahan would do after he left. They talked about stages of grief over a loss—denial, anger, and resignation—and how unemployment was like divorce or a death in the family. Callahan said he wanted to do some carpentry again, now that he would have the time for it.

Did Nick want to do some work on Fred's house? Fred had all the tools. Nick liked the sound of it. It was the final, conclusive stroke, the final act of friendship—and that's what closed this deal. Neither studies nor financing tricks, neither time pressure nor a sense of obligation to please one's manager—nothing but the perception of loyalty between two irascible human beings. With that offer of work, Fred ensured this deal. There was no turning back when it became this personal. After another drink, they said their good-byes, and their words meant more than most good-byes, a farewell to a relationship that had lasted years.

In the car with Bruno, Fred was glowing.

"We'll have to bend the rules," Fred told Bruno, and then he chuckled, angry at Nick Callahan and yet filled with admiration at the same time. "He's an asshole, isn't he?"

They turned to each other and did a high five, their elbows bent in the cramped space above their heads.

"I hope this gets you to President's Club, buddy," Bruno said. It would.

"I owe you," Fred said, elated.

When you were selling, everything became sales. What had he done? Nothing, absolutely nothing. He shared lunch and conversation with another man of his generation and somehow a machine was sold. It was magic, once it was done. It seemed to happen all on its own, as effortless as breath. The act of persuasion was happening everywhere, at all times—the husband smiling at the back door, the child crying in his room, the candidate chanting at his convention—all the way back to the apple in the Garden, that first act of persuasion to set history in motion. First the Creation and then the Sale. Selling was as elemental as the flow of water and air, as old as humanity's most enduring myths. In certain moods, Fred would have nodded if he'd been told the sky sold rain to the earth, the sun sold light to the moon.

Fred regained once again the feeling of total confidence he loved—a momentum, a force, which preceded the salesman on a call like the buffer of air riding the nose of a subway train. In that state of mind the salesman was like an athlete playing *in the zone*. He could do no wrong, and customers knew the salesman felt irresistible, as if he were doing so well it didn't really matter if he made a particular sale. What sold a product wasn't reason, it was this amiable emotion, illuminating a man's face. People recognized the mystery of that smile—as if the salesman had solved the riddle of life and was holding it back, teasing them, hinting how they might have some of it. They wanted to buy from somebody in that state. They wanted their share of it.

This force might last a day. It might last seven years. To call it a streak diminished it and categorized it among the aleatory gifts, whereas what he attained in his best moments seemed much more fundamental in its power to change the way things looked and felt and tasted. If you took it to its extreme, a salesman really wanted what actors, singers, presidents, comedians, swamis, and lovers wanted—to light up a room simply by walking into it. Fred wasn't sure he could illuminate a room by smiling, at least not a *large* room, but when he had this feeling, everything looked a whole lot brighter to *him*.

And where did it come from? From the act of selling office equipment? From one man facing another across a table? There was no way he could explain how one plus one added up to four hundred thousand in this game. It was one of those risible secrets of life, how you could get this sort of buzz off the act of selling a box that churned out paper and black powder in the grip of static electricity. Yet Fred's life was more than this machine. It was more than this company. It was more than this business. And this force was more than a matter of a single deal in a single sales year. Beyond and behind the financial deals and the copies per minute and all that heated paper, there was a charm, an energy. It transformed a salesman from a huckster with a pocket comb and a shoeshine into an engine of the free market. Reducing it to words and numbers was like trying to capture the Mona Lisa's smile by calculating the X and Y coordinates of its curve.

At home that night Fred collapsed. His entire year was winding down. He still needed to finalize the deal with Callahan and do all the petty things required to make sure none of the orders would get canceled. He'd done it, though. He'd succeeded. He'd made trip. Somehow, it felt incomplete and insubstantial, as it did every year during these shortest days of winter. There was never any fanfare for this kind of triumph, no ribbon you snapped as you sprinted past the finish line, no bottle of champagne poured over your head, no high-heeled young woman with an armful of American Beauties and a kiss. You won the game, and then what—you came home, ate a bag of M & M's and some chicken wings, watched Larry King, and went to bed. You had to wait until the following year to celebrate—a Gold Medal breakfast in January, a glitzy ceremony in February, and then Palm Springs in May. It was all so delayed—there seemed no emotional link between the victory and the delirium. Besides, Frank would still be worried about the district as a whole for another week, and though he might give Fred a flashy kiss on the forehead, he wouldn't have time to lean back in his chair and look at Fred with wonder and say, *How have you done it, Fred? How have you made President's Club*

*every year for more than a decade? You're a hero, Fred. You are.* If Fred
could have heard those words from Frank, then somehow the
whole year, with its superimposed cycles of prospecting and calling and selling and closing, would have seemed worth it. As it was,
on the evening of victories like this one, he simply wondered if this
was all his life amounted to, this crushing drive to get orders all
year, followed by a little trip in the spring as a reward. There was,
of course, the paycheck to consider, but sometimes it seemed
certain key people at American Express and Visa and MasterCard
had all come to take Fred's paycheck for granted.

"So you going to President's Club?" Christopher asked him.

"Yeah."

"Darn," his son said. He never liked to hear of his father's plans
to travel. He was wearing a new pair of basketball shoes.

"Why'd you get those new shoes?" Fred asked, ever alert for
new expenditures, especially with Christmas a few days away. He
was wondering why they hadn't been saved for under the tree.

"They're nice!" Kylene said.

"No, they're not. They're too high on the ankle."

Kathy looked at her husband, smiling. No matter how they
spent their money, there was always something wrong with what
they bought. Fred noticed Kathy's look—and he recognized an
opportunity to reverse directions.

"Yeah, you're right. They're fine," Fred said. He wanted to fall
to the floor and close his eyes. He had a headache. He was a
success. He was a wreck. With both pride and weariness in his
voice, he said: "Hey Kathy! I had two Bloody Marys, two gin-and-
tonics, and a sambuca. I'm a mess. I've got a headache."

He was proud of his pain. He was exhausted, and it *was* an
accomplishment, considering it was the price he paid for closing
the Bedford deal. He'd collapsed, victorious, on the field of battle.
It was the sort of victory Coach Lombardi would have loved.

Coach Pacetta certainly did. But would either of them have paid much heed to their most valuable player's wife? Kathy had a headache too.

*6.*

SOME OF THE other managers were still waiting to make trip, still hoping for the impossible. A few nights before Christmas Rob Onorato discovered he couldn't swallow. He told Fred he was so nervous that evening, he couldn't get his throat muscles to work. It seemed more than a boast. Rob looked worn out, puffy around the eyes, everything about him slightly out of focus, a little blurred and smeared.

On the morning before he hoped to close the Goodyear order, Rob invited Fred into his office. The little silver inflatable Goodyear blimp hanging from Rob's ceiling looked wilted and soft. The anachronistic motto across his wall was as blatant as ever: *Greed Is Good!* The large poster of a Porsche hung on Rob's wall, an imaginary incentive, a summary visualization of life's possibilities. Fred's little photographs of his wife and children on his desk served the same role in his own life, but it seemed much harder to link those human faces with a number at the end of the year. It was so much easier to do it with a red Porsche. They were talking about the following year, who would get what kind of assignment. Rob hadn't eaten anything for days. This was serious. Rob lived for food. He related to people, cities, states, and continents through his palate. He remembered significant days of his life by reminding himself what sandwiches he'd consumed on those days. When Rob stopped eating, people stood aside and gave him the right of way.

The morning sun shone directly, horizontally, through Rob's windows. The folds of his shirt cast stark shadows in the warm sunlight. As Rob was leaning back in his chair, talking casually, apparently at ease, he did something Fred had never seen anyone do. At one moment Rob was talking rationally about job changes. The next moment he turned into a spastic, terrified object of prey. As he glanced down at his own shirt, he sprang from his chair and started hopping around behind his desk, flailing at the shadowed folds of the starched cotton pinpoint fabric. He was gasping with a guttural, growling shriek as he slapped the front of his shirt. The two things didn't seem to belong together—the animal howl and the refined sartorial eagerness to smooth the shadows out of that fabric. Fred shrank back, caught up into the hallucinatory shock of the moment. Suddenly Rob dropped his arms, sighed, and sank into his chair, like a rag doll suddenly released from the grip of a spoiled child. He was still panting. He told Fred he'd thought a spider was crawling up his shirt.

It was a new December phenomenon. Would there be no end to these year-end wonders? Is this what Pacetta wanted from his people? Was he really willing to push people beyond the edge into this surreal world where discontent became madness, where the normal rules, the normal laws of physics and perception and trust, seemed to be suspended? For what? To sell a few more copiers and win the Big Game? Did he want to inspire people to work so hard, to care so much about the fate of the big deal, the Big Game, that they hallucinated their anxieties into creatures apparently less frightening than the idea of failure itself? Fred and Rob were exactly alike (with the admitted exception that Fred didn't see things crawling up his shirt). They wanted to exhaust themselves as an act of service and self-sacrifice. They liked to think of themselves as capable of having nervous breakdowns from the effort of selling copiers. They wanted to take everything to an extreme, in the way they worked and the way they played. They wanted to fancy themselves in a class with van Gogh in his cell, or Sir Edmund Hillary on his mountain of ice, or Saint Anthony in the desert. They might laugh at themselves over a beer and remind themselves that, after all, they weren't one of the desert fathers, eating locusts and seeking illumination in a cave. An undernourished saint had a passable excuse to imagine things clinging to his button-down loincloth. Frightening visions seemed, well, less appropriate for an office equipment salesman.

Later that day Fred discovered Libby wanted to put him to work. Now had come the time for penance, the time to repay Libby for everything she believed Fred had tried to do to her—a time to repay her for the favor she'd done for Fred with the ten orders. Now he would have to become a worker for Libby, and he didn't hesitate to do it, because he wanted to solidify the Crawford Manufacturing order.

Ostensibly, Libby didn't like the way the riggers installed many of her copiers. She wanted a white-collar salesperson to help move a new copier into place at her building. Diane didn't have the muscle for it, and therefore the duty rolled to Fred. So that afternoon Fred arrived and found the new copier in a hall near the loading dock, still packed in cardboard, back near the dumpsters and boxes of solvent in wire-mesh cages. He got a foothold behind the machine and started shouldering it forward. The wheels squealed as he moved it out through carpeted offices, halls, the reception area itself. The glass doors to the executive suite were locked. The receptionist handed him a knife from her drawer: *You just wedge this in up at the top. It'll work. Try it.*

He worked the knife between the door and the frame, and finally it gave. He arrived at the executive suite with his squealing cargo. He was sweating and panting, trying not to crush water fountains with his unruly load. He'd never used a knife to open a door before. He felt like a burglar. He could almost hear Libby whispering to him: *This is what you get for trying to slam that Citadel deal. Now we're even, Fred.*

He left the copier in the lunchroom, where it was to be installed in place of an identical machine that looked as new as the model Fred had just delivered to the room. *The big deals just keep on churning,* as Pacetta might have sung it—it was a beautiful sight, a new machine replacing another apparently new machine. Fred did his duty. He accepted his penance. He didn't complain to anyone about it. He did it, and then it was over. But in the car, driving back to the office, he launched into one of his manic soliloquies. With the hills and forests and grassy berms flashing past him, the other cars receding behind him, he started talking to himself, to the ghosts of other people not present in the car, the specters of all the people who haunted him that year—Larry, Frank, Nancy, and all the others. He vented all the tension building within him through August, September, October, November—just the way Rob, in his own way, visualized his own horror as a spider scaling the buttons of his white shirt. He talked as he drove, doing his own voice and performing their voices as well, talking to the others by talking to himself. It was a rapid, ceaseless riff, lasting three, four, five, six minutes with hardly a pause for breath.

"So what's the problem, Larry? They're building a building, Fred. We have to wait until the building is done before we can install. Okay, Larry. Fine. What, three years from now? How can Bruno be sick? He's twenty-eight. I'm here, aren't I? I've got a sore throat. My stomach hurts. Why am I here? You're an asshole, Fred. Let's interview the new job candidates. I want Sal. I want Serena. No. Then why am I interviewing them, huh, Frank? I want Pat to be in the interviews, Fred. Why? Is she going to be the new DM? Pat has no business being in on my interviews. Why? I don't care. I really don't care. Here we go, Larry. Here we go. (He starts doing an effeminate voice of a customer Larry wants him to see.) Fred, I called him and he isn't there. Fred. Fred! Breakthrough! Lunch! Like he's even going to ask about the 5100. Yeah, sure, Larry. Didjya? Did you ask? Did you ask a direct question? Did you ask them if they want it? No? Oh, why's that? Didn't have a chance, Fred. I walked away. God Almighty! Printing systems set up the lunch and they wanted somebody to lead the discussion. That's all. What did *you* do, Larry? I didn't think it was a good time to ask, Fred. The message said he could only give us half an hour. There's your answer right there, Larry! Are you blind? (He coughs several times, unable to speak, and then recovers.) There's your answer! Only half an hour! Hi, Larry. Oh, you got the order? Ten to one there's a wrinkle in there somewhere. I forgot the uplift! I forgot, Fred! Wow. I got the order at twelve fifty-nine P.M. on December thirty-first. Now, Fred, get the machine delivered this year. Okay, Larry. Frank will want to party until three. He'll turn up the music. You think I want to go to a party? I think it's great music, Frank, but I want to go home. You've whipped me for twelve months. I'd love to turn in my resignation right now. I'd love to walk in there with it on paper. I'm waiting for that day. This isn't the way life should be. But it is. Everywhere. It isn't just Frank. That's the problem. Even lawyers have to make deadlines. Is Nancy working? Where's Nancy? Out shopping for Christmas presents? Nancy? Did you have a rough year earning your ninety thousand? I may end up being a parking attendant in my life. I have a hunch. That's what's going to happen. I can feel it. A parking attendant."

He was a success. He did it the way he'd done it every year for more than a decade. He knew how. It was no secret. He was willing to go to almost any length to get and keep an order. It was what they all did. Frank did it. He did it. His best people did it. They put their health and sanity in hock, and they accomplished their mission, and then in January they pulled themselves together and started the process all over again. Year after year. It never ended, unless you got promoted off the front lines or quit. People were exceeding their budgets by huge margins, making good money, and feeling it wasn't quite worth it. And yet they kept coming back for more, addicted to what Frank Pacetta had created—the notion they were doing something inexpressibly more significant than earning a paycheck. Fred had found his Grail again and again in the closing calls at Wellco and Smith Brewer and Bedford Tele-communications. He'd sipped his *elixir vitae* from that cup and felt the little rush of euphoria and well-being that followed a success-ful close. And he would enjoy the abundance in his life that resulted from the chase, the successful quest, in the form of a paycheck, with commission and bonus. It was going to ensure his family's prosperity for yet another year. But it was getting old, the way he'd been doing it. He didn't want to keep slam-dunking equipment as the snow fell every year for the rest of his life. Once it was done, it left a bad taste. There was no peak of joy to make it seem as if everything had come together. The big struggles just melted into smaller ones, and soon the new year was upon them, cold and inert, with a whole new truckload of ordeals waiting to be rigged into their lives. He wanted to do things differently. He wanted to live a different kind of life. He wanted to be a different sort of person.

In the final days of December, after Fred pushed his team over the top, if not over the edge, all the others frantically pushed toward their own goals, some winning, some failing. One rep arranged to have delivery trucks follow her to calls on customers who hadn't yet signed an order. She talked to the customer; he glanced out the window during the call, saw the Xerox truck circling his building, and looked at her and said, "You're a little presumptuous, aren't you?" Usually it worked.

Other reps handed out guarantee letters, giving customers the option to sign an order with an escape option if they decided— several months later—they didn't like the machine or couldn't afford it. Pacetta used this technique himself to close a huge deal at one of the district's biggest customers, helping to push the whole district over the top at the last minute. It was a great way to get the machines onto the premises before the end of December, but when the orders started falling apart three months later, or a year later, nobody bothered to recall the gold ribbons and commendations and recognition in January and February. The reps and sales managers had already taken their place among the heralded winners at the awards ceremonies, and some of them would have moved on to other jobs by then. Under Pacetta, you did what it took to secure the business—or at least the appearance of business—before the year ended.

Everyone worked late every night during the week and on Saturdays, getting orders booked. Pacetta was everywhere, upstairs, downstairs, on calls, on the phone. Though Fred should have been relaxed, enjoying his victory, he was as agitated as everyone else. *If you had to bet on it, when do you think Fred is going to die,* Pat Elizondo asked her husband. *Any day now, as far as I can tell.* One of Pat's reps begged to be fired, as if that would put her out of misery. Pacetta came out of his office, put his hand on her shoulder, and talked her out of it, as if he were talking her off a ledge twenty stories up.

Everywhere reps rushed to make last-minute deals with customers. Pat herself went on a last-minute call to Akron, where one of her customers was refusing to let a machine be installed. When he got her into his office, he sat down and started screaming at her:

*You salespeople are all alike! All you care about is slamming the machines! I'm not going to do it!* She looked at him calmly, knowing how few days were left in her year, and said, *All you purchasing agents are all alike. All you care about is money under the table.* He went pale, leaned back in his chair, and completed the deal. They got the order, and several months later Pat read in a local newspaper that the man was charged with graft. Her remark had been pure luck, a successful bluff.

Fred spent the remaining days of December shoring up his orders and facing what he imagined to be one of the most delicate decisions of his year. He forced himself to think of it as just another business risk, just another minor venture into the danger zone Pacetta liked everyone to imagine they explored and exploited near the year's conclusion. Fred told Nick Callahan he would pass along to the Cleveland partnership a request to bend the rules and keep the machine—against Xerox policy—until after January began, and then have it delivered to Bedford Telecommunications. Bruno wanted no part of this request. He didn't need the deal, and Fred didn't need the installation. They both would get credit for the order alone. Yet without some kind of rule-bending, Pacetta wouldn't get credit. This way Callahan could feel as if he'd evened some old score with Pacetta, and Pacetta would still get credit for the install. It was what the customer wanted. It satisfied the customer—and that's what they were being told to do, day after day. Yet potentially it was a career-busting way to bend the rules. Fred wanted to do it for Pacetta. He felt he owed it to his boss, and he wanted Pacetta to feel he owed Fred.

To get away with something like this yields a sort of wicked joy, in its own way—just like baking extra costs into a contract or getting a customer to sign an agreement he doesn't fully understand. It's an integral part of selling—the magic act, the sleight of hand, the bluff and curve ball and camouflage. Is it wrong? A salesman wonders why people ask this question of his profession, when few feel the need to ask it of certain other gifted people. It's fine for an artist or an actor or a rock star to do reprehensible things because he's seized, he's a vessel of truth, he's a lightning rod of higher powers, and he can no more be held responsible for his depredations than be credited with his inspiration. Like a salesman, the poet seizes his listener's mind and molds it to his warped and yet interesting vision of things. The poet has an accepted alibi for doing it—ostensibly, he's trying to speak the truth. In actuality, a poet may be, like John Donne, trying to sweet-talk a young woman into bed. But he's a poet, and he's allowed to do these things, as long as he does them in a beautiful way.

Sometimes a salesman is inspired too. The problem is, when a salesman does something we don't approve, more often than not, he does it to the rest of us. The common guy is often the one getting tricked. And a salesman isn't giving birth to a vision of beauty and truth—he's peddling gearboxes or houses or copiers. He's taking money from us. We resent it when this sort of artful talent directs its amoral force into our faces and hearts. If someone else happened to be the object of prey, if it were always happening somewhere else, then maybe it would be amusing and excusable and an entertaining form of artistry. But salesmen don't get that sort of clemency. They have to ride this appetite that distinguishes between winning and losing, but not always between right and wrong, because a lot of people depend on them to get the job done—shareholders, employees, and everyone who hitches a ride on an economy kept alive by the continued act of buying and selling. Yet nobody out there is going to forgive a salesman the darker side of his life the way people might forgive Robert Frost for being a son of a bitch simply because that was the price a man paid for knowing how to make words sing. Salesmen can make words sing too.

In this situation, though, the customer is getting what he wants and Fred's the one at risk. By associating himself with Nick Callahan's request Fred's the only one giving up anything. What he's giving up is his sense of job security. Yet he feels no remorse because he's doing what his customer wants him to do. It's only a way of making the customer happy, and if the customer doesn't care about paying for a copier while it sits somewhere in a warehouse, then why should Xerox object to the arrangement? He's just trying to make everybody happy, just trying to do his job. His customer satisfaction record was almost spotless.

"Don't do anything stupid, Fred," Bruno said.

"I would have Xerox get rid of me before you."

"Why do this?"

"Because I want the install." He wanted it because Pacetta needed as many installations as he could get. Yet wouldn't Pacetta get to share all the deal's benefits and none of its risks?

"You hang yourself."

"I don't care. Maybe it's the best thing for me. I'll tell Xerox, *You guys gave me the title. I do my best for you. If you want to hang me, it's only because I wanted to do my job.*"

Besides, it wasn't his decision. It was something only the partnership—Tom Bill, Tom Haywood, and Frank Pacetta—could approve. Besides, the customer had authorized the dock installation and had requested the delay until after the first of the year. In all his years with the company, Fred had only one letter of reprimand in his file, on a minor issue. He was as clean as anyone could get in sales. He wasn't afraid. He had the strength of a certain sort of righteousness under all his persistence and cunning and bravado. No matter how he would be punished—if the installation tactic was discovered—he didn't care. He felt he was doing the best thing for everyone involved, despite the rules, even if it violated the sort of accounting practices his company followed to make sure a customer got exactly what he paid for, as soon as he started paying for it.

Before Pacetta arrived in Cleveland, as Fred understood it, people were fired for doing things like this *without the customer's permission.* Xerox didn't want customers paying for a copier when the copier wasn't on the customer's premises, even if the buyer requested this temporary arrangement, for convenience. It was a paper installation, and it wasn't a fair exchange in anyone's book. Yet in this case it seemed like the best thing to do—it would please Nick Callahan, and it would get Xerox the business. In reality, Fred was making himself vulnerable to attack from people higher up in the company simply to help Frank Pacetta win this year's game rather than lose it. Fred had no choice but to make Pacetta happy if he wanted the kind of career support his boss showed to Pat Elizondo and Bruno Biasiotta and all the other favorites. To ensure himself a future—in this world defined by Pacetta—he had to put his future at risk. It was a strange wager. You put a hundred dollars in the pot in order to get your hundred dollars back. The odds were one to one. Risk your future to ensure it will happen. And somehow this made Fred feel briefly as if he were gaining something in life. Pacetta had become more than a boss to Fred. He was a friend, a brother, a surrogate father, a godfather. He felt he had no choice but to please this man who had done so much to get Fred's motor started every morning of every day of the week.

Once everything was set up, Fred got the call from Nick Callahan.

"The brass ring? We owe you a big one. Hey, that's great. What should we do? Tonight, you don't have free time, do you? We could meet you. Let's kill some brain cells."

At last, the entire district was on a roll. Printing systems orders were coming in. All the teams were getting the signatures they needed. Frank was rushing through the bullpen, high on the money his people were ringing up. "Ring the bell! We've written five million today alone! Is this miraculous? These kids are unbelievable." The entire district was bringing it over the top, in one last paroxysm of selling and installation. The frenzy continued until the final district meeting, just before Christmas, when everyone gathered in the amphitheater by midafternoon. Many of them had been drinking since lunch. The ones who had made their budgets looked as if that longed-for illumination had descended upon them. The rest looked as if they'd lost their way in a very dark wood midway through their lives. Nancy Woodard told the woman sitting beside her that she planned to burn all evidence in her files that the year existed, with the exception of one day on the calendar, the day she got married. Some of the reps had so much to drink, they had trouble speaking.

For two days before this meeting, Fred and Diane made calls at her other accounts, trying to get her enough orders to put her at or near the top of all the reps in the district. She had more than enough to make Palm Springs, but they wanted more. They wanted to set records. But they didn't have what she needed for that. When they arrived in lobbies, she rushed off to the rest room. Fred figured she was either throwing up from the stress or having some other equally inconvenient bodily response, but the details were the last thing he wanted to know. Diane was not the type to talk about it either. He had heard a rumor she once ruled out a second date with one man because he served her wine in the wrong kind of glass.

So because they were rushing around the city making last-minute cold calls, they arrived late at the district meeting. The hype, the Fluff, was in full swing. Santa Claus had arrived already—Paul MacKinnon in a portly red suit and a white beard, with a large bag. On the stage were arrayed the most expensive prizes awarded that year to the people with the best performance: a color television set, a Sony Discman compact disk player, a cordless telephone, an answering machine, a 35-mm camera, a Sony boom box, a General Electric boom box with detachable speakers, gift certificates to the Ritz Carlton, a baby walker, and a Mont Blanc pen. As MacKinnon came into the room, Pacetta led the chant: "Santa Claus is coming to town. We want Santa. We want Santa. We want Santa."

"I'm just a humble little guy from the North Pole!" MacKinnon said. "Merry Christmas! Ho ho ho!"

Frank spoke to the group in his Brooklyn accent, asking for one last push for installations after the Christmas break: "Who's got a bonus on the line? No retreat and no surrender. I know you lip-synch what I say because I've been saying it for four years. An extra fifty thousand from each team gets us there. We ran out of order forms this year. That was a first. It will be a spectacular, spectacular year. You're very, very special people. We'll be first in everything. Merry Christmas."

As Pacetta and MacKinnon called out the district's top performers, they walked, sprinted, stumbled, and wandered to the front of the room and picked through the awards. This was where, in their lives, the emotional mechanics of capitalism glowed with all the enchanted colors of Christmas Eve, where the line between gifts and earnings became impossible to draw, where it was easy to forget how much work it took to win such modest rewards, where the material possession became more important for what it *signified* than for what it could do.

All year long, at these ceremonies, reps accept these gifts with a universal spirit of delight and gratitude. It's always the same ritual. One by one, reps go up and linger among the televisions and boom boxes and CD players. One rep takes his time, picking up one item and then another, finally settling on the cable-ready color television. Another wastes no time, heads straight for the travel vouchers. A third wants the stationary exercise bike. Some of them joke about the whole thing: "I told my wife, before I left this morning, *Honey, I might be bringing home a toaster tonight!*" But most of them take it as seriously as they take anything else in their work lives.

When her time arrives this year, Diane Burley knows exactly what she wants. She remembers the bike she rode as a child, coated with yellow house paint. She picks the ten-speed. She looks as if she's entered her true element, her chin raised, her eyes on the front of the room, a proud woman determined to overcome all the heartbreak of her childhood, not through therapy or faith but by selling copiers and working hard. Her face is filled with a steady, confident happiness that comes from wanting and not having and finally getting. In that face could be seen, as nowhere else in the district, the most benign expression of what made Pacetta a success—he knew how to put that look on people's faces. He knew how to turn bicycles and CD players into talismans of emotional and social transformation, how to make personal sacrifice into a wellspring of temporary glory. He knew how to locate another human being's most private wound and apply pressure to it. He could inflame it or pretend to heal it. Diane was one of the ones who felt healed. This year she made trip *and* earned the dream of her childhood. It was a triumph, both material and emotional. She could have bought a bicycle years ago, but it wouldn't have been the same. She was being paid for her work, but the reward was a prize, too—both earned and freely given, like a parent's love—and that's where the magic resided. For her, this gift of a bicycle was a quarter century late, but not *too* late.

That night Pacetta invited all the managers and their wives to cocktails at his house and dinner at a Hudson restaurant. In his home he spoke to everyone again, thanking them all, assembled in his family room: "It's been a great four years. I want to thank you all." It sounded to everyone like an announcement he'd be leaving the district. During dinner Pacetta didn't break into song. No one threw food. Rob tossed a sugar cube at Fred, across the table, but that was all. The era was ending. It wasn't the same anymore. They returned to Pacetta's house after dinner for more drinks, and everyone headed home in a snowstorm.

Driving the hour back to his home with Kathy, Fred felt warm and satisfied. He told Kathy he felt good about his success, but it was a flat feeling. His team would achieve more than a hundred and thirty percent of its budget for the year. He would win President's Club. Pacetta would make his budget too, thanks to Fred's effort. But it didn't feel the same. It wasn't the same as it used to be. He'd tasted victory once more, though he wondered if anything important would change because of it.

# A NEW LIFE

## 1.

IT WAS TIME to relax, to celebrate, to move on. You never admitted any of this, though. The selling never stops! The mission never ends! You put up a good front of earnest and strenuous work early in the year. You shot for a not unreasonable budget in January, February, and March. Yet you didn't take it seriously. Few machines got sold. In the sales calendar, January was the month of rebirth, not April. As Larry Tyler put it: "All your sins are washed away. As bad as it is, whatever it is, it never lasts longer than twelve months." Now was the time to plan a future, if not an escape.

Fred proved himself with his year-end results. Now, in return, he wanted more than money. He wanted compensation for two decades of faithful service. He wanted compensation in the form of a new position. He kept talking to people about becoming a stockbroker, but he intended to go no further with it until he knew for sure he wouldn't get a better job at Xerox. He decided if he didn't get another job in the new year he would leave the company. He would quit making calls to stockbrokers he knew, and instead he would *become* one.

He told everyone he would do it—Frank, Pat, Rob, Kathy, even some of his customers—and they sympathized. They knew he needed a change. He looked upon it as a matter of almost physical survival. The job of sales manager was the most taxing job in the entire sales organization, and he didn't believe he could withstand another year of it, along with the partying to make it endurable.

He was nervous about his future. What about Frank? Was he leaving? With typical arrogance, Frank said he wanted to run something someday—Xerox itself or some other company. He was telling Rochester he didn't want to move far from Cleveland. How did this add up, exactly? He wanted a club membership. He wanted a bigger title. He wanted more responsibility. He wanted to be a king, the way he was a king in Cleveland. He would have to wait and see what they offered him. But where could he go? What *could* they offer him?

Fred refused to leave Cleveland. Was there another job for him in the district? Frank thought Fred was doing a tremendous job right where he was. It was Fred's choice. What did he want? Frank would create a job for him. Pacetta had been hinting this for a year now. So where was the new job? Why wasn't he in it right now, in January? Fred had risked everything for Pacetta. He'd done what he felt he needed to do to make Pacetta himself successful; he'd taken himself over the edge at Smith Brewer and Wellco and Bedford Telecommunications. He'd played the game the way he believed Pacetta wanted him to play it, and he'd been lucky. No one was making a stink about anything that happened in the previous year, except the amount of money Pacetta spent to entertain his people and his customers. Now where was Fred's reward? Why didn't Pacetta have a new job lined up already?

Pacetta asked him: Did Fred want to become a third national account manager in Cleveland? No, because he wouldn't get any of the cream accounts. Those would stay with the two current NAMs. Well, as it turned out, there was talk that one of them might be moving into a new job. It wasn't a sure thing yet. Nothing was finalized. There were other people who would want the job too. Fred didn't allow himself to feel any real hope, but it gave him enough reason to stick it out and stay at Xerox at least as long as Pacetta stayed.

Everyone expected Pacetta to leave in the first half of the year. As months passed, Pacetta remained in Cleveland. Early in January Fred heard Pacetta was offered a job with Xerox in Italy—a curious offer to a man who said he wanted to stay close to Cleveland—but it fell apart within a week, and Pacetta was both disheartened and peeved. Then the previous year's results were finally tallied, and Pat Elizondo shared with certain people the sheet from corporate, showing that the Cleveland district had come up short of a clear profit. She pointed out that the Cleveland number was actually the absolute minimum the district needed to achieve a profit, a glaringly even figure. This meant, to her, that corporate had rounded the number up, as they sometimes did as a favor for hardworking district managers, to give Pacetta a satisfactory showing. The number said it all: They were generous enough to give Pacetta the nudge he needed to make his nut, but they did it in a way that told everyone else he needed their help—because they could have made the number even a little higher, making it look more realistic, a little higher than the target. Nobody, after all, hit his target exactly on the dot.

No one argued with Pacetta's ability to motivate people to sell more copiers than ever before, but he had this lingering habit of spending too much money on customer entertainment and district parties and recognition meetings and customer junkets. He was a great motivator, but what about the bottom line? In Elizondo's view, the transparently rigged number on the ranking sheet made it clear that corporate wanted everyone to know Pacetta's short-comings. It was as if they wanted to show that this man, who had the gall to try to dictate the terms of his own promotion—a club membership, a vice presidency, a spot with almost total empower-ment to do things his own way—did have his weaknesses, after all. Pat Elizondo recognized it as a slam against Pacetta, and in a vicarious way she felt as hurt by the number as he did, because she thought of him as a colorful motivator, a sort of Bobby Knight, a coach some people loved and others hated. If they were going to doctor his results, why didn't they do it in a way that made it look more believable?

In the midst of all this, Fred expected Pacetta to stay in Cleve-land for the rest of the year—a delightful prospect. If he didn't get a new job, he'd probably be working for Pacetta, he was happy to learn. In one of his quieter moods, Pacetta came into Fred's office, looked out the window, and said, "The early pioneers did some things for this country, Fred. But they all died." And then he left the room, his head bowed. Fred chuckled at the phony drama of it, and then he felt sad. He would miss even these moments of melodramatic self-pity if Pacetta left.

Undaunted, Pacetta organized a series of celebrations to reward his people for their performance in the previous year. During the first celebration, the Gold Medal ceremony, as Pacetta called it, he stood before the group and lifted to his nose a computer printout of the district's results for the previous year. He sniffed the paper and grinned, telling everyone they installed more equipment than any other Xerox district during the last four months of the year. In December they topped two hundred percent of their plan for the month. He handed out gold medals, which resembled Olympic gold medals, to everyone who attained a certain percentage over plan for the year.

Halfway through the year's first quarter, the district held its annual Academy Awards recognition party, the biggest and flashiest and most expensive party of the year for Xerox people in Cleveland. It was one of Frank's unique inventions, a night when everyone was recognized for the work he or she did during the previous year. The night when sales was recognized as an acting job, and the most superlative actors and actresses were honored for their roles. Spouses were invited—unusual for a district gathering. At this party Frank did his finest job of recognizing almost everyone in the district for the effort they put forward. Limousines arrived at the houses of the managers, and inside the limousines the honored couples found a bottle of champagne, hors d'oeuvres, and a personal note of thanks from Pacetta. Always the iconoclast, always the outsider, Fred drove in his own car to the party, at an eastside convention center. But the other, younger managers welcomed the limousine.

Inside the ballroom the impression was of an environment halfway between elegance and glitz. Everything looked black—the evening wear, the walls, the night outside. White Christmas lights were strung everywhere, though the holiday season was long gone. The tables were covered with shiny bolts of reflective silver fabric. Candles burned in hurricane lamps. Everyone gravitated to the bar in the half of the huge ballroom designed for cocktails and quick meals of meatballs, egg rolls, and an endless supply of other hot food from the steaming chafing dishes on the shimmering tablecloths. In the next room, completely open to the party room, chairs were arranged auditorium-style, facing the stage and a huge screen, onto which the happy, shiny faces of district people were being projected, a hundred times larger than life—the faces of everyone in the district, down to the support and secretarial help. Spotlights swept the room. People stood in the shadows, then were illuminated for a brief moment before the shadows flooded back over them. Bruce Springsteen sang over the loudspeakers: *In a world without pity, do you think I'm asking too much?*

Pacetta took the stage. He was so thin in his black tux, he looked like an inky inverted exclamation point planted on the floorboards. The awards ceremony proceeded with twenty-foot images of people and their spouses and babies projected onto the screen. In the smiles of these magnified faces the teeth looked as big as a row of white encyclopedias or Bibles. The thrill spread through the audience as various couples saw themselves on that huge screen, famous for fifteen minutes in their own parochial way, like extras in a blockbuster movie. The whole evening was designed to create the illusion of glory, and it worked. As forced as the production seemed, the music, the photography, the tuxedos, the vodka and scotch and gin, all fused to create an exhilaration that seized everyone, even the most skeptical spouses. Everyone surrendered to the sense that what they were experiencing here was unique, exclusive, and precious.

"Fred! Freddie, come on up!" Pacetta shouted from the stage, after most of the other sales managers had been summoned up front. "These people did a lot. Caring and pride are very important things. I thank all of you very much. You people kicked some serious butt last year. I appreciate that."

For another half hour, the people who cared enough to kick serious butt were called to the stage and given awards for everything from their sales performance to their efforts in other areas, such as customer satisfaction. Pat Elizondo was called up for recognition in this particular category, with Simon and Garfunkel singing in the background. *Just trying to keep my customers satisfied, satisfied*... By the time she reached the stage, she was singing the song herself, and so were all the others lingering onstage from previous awards. The recognition party had melted into another sing-along and soon would melt back into the Academy Awards. Everything was timed and choreographed. Finally the Blue Max winners were announced. This was the biggest award for the evening, in which everything was taken into account—not only the employee's percentage of budget, but all aspects of individual performance. Fred Thomas was one of the first called to the stage, followed by Ron Nelson, Bruno, Pat, John, and several others. "Danger Zone" played over the sound system. At the end of the ceremony, waitresses emerged from doors in the back of the room bearing trays of champagne flutes, sparkling and gold.

People drank and danced past midnight. Soon the last stragglers climbed back into their waiting limousines. Fred returned to his own car, and a few others decided to ride with him—Ron Nelson and Rob Onorato. One of the other printing systems reps, who had had less to drink than the rest, drove all the way to Ron's house and then Rob's. They sang all the way home, with the radio blasting, at speeds close to a hundred on the highway, car doors opening and closing, all the windows down. After they dropped off the others, Fred asked Kathy to drive the rest of the way to their own house. This was a first—he was letting her take control. As soon as she took the wheel, Fred lay down in back. He was letting Kathy drive him around. She couldn't believe it. Maybe something *was* going to change this year.

As she drove, she thought: *We're too old for this. This is high school. This is college. This isn't for people in their forties.* She wanted to tell Fred she couldn't believe they were still doing things they'd done in college. But he was sound asleep.

2.

PALM SPRINGS SEEMS vaguely unreal. The skies are brilliant, as blue and promising as the bubble of water in a pregnancy test. Circle down to the little airport in the valley, and from the air it looks as if there's nothing below but mountains and desert and little drab patches of arid civilization, where human life struggles to survive maybe even a little harder than it does in Trenton or Gary or Cleveland. But once you are on the ground, once you are on the way through the dreary commercial strips, something unfamiliar emerges. It's one of those communities where the business sector seems to cling like a parasite around the edges of resort and residential tracts—the inverse of most metropolitan areas, where the suburbs, the bedroom communities, are handmaidens to the commercial and industrial core of the local economy. Here, it seems more important to play than to work.

In light of this, things begin to assume an *Alice in Wonderland* aura of dreamy novelty. It takes a while to figure out why things seem surreal, until it becomes clear this is a world of effortless money, a realm where many people don't need to work—a place of superabundance, where accumulated money multiplies by itself, without human sweat or ingenuity. This is the Promised Land of a capitalist society. This is a place where people live off the earnings of their investments, free to do whatever they want with their lives—and yet, perversely, it seems many of them continue working, making movies, making megadeals, making *more* money, doing whatever they did before they achieved independent wealth. In reality, they have all the time in the world to do whatever they please.

Fred and Kathy, on the other hand, have three days they will cram with swimming and partying and golf. Here the hours become more precious than ever. With the car windows down, the sweetness of cut lawns and sage and the clean, fresh scent of desert air enter the car, thousands of miles from the humid hills of Ohio. Everywhere the desert is turned into an oasis, with road runners on golf courses, jack rabbits in backyards. Oleanders, pomegranates, azaleas, bougainvilleas, palms, cactus, hibiscus—all the plant life seems to bear either flowers or fruit. The trees look exotic and tropical, dropping pecans, lemons, oranges, and dates into the grass.

Once into the foothills of the Santa Rosa Mountains, turning onto Frank Sinatra Drive, the President's Club winners wind up the brown hillside and gaze back on the valley as it drops below. Its vast plantations of windmills, looking like beds of needles from a certain distance, generate electricity for those who live here, harvesting light and heat from the wind. When they reach the Ritz-Carlton Rancho Mirage, they see suites stretching low along a high ridge, with a view of the entire valley—palms, sage, mesquite, salt cedars, the populated miles in the valley, and in the distance, the snow-capped mountains surrounding the dry flatland. They aren't too far above sea level on this hill, yet it feels as if this is some kind of ultimate psychological altitude above which they cannot rise.

It's a hundred degrees when Fred and Kathy check in. The air's so dry that when a key is inserted into the lock of a room, a spark of static electricity jumps between the tip of the key and the hole in the lock. It's a relief to be here, to know that three days of fun await—a complete escape from the grind, from the midyear tensions, from almost every aspect of daily work and responsibility.

Other people do the work now. Every member of the Ritz-Carlton staff is solicitous, polite, and ready to fetch anything for anyone, demurring at tips with self-effacing gestures, backing out the door. The halls and rooms are furnished with Victorian-era mahogany antiques from England. Original oil paintings by obscure nineteenth-century painters hang on the damask walls. In the television cabinet for each room is an elaborate personal snack bar. In the booklets listing local attractions and events are advertisements for plastic surgery—collagen injection, chemical peels and dermabrasion, reshaping and liposuction. At the bottom of each ad is the name of the surgeon as well as a reminder: "Limousine service available." They've come a long way from Cleveland. This is more than another world. It's like tasting life as another, higher species might choose to enjoy it.

The night before he left Cleveland, Fred was so wired, so eager to leave his work behind, he couldn't bring himself to go to bed, even by midnight. He took out the garbage around twelve-thirty. An hour later, he replaced a lightbulb in the streetlamp at the end of his driveway. At two-thirty, he climbed into bed. Three hours later he awoke, sprang out of bed, and started loading bags into the car. Even now, he was so energized, so euphoric about being here, that he didn't feel weary.

In preparation for Palm Springs, he had run seven miles a night to burn his waist back down to a size thirty-four. He bought a treadmill, which he placed in his basement. Kathy, already as slim as any wife in the district, ran diligently day after day, trying to trim a fraction of an inch from her thighs. Palm Springs would be fun, but it would also be a contest—a popularity contest, a drinking contest, a poolside bathing-suit contest. Everyone would be comparing notes, and so everyone worked hard to be at his or her physical peak during those three days under the Southwest sun. Many people in the district made regular trips to tanning booths, though Fred and Kathy drew the line at that. They bought new clothes. They watched their diets. They ran like rabbits. The tan could wait. Now that they'd arrived, they both looked slim, rested, younger than they'd looked six months earlier. All of this for three brief days of California dreaming.

Though half of Fred's team made trip, only one rep on Fred's team—Diane Burley—has arrived in Palm Springs with him. Though Bruno made President's Club, he isn't in Palm Springs, because his wife gave birth to their new baby, Gabriella, and they wanted to stay home with the infant. Nancy Woodard planned to celebrate her own efforts with her husband at home, since she wasn't allowed to go. Larry Tyler planned to go in to the district office and work both Saturday and Sunday of the President's Club weekend. One group of losing reps decided to hold a Vice President's Club celebration in Cleveland, with a few cases of beer from a corner convenience store.

The last thing Fred wants is for this vacation to be a contest between himself and his wife. He wants to believe he's on the verge of a new life, both at work and at home. Kathy doesn't believe it, but he wants to tell her how he feels, that he wants to make a change. He wants Palm Springs to initiate a new life for both of them. He wants it to begin here. Their wedding anniversary will fall on one of the nights they're in California, and he plans to give her a new set of Taylor Made metalwood golf clubs. He talked with Pacetta about how to present them to her, and Pacetta suggested Fred simply put them in Kathy's bag, without her knowledge, and let her find them the first time she went out for eighteen holes on one of the desert courses.

After they check in, Fred and Kathy go first to their room and then join the others outside at the pool, where Cleveland people are comparing notes: *I tanned three days before I got here. I tanned seven days. Oh, come on. You tanned five days. No, seven days.* Frank Pacetta arrives at poolside about the time Fred and Kathy do, though Pacetta took a different flight. He and Fred look as they looked at every other President's Club. Their bodies—arms, legs, torso, even their backs—are entirely carpeted with a layer of hair. On other trips, before the two of them disrobed, people were known to place bets on which of them was hairier. Only a few of the Cleveland people are at the pool, though there will be more than a hundred attending on this weekend from districts in the same division as Cleveland. Xerox staggers the arrival of different parts of the company throughout the month so that no single group becomes too large for the resort to handle effectively.


Fred's surprised when he discovers the theme for the outdoor bash is Arab, as if the whole event had been designed with his Lebanese lineage in mind. As they walk outside and down the steps to a broad sward of grass, which looks as if it had been unrolled like plush Persian carpet onto the sandy hillside, they see what would appear to be a cocktail party for a sheik. Tents are pitched on the periphery of the grass, with tables serving drinks and food set up at intervals. Clusters of people are gathered everywhere, and everything seems to be in a state of motion. A belly dancer in blue silk with finger cymbals stretches her legs by the steps. A man wears a purple turban with gold spangles. Under her tent a palm reader scrutinizes a young woman's hand. A snake charmer sways between tables of food with a python wrapped around her neck and waist. She has two snakes: Mephistopheles and Lady Godiva. People play tambourines and guitars onstage near one of the wet bars. In the distance, miles away over the top of the tents, Fred can see across the Coachella Valley to the pristine snowpeaks of the mountains beyond the cultivated lowland. Treasure chests, magic lanterns, Persian carpets—nothing has been spared. Up on the hill, people are riding a camel. Occasionally a fragrance of camel pelt seems to drift down into the Xerox throng.

As a joke, Kathy has her palm read. The reader, Jamie, tells her: "You do a lot of thinking. You have strong opinions about things. You have more mental than physical energy. Not a lot of strength. You analyze your feelings a lot. You have a good marriage, though. You're very creative. But are you doing anything with it?"

When it's Fred's turn, she tells him: "You have a strongly developed will. You have good stick-to-itiveness. Good strong life line. A lot of energy. You have an unpredictable temperament. You have good mental focus. You have good management skills. You integrate your intuition and logic."

"You're right. That's true. I go with my gut feelings," Fred says.

"You have a strong sense of purpose. Here's your heart line. It's straight but short. Your ambition line and your life line are the same."

"I'll be rich," Fred says, trying to prompt her agreement.

"I don't know. I think it means your career is your life."

"But can I pay off my Visa bill?" Fred asks, and she laughs.

"Probably so."

That's a relief. The evening progresses according to the Pacetta Laws of Celebration. The cocktail party becomes a dancing party, with a band playing numbers from the sixties, mostly surfer music. Then, as the drinking becomes heavier, a few of the Cleveland people start singing Pacetta's favorite oldies: "My Girl," "Ohio," "Wooden Ships," "The Weight." It's only ten o'clock when the management asks everyone to disperse. Others at the hotel want to sleep. They have early tee times and many of them are much older than the Cleveland crowd. As the wife of one manager puts it, slipping through the dining room to get outside: "I have to pass though my father's generation to get somewhere in this place."

Many of the younger reps assemble at the hot tub near the pool, displaying their slimmed-down figures and new bathing suits. Ron

Nelson stands beside the pool, looking as if his taut, hairless body is molded from polymers. He spent many months weightlifting for this moment. When things get a little too noisy at the Jacuzzi, a pair of cowed-looking waiters come forth and say, "Our practices are peace and quiet by ten P.M." On the cement lies a broken tequila bottle.

Fred's upset because much of his luggage still hasn't arrived from the airport, so he finds the office of the group who organized the entire President's Club event, and he starts to badger a woman who's getting ready to go home. He's mad. He's going to get something out of this. After five minutes of his abuse, the young woman picks up the telephone and calls her boss at home, who says he will look into it.

"You know I'm having fun with you. I'm drunk," Fred says. "But I really do need my luggage. And I will give you guys a negative rating when it's all over."

Fred returns to his room and takes off his trousers and lies on the bed in his boxer shorts, phoning the airport again. Kathy arrives a few minutes later, and then John Kitowski shows up, just before the luggage is delivered to their door. Fred's still stretched on the bed, undressed.

"He's so involved, he's oblivious," Kathy says.

"I had four conversations with this guy," Fred says, having found a mission to pursue even on vacation. "He told me I was on Delta. I told him I was on American. We weren't getting anywhere."

"I think you should go around tomorrow dressed just like this," John says. "You should say, *I've been robbed.*"

"You hear what that girl told me?" Fred asks. "She said, *Mr. Thomas, we're going to give you a free T-shirt.*"

When the luggage finally arrives, Fred announces, "It's all because I got riled up."

The boy who delivers the luggage opens the minibar for them.

Everyone looks inside: Bloody Mary mix, tanning lotion, a disposable flash camera, jelly beans, pistachio nuts, Tylenol, a bottle opener, gourmet flat bread, a deck of Ritz-Carlton cards, diet cola, club soda, Sprite, ginger ale, gin, bourbon, tonic water, almonds, popcorn, shortbread, skin moisturizer, along with twenty other items, all costing far more than they would cost anywhere else.

Fred puts on his slacks again as others arrive in the room. They tell the story of what happened in the lounge: Pacetta showed up dripping wet in his bathing suit, along with some of the managers and their wives. They refused to wait on Frank because he tried to get another sing-along started in the lounge, where many of the other patrons were dressed in evening wear and Armani suits.

Fred's trying to kill a moth with his tennis racket. Now people are sprawled on the bed, and he's in motion. Yet for all his energy, Fred looks grim. They are eating freely from his snack bar. Finally, he gives up and walks to the snack bar and starts tossing snacks into the air, like a bride tossing her garter.

"Anything your heart desires, hon! Because your next paycheck is coming to me this time, sweetie," he says. "What would you like?"

"Nothing," Kathy says.

"How come?"

"I'm full, Fred."

"If you want some cookies, please don't hesitate."

One of the other managers, who arrives late in Fred's room, bounds out, announcing as he leaves: "I love this country!"


The three days passed with tennis and golf and sunbathing at the pool, where a young Ritz-Carlton worker walked around to each sunbather, carrying a small spray can of the sort used to mist tropical house plants. They called him the Spritzer. He would ask each bather if he or she would like to be "spritzed," to cool off from the heat. It was typical of the resort—at night a Godiva chocolate on the pillow and during the day a personal mist of soothing vapor for the extremities.

On the second morning of the trip, Pat Elizondo and John Kitowski rented a hot-air balloon and took a few reps up for a flight over the desert. They arrived at the site just after dawn; another yellow-and-red balloon was already in the air above them. As the group climbed into the balloon, the heat from the bellowing gas jets was searing. As they rose into the air, they were awed by the shrinking view of scrub bush, pomegranates, and salt stains on the desert floor. They floated over housing developments, out over the groves of date palms with paper bags covering the fruit, then citrus trees, and by the time they reached their cruising altitude, they could see four or five other balloons in the air at the same time—green, blue, red, and gray. It wasn't enough to be in Palm Springs, far from the turmoil of distant cities. They wanted to escape gravity itself.

Pat spit over the side of the balloon to see how long it took for something to reach the ground, and then she noticed the modest houses of migrant workers in the onion patches below her, not far from the polo fields. The pecan trees' spiky leaves looked plastic when viewed from so high. Somewhere a rooster crowed. Cows grazed. The flames bellowed and hissed above their heads; the balloon swelled and lifted. When they hit the soil, the smell of onions and sage and dust returned, and with it the pickup truck to deliver them back to the launch site, where iced bottles of champagne awaited.

It was only eight o'clock in the morning. It was going to be a long, forgetful day. *We aren't leaving until we're heaving. Keep it going or suffer the consequences!* For all the unbridled, headlong determination to keep the levity going, these President Club events were tame compared with the ones many of them remembered from a decade earlier. At those three-day parties, marriages fell apart. People became completely uncontrollable. In front of the entire crowd one year, a district manager's wife burst into the ballroom and slapped her husband because of the affair he was having with one of his sales reps, there, in the hotel, during the trip. People went three days without sleep, the better to keep it going. In Hawaii back then, helicopters flew over the entire crowd, showering people with an endless rain of flowers—hibiscus, bougainvilleas, begonias. It was like some kind of afterlife for sybarites, effortless and voluptuous and free.

Now it was up to small groups like this one to keep the sense of excess alive. In the course of an hour and a half, Pat's group of six people finished five bottles of champagne. At breakfast, after this, there would be more champagne. There was an entire day of drinking and swimming and volleyball ahead of them after the meal, and they ate quickly, once they returned to the hotel dining room. They didn't want to miss a thing.

After their first full day in Palm Springs, Fred makes reservations for his anniversary dinner at Wally's, a restaurant not far from the resort. When they arrive and are seated, a waiter named Ramone brings their drinks. Lamps on each table cast a warm glow on the faces of diners.

"This could be my last President's Club," Fred says.

"You always say that, Fred."

"This is a special night. Whatever your heart desires, I'm buying. You know I love you, Kathy. You know I—"

She smiles her skeptical smile, but says nothing.

They order a bottle of Asti Spumante for a toast. When Ramone brings the bottle to the table, he's unable to pop the cork. It's all

Fred and Kathy can do to keep from breaking into laughter. Ramone tells them it's the first time he's ever had this much trouble with a bottle. He motions to another waiter, who scurries over to their table but does no better. A third waiter arrives, and then a fourth, who finally manages to wrest the cork from the bottle's neck with a loud pop. Fred and Kathy applaud. The successful waiter takes a bow.

"Happy nineteenth. Who'd have ever thought we'd be in Palm Springs?" he says.

After she takes a sip, Kathy crosses her arms. It isn't the sort of body language Fred wants to see. He tells her this year will be a turning point in their lives. Things are going to change—on the job, and at home. He wants to make a new beginning.

It's clear Kathy's reluctant to put much faith in dinner conversations with Fred, even during a little celebration of their wedding anniversary like this one. She's listened to Fred for years, and she will continue to listen, but she isn't going to accept these declarations as any different from the ones he makes year after year, the same good-natured and yet merely provisional commitments. She studies him for a moment and then leans forward, her arms still crossed.

"When you think like this, it seems so nice. But it could all change in a split second. You could be saying just the opposite in an hour. So your words don't mean anything."

Fred doesn't understand. He means what he says. He intends to change his life. He's grown beyond his job, and he needs more of a challenge, more responsibility, and less pressure to make the thirty-day deadlines. He wants to live without constantly pushing himself over the edge at the conclusion of the year. Kathy wants to believe him, but she doesn't want her heart broken yet again if she allows herself to hope for things based on what he promises.

"If I were to ask you to make a list—this would have to be going back in time—a list of what would bring you happiness, what would you say? Your total happiness in life," she asks.

Fred ruminates a minute, sipping his wine.

"It's hard to answer. To find peace of mind, I guess."

"Go back to before we were married."

"Always to be in a win-lose situation, and I know it, and for me to rise to a level and win, and then find peace of mind."

"It wouldn't be love, a wife, home, children, security—"

"Part of the win-lose is for my wife to realize that I did sacrifice—for whatever good comes out of what I've done—for you to realize that I did it, that I made sacrifices, for those other things. For my wife and children. I like being the martyr, I guess."

She agrees.

"It goes back to the challenge of the win-lose. I have to win," he says. "I think I'm playing a ball game every day. Maybe the only long-term goal I can accept is leaving the kids in a situation where it's easier for them than it was for us. That's the long-term win."

Even as he says it, he knows this isn't entirely true. He does want more than this from his life now—he knows if his life doesn't become more than a game, he'll lose something bigger than a score. He can't win a game that never ends. But he still hasn't found the words to say what he wants. He's never felt entirely confident with words, except on a sales call. At times like these, his emotions never seem to fit into them properly.

As she listens, Kathy wonders how a man could turn his entire life into a game, a playing field. Is that all there is? Winning? Victory? Triumph? The sheer animal pleasure of winning is invigorating, but what does it mean? The loser feels like nothing, and the winner takes all. Kathy feels that sort of win has almost no significance in the way human life is actually lived, where winning and losing are tendencies toward greater or lesser achievement on an infinite scale of quality. The line between winning and losing, black and white, good and bad, virtuous and vicious, is never clear. Life is lived on an endless spectrum with Better at one end and Worse at the other. When Fred spends his life trying desperately not to lose, he forgets that, to a greater or lesser degree, he's always winning compared with some people, and always losing compared with others. Kathy wonders why he can't understand there are no absolutes, no enemies, no opposing teams, no finish lines, in his personal life. And though he does his job with more excellence and shrewdness than most, he never admits it to himself, never gives himself credit for how hard he works, because he's afraid he'll ease off. He's afraid he'll lose. Yet shouldn't a human life be more than an endless effort to avoid failure?

They talk casually as they eat, and once they've finished their meals, they talk quietly about Kathy's father. The conversation goes straight to Kathy's heart. Her father was the king of his house. He kept peace with Kathy's mother and his children, and Kathy looks back upon that time as a personal Golden Age in comparison with the turmoil of her own life. It was the same for Fred—she talks about how wonderful Fred's own father was, working two jobs each day for a portion of his life, never complaining, never ranting and raving. Kathy's eyes fill with tears at these memories of tenderness, these examples of gentle masculine strength. What happened in all the years between two generations? Has sales become a more brutal kind of work, or is it just Fred who's unwittingly become more callous?

"Your father did show a lot of affection," Fred says.

"Maybe because he felt it," Kathy says, tears inching down her cheeks.

"He would hug and kiss your mother every time he left the house and came home," Fred says, making it worse without realizing it.

All of a sudden, in tears, Kathy stands and walks toward the rest room near the restaurant's entrance. At first, Fred wonders if she's leaving the building. When she returns, Fred takes a few more bites from his meal, looks at her with sheepish eyes. As he speaks to her, his words are one of his most candid, heartfelt attempts at persuasion. Nothing else is worthy of the occasion because it is, in many ways, yet another movement in his toughest sale—a sale in which he keeps coming back for another demonstration, again and again, without ever seeming to settle on a firm contract between himself and this woman on the other side of the table.

"Kathy, I really do love you. I love you so much, you don't know. Maybe I keep thinking I'll win the short-term game. If I can keep winning it—maybe that's why I stay. Maybe that's why I keep doing what I'm doing. I think of the things we did when we dated, loving each other, driving the Fiat, there's a box full of letters I wrote you. We had every opportunity to go our separate ways, and we didn't. In high school, in college. The rotten things I've done are just a part of life. Most people have done those things. I think we are very, very good people. I think our kids are great because of you, not me. I know that. They love you far more than they love me. I think in the end they'll understand the whole thing. I hope so, because I know in the end I'll bear the brunt of it all, of what's happened between us. Maybe that's the sacrifice you're making—that you accept how bad I am."

She sits in silence, unable to speak, or unwilling. Her arms are crossed again. A smile has frozen on her face, and her eyes look vacant. She refuses to be moved. It's too dangerous to feel things at moments such as these, because such moments have proven so rare. It's too risky to surrender to Fred's words. She wants proof. She wants action.

"Are you done with your speech, Fred? All those beautiful words. But my level of trust—"

"That's your problem. Not mine. We're both losers if we can't stay together, Kathy."

"I'm not so sure of that, Fred."

"I guess I'm not feeling sorry for myself," he says. "I don't know what else I can say."

There is nothing he *can* say. Kathy knows the duplicity of language—how it amounts to nothing binding, usually nothing more than the evidence of some passing emotion. No matter how many words Fred offers her, they mean nothing compared with simple physical gestures—help with the dishes, a hand on her shoulder, a dance after midnight downtown at the Flats. Words count for nothing compared with a simple movement from point A to point B. If he came home and announced he'd been hired somewhere else at half the salary, she'd be a little disheartened and yet tremendously impressed—Fred would be doing something rather than talking about it. There was hope when he took action. Hopelessness came from too much talk. There's a feeling of physical relief when you watch a building implode or a brick wall crumble under a hammer, because everything that serves as habitation also serves as confinement. Almost any change—a real change, even for the worse—would be better than simply talking about it. She doesn't want to chance an unqualified faith in his words. She could be hurt too badly if she let herself be drawn in. She's afraid his marriage—*their* marriage—has become just another game he's trying to win. Conversation is always a gambit with Fred. When they drift into the realm of words, she's reluctant to go where he wants to lead her. She feels she's being tricked. Yet when he touches her, she believes in the feeling it conveys. Yet they can't live together in total silence. She needs to see some of the things he promises actually come true.

They pay the bill and rise from the table. As they leave the restaurant, Kathy ducks into the rest room one last time to dry her eyes. Outside, they drive to the Marriott Desert Springs and find many of the Cleveland people assembled at a bar frequented by a younger crowd. Within the hour, Kathy's smile resumes a natural life of its own.

After visiting with Pacetta and some of the wives for an hour, Fred asks Kathy to dance. This is what she wants—a dance, a genuine touch. This modest gesture, without ambiguity, without any multiple layers of meaning and intent, means more to her than any of Fred's words at dinner. He never asks her to dance anymore. So they sidle through the crowd and take the floor, while Prince sings and dances on the video screen behind them. Fred is not a graceful dancer and doesn't pretend to be. But the two of them joke about his awkward, self-conscious moves, and he wears a self-deprecating grin. Fred has quit talking and started doing something. It's only a dance, but it means more than all their talk over dinner.

The next morning, when they head for the golf course, Fred slips the new clubs into Kathy's bag. When the bag is brought to her at the hotel, she sees the new woods in her bag and says, "This isn't mine. It can't be mine."

"See Kathy! See the tag! They're your clubs!" Fred says, trying to fool her, delaying the surprise.

"But there must be some mix-up," she says.

"Kathy, what does it say on your bag? Kathy Thomas, right? They're yours!"

It isn't until they reach the golf course and Kathy hits her drive—a beautiful long ball straight down the middle of the fairway—that Fred grins at her and announces, "Happy anniversary, honey." Now she understands, and she's pleased he went to the trouble to bring her these clubs and keep it a secret. Yet all the while she watches Fred put on a show for Pacetta and the others— always playing a good-boy role for an audience, even when he presents his wife with a gift. He could have done it in private, but then he wouldn't have gotten any credit from his co-workers for being such a thoughtful husband. Fred was always playing a game, always making every gesture work on two or three levels, getting the most out of everything he did.

Still, it *was* a nice gift. She takes the driver from her bag again to give it a swing, feeling the little twinge of nervous hope it offers her, trying not to count on anything new, trying not to feel too confident, trying not to jinx what it might allow her to do.

During these eighteen holes Kathy hit a few great balls. When she drove it, the ball sailed higher and higher, rising into the sky, a little wingless bird, until at last it began its descent. She kept chasing the ball to see what might happen next, and on this particular day her game didn't completely disappoint her. Sometimes, when it landed, it seemed this ball could have found no better resting place in the world, until a few minutes later it took flight again, pulling everyone's gaze and one woman's hopes onward into the green distance ahead. In this game, no matter how bad it got, for better or worse, there would always be one or two shots that made the rest of the day endurable. Sometimes one or two good shots were all it took to keep the hope alive.

*3.*

PACETTA SAID THE new job was a done deal. The NAM job was opening up in Cleveland, and Fred would get it. But after phone conversations with people higher up, Pacetta realized Fred was being overlooked for the new spot. He started making more phone calls, telling people in Rochester about Fred, insisting he get the NAM position. Even though the new NAM wouldn't answer to Frank, whoever got the job would be miserable if he didn't have the backing of the Cleveland district manager. This was the loyalty Fred hoped to get from Pacetta in return for all Fred's loyal service to him. As long as he was district manager, he'd have a say on who came into his district. Finally Fred himself called the man who would be his boss in Chicago and made a plea himself—he knew the accounts. He'd been the major accounts sales manager. All the arguments were in his favor.

At last Fred was invited to Chicago for a job interview. When he got there, he realized it was a formality. He ran into the two interviewers, by accident, in the lunchroom of the Xerox office there. They talked about basketball, and they shared lunch. At that point, Fred suspected either he was completely out of the running or they had already decided in his favor. They wouldn't be so casual with someone if things were still uncertain either way. They went through with the formal interview, but it wasn't a series of questions and answers. It was warm, easy, open-ended. At the end of the talk, when it was clear the time had come for Fred to leave, they handed him a letter. He had no idea it worked this way—they hand you a letter, you get the job, just like that? This was the salary, this the bonus. He'd get the job by the end of June. The job was his. He could hardly believe it.

When he returned to Cleveland, Kathy was overjoyed, and yet she wasn't surprised to see Fred expressing doubts now about the move. He wondered if he'd done the right thing. A few nights later they went to a cocktail party where he met some stockbrokers, and by the end of the party he was moping about how he'd missed his chance at selling stock. His predecessor in the NAM job had been a sophisticated, multilingual, cosmopolitan figure among the home-grown sales people in the district. Fred couldn't live up to that manner, that polish. She told him not to worry. He had his own style. He was a more genuine person than anyone in the district. He would do well.

It *was* hard to believe. Finally what he promised, well, it *happened*. His life had changed. Her own life wasn't changing so much yet, but she knew enough to allow more time for that, since Fred only recently entered his new role. However she could see the dawn of something hopeful in her husband's eyes, and that, at least, was a start. It would take him months, maybe more, to unwind from the pace of two previous decades—to start setting his clock radio for six instead of five, to get used to coming home before, rather than after, the dinner hour.

"I think this new job could help this marriage immensely," she told Fred.

"Thanks a lot," he said, laughing, as he finished his dinner at the table.

Life *was* changing. *Fred* was changing. At a district meeting, Frank and the others rented a money machine—the same one Fred saw at the Marriott, where people entered a glass cage to reach for fluttering, windblown cash—and they brought it to the amphitheater and asked reps to get inside, if only as an amusement to keep people awake during lulls in the meeting. Fred stood in the back of the room. Now he had his chance to get inside that machine. But he'd outgrown it. He didn't think it was right for a manager to divert money from the pockets of his reps. He made a conscious decision to require more of himself than to be a man in a money cage—though it hurt a little to see all those fifty-dollar notes going into so many other hands. It *was* his job, after all, to pay the bills.

Fred's new step forward gave Kathy a surge of energy, though at first she envied her husband. It was as if he'd gotten *his* reward for all the years the two of them had put into his career. Where was hers? Where was the recognition for everything she'd been through? Fred got his promotion and title and a set of new challenges, but in what way was Kathy entering a new realm, except vicariously, through her husband?

She wanted to get a full-time situation in Lorain, teaching grade school to disadvantaged children. With this job she could get paid for doing something meaningful. She applied at the school where she did her student teaching, a school serving mostly underprivileged minorities. It was located in a section of Lorain plagued by the problems usually found in larger metropolitan inner cities: drugs, crime, broken families, and a general state of hopelessness. But a tax levy failed, and the job wasn't available. She didn't dismiss her hope for that job. It wasn't just an idle self-gratifying daydream of a comfortable woman. She planned to substitute teach again, one or two or three days a week, on demand, until a full-time job became available. And as she took more calls, she *got* more calls. It was becoming a steady process—maybe even the beginnings of a career.

It was something real. There wasn't much money in it, but it had a future. Kathy didn't completely abandon her other dreams. One day early in August she was running on the treadmill in the basement. As she ran, all the rules for her game show occurred to her in an instant. She understood how it would be set up visually, the way the contestants would be scored, the kinds of questions they would be asked. Until this moment she hadn't been able to sit down and write an outline of how the show would work. Suddenly, after more than a year of incubation, the whole idea became plausible to her. All she needed to do was put it on paper.

Then, a few days later, in her doctor's office, she picked up a magazine to pass the time. She paused halfway through the publication when she found a profile of the author of *Life's Little Instruction Book*. She was always interested in self-help books, little volumes that talked about self-motivation and success. This book offered humorous and inspirational aphorisms and affirmations on how to succeed. As Kathy scanned the article, she came to a passage that described how the author once had an idea for a game show and almost convinced people in Hollywood to produce it. She called the publisher. But she wasn't able to get a phone number for the author, whom she really wanted to approach for assistance with her idea. But it didn't matter. She needed to finish getting the idea down on paper first. Simply taking action, no matter what happened with it, exhilarated her and gave her a sense of control over her own life.

With all her new enthusiasm and confidence, she decided to see if she could patent her idea for the toy ballpoint pen. She wrote and requested nondisclosure forms from the patent office, and Fred helped her arrange a meeting with three engineers at Case Western to discuss building a prototype. He was there at her side when she needed him. He wasn't mocking her now. He wasn't talking about how much it would cost. Her confidence was higher than ever. It carried over into everything she did. She took her children to Cedar Point Amusement Park. She had an ulterior motive. She wanted to prove something to herself. All week, she told herself she was going to ride the biggest roller coasters at Cedar Point, for the first time in her life.

Finally, after several hours at the park, she gained enough courage to climb onto the Mean Streak. It was huge, with slopes like a canyon's, but she had an idea, and she intended to test it—if she pretended to be driving the car she was riding, she suspected, the ride wouldn't be so bad. If in her mind she could convince herself she was in control, it would be fun. And it worked. She tried the Magnum, and it worked again. She learned to anticipate and mentally push herself into each fall and rise, feeling as if she were making things happen before they actually happened, developing an appetite for the next wave of weightlessness before it arrived, so that she felt as if she were the cause rather than the effect of the situation, even if she had no control over anything but her own mind and stomach.

It was a thrill to be thrown into the sky, the wind in her hair, the view of the tiny trees from the highest peaks, the sensation of riding toward the clouds and then falling to earth as fast as a skydiver. She rode all four roller coasters, looking forward to each fall and twist and corkscrew, anticipating what would happen a few seconds before it did, hungry for each jolting plummet through the air. In a way, she *was* in control. She faced the worst, and she mastered it. With the right attitude, it seemed, nothing was impossible. It was only a mental trick, a way of pretending to be in control, a willingness to go along for the ride. Yet it changed things.

Both their lives were like that. Fred hadn't escaped Xerox, any more than Kathy had sold her game show. Certainly, the two of them weren't entering a second honeymoon. But things *were* different—it was just that they had to be alert to those changes. They had to fight not to take for granted the little victories.

One thing was undeniable: At last Kathy could hold up a transcript of Fred's romantic speculations and look at the real world and see the two things match up, or at least bear a passing resemblance to each other. There'd been more truth than embellishment in his declarations at Palm Springs. What he'd predicted, at least in part, had come to pass.

After only a few weeks of his new assignment, Fred began to realize his good fortune. His office was moved to another part of the building, farther from the hubbub of the weekly grind. He began to establish his own schedule, his own goals, his own sense of achievement. He missed being a part of the group. Slowly, as he outgrew the ache of separation, he gained a sense of control over his life he'd never experienced before. His entire approach to a day in the office began to change; he came in at a reasonable hour and went home at five, night after night.

Fred watched the other sales managers in meetings and talking together in the halls and in their offices. He listened as Rob Onorato stuttered through his conversations, not finishing sentences, trying to follow four lines of thought simultaneously. Fred found himself becoming more coherent, more organized, more deliberative. He remembered his frenetic days as a sales manager with all the amused hindsight of a man looking back at a land or a time he'd escaped for good, though at the time he was living that former life he'd had no clear impression of his state of mind. It startled him to realize that he hadn't known how discombobulated he seemed to other people, that he'd had no way of stepping outside his own consciousness and observing it rationally. It was obvious to everyone else, but this condition of desperate over-achievement had a curious property—it tended to disguise itself in such a way that the overachiever himself had no way to recognize the symptoms of what, to others, looked like a disease. Fred felt that by becoming a national account manager, he was recovering from some condition he didn't fully comprehend. He felt the relief of someone who survives a fever and knows, as if for the first time, the pleasure of merely walking outdoors and smiling into the steadying coolness of an April breeze.

In his first few months on the job Fred began to apply himself. Week after week, he made dozens of phone calls and trips to Detroit, and other cities, to line up a deal for color copiers. The amount of time he needed to wait before closing the deal made him feel insecure; it made him want to be all over the world again, calling on three customers every day. And yet he knew it was the only way to do business. He wasn't slam-dunking equipment. He was doing things the quality way, step by step, figuring out exactly what was in the customer's best interest. After months of work, his effort culminated in the first of a series of complicated and delicate meetings between Xerox corporate executives and one of the district's most important customers.

Around the dinner hour on this same afternoon, standing in the kitchen, Kathy heard the unmistakable sound of someone honking a car horn, a block away, as he drove down Tradewinds Drive. Who was that horse's ass? As the honking got louder and louder, she went to the window and saw Fred pull into the driveway. Oh, it was *her* horse's ass. She smiled. Fred was telling her in his own way that he'd done something good. It was pure Fred Thomas, amusing and a little annoying and touching all at once, like the absurd buzzing of a kazoo at midnight. Fred laughed a little more now. He made *her* laugh a little more. He was surprising her. He was starting to come home on time.

## 4.

IT WAS FUNNY. They were giving Fred a going-away party, but where was he going? He wasn't leaving, exactly, but he wasn't staying either. He was still working alongside everyone else in the district, though he wasn't working as part of the team. His new boss had an office in Chicago. Fred was on his own.

When he and Kathy arrived at Pacetta's house on a Saturday night, Pacetta shoved a video camera into their faces. He was taping the whole gathering in the backyard on the deck, intending to preserve the entire party for Fred's own personal video archive. Pacetta kept stumbling backward, doing a running monologue, as

Fred and Kathy moved around the corner of the house and up onto the deck.

The caterers had set up a tent and were serving drinks, and most of the guests had already arrived. Everyone knew this would be one of their final celebrations together as a team. They were determined to have fun. Fred was the lucky one. He had been in Cleveland before all of them, and he had made it through the door into his own future ahead of them all. It was fitting he be the one honored, in a way, for what they'd all done together.

Everything was in flux as this year came to a close. Pacetta had had two opportunities to join the corporate staff and had refused both of them. Instead he asked to be district manager in Columbus, a smaller district close to this region he loved. Though it was little more than a lateral move to a smaller district, Pacetta could run things there—he could continue to be a king. Pat Elizondo was inheriting his throne in Cleveland. Rob Onorato was running Fred's old team with great success. Bruno was still working as a high-volume specialist. Stalled in his effort to become a sales manager, Bruno was looking outside Xerox at other opportunities. Nancy Woodard was having a tough year again, making few sales to the nonuser accounts in her second and last year in that territory, and though her husband was still hunting for a job, they had bought a new home, fully confident in her earnings at Xerox. Soon after Pacetta's departure was announced, Larry Tyler was promoted to Key Account Manager, a role similar in some ways to Fred's, allowing Larry to sell the entire range of Xerox products to a small number of important accounts.

Diane Burley was having another record-setting year as a sales rep, still one of the top performers in the district, even though she'd quit speaking to Libby Jones at Crawford Manufacturing and was taken off the account. Their friendship had ended in an aborted effort to sell five 5100s to Libby—including the one Diane and Fred had tried to install at Citadel for almost two years. After Diane and Rob approached other people at Crawford with their proposal, Libby composed a masterly counterproposal, arguing that her company didn't need the new machines, that they ought to simply make the final payments on the old machines and keep them for three or four more years. In other words, she called a halt to the churning. She phoned users around the country to get their testimonials on how happy they were to buy these machines and keep them beyond the leasing period. Libby won the battle. In effect, she did what every smart Xerox buyer needed to do—she stopped the churning by doing her homework. It was the quality way to be a customer.

Fred milled through the crowd and noticed the roast suckling pig on a table under the tent.

"I've got to get a shot of the pig," Frank said, the camcorder on his shoulder. "The caterer threw in the pig for an appetizer. It's a baby big. A suckling pig. That's a special for me."

Free pig. The party was costing big scoots. He deserved a free pig. Yet who among them believed the pig was free? Nothing was free in a real deal. The cost of that pork was baked into the barbecue somewhere, wasn't it?

At dinner Kathy sat next to Pat Elizondo. She told Pat how she mastered all the rides at Cedar Point. Pat said she wept on the Mean Streak.

"When I get off that ride, I always check to see if my pants are wet. There were, like, flies in my mouth," Pat said.

"It's true," Kathy said. "You come off these rides and pick the bugs out of your teeth."

"And then you say, Let's do it again," Pat said.

One of the caterers brought the main course: pasta, featuring a red sauce with clams, mussels, lobster, oysters, and scallops. The sound of laughter swelled over the tables, filling all the downstairs rooms, rumbling in the floor of the upper halls. Outside, it grew dark. Inside, the party distilled itself to the basic elements: candlelight, laughter, friendship, food, and wine. On the stereo in the family room, Neil Young sang one of his plaintive, dissonant ballads.

As dinner ended, everyone could hear, between songs on the stereo, the sound of crickets and peepers, a steady chirping that spoke of other sylvan places, weekends on a lake, honeymoons in rented cabins. Hudson *was* a beautiful place to live. Strewn across the tables were bowls of empty mussel and clam shells, pepper shakers, long-stemmed glasses with a red coin of wine drying in the bottom. Outside, dessert was being prepared—crepes smothered with Grand Marnier. The flames from the crepe pan illuminated the chef's nose, and a thousand small leaves over his head appeared in relief against the dense and dark woods behind Pacetta's house.

"You know what a Hudson wife makes for dinner?" someone asked.

"No, what?"

"Reservations."

Inside, Fred lifted Kathy into the air as everyone pushed aside the furniture and danced in the family room. He felt comfortable here, with a buzz from the drinks, with people close to his age, with music he enjoyed on the CD player. And soon he was going to be the center of attention. Much as he pretended to hate it, he could think of few things in life better than being honored at a party like this, organized by a man he liked and respected more than anyone else he'd served at Xerox. The stereo was blaring Pacetta's favorite oldies. As John Mellencamp's new CD started playing, most of the managers gathered on the deck to confer on how to honor Fred. Everyone who wasn't out on the deck gathered in the family room and found a place on the loveseats or on the floor or on the cream-colored sofa with a raised herringbone pattern in the fabric. It was a large room, with a hearth along one wall, large windows, a big-screen television, a wet bar, and a reproduction of what appeared to be a Remington sculpture of drunken-looking cowboys riding at full gallop, possibly toward a herd of docile, unsuspecting cows. When the managers came back into the room, Rob Onorato took command, asking Fred to sit in an armchair he placed in front of the fireplace.

"Fred, you've touched each one of us on the management staff—"

"He touched me a lot!" one of the wives said.

The room burst into laughter.

"Each of the management staff will share an experience tonight. I'll go first. Not only did I have the honor of working with Fred, I worked *for* Fred for six months. There was one account we needed for President's Club one year. We're sitting at the table with the senior VP and our contact. I brought Fred in for support and guidance and vision. In the meeting, he's, like, *When you gonna order, order, order? Can we install, install, install? We need the order, order, order, the order.*"

Everyone laughed, and Rob timed his delivery to hit the quiet lulls.

"But we have a pretty good call, anyway. Now, Fred, as wild as he is, is also a pretty sensitive guy. As we're leaving the call, my contact pulls me aside and says, *Rob, I'll tell you what, your proposal looks great, your product looks great, your pricing's great, but I can't stand this Fred Thomas.* She said, *If you wanna get the deal, I'll leave it to you, but just don't bring him here anymore.*"

More laughter, and scattered clapping.

"So we go out and fire up the Toyota Camry. We pop in a

Grateful Dead tape, and we get to Mama Santo's for lunch. I say, *Fred, you are a tremendous leader. You have great vision. But please don't ever go there again. This lady hates your guts.* So as we're eating pizza, Fred looks up with his sad puppy eyes and says, *Does she really hate me?* I said, *Fred, as the day is long, she hates you, and don't ever go back there again.* And then all the way back to the district, every few minutes, Fred would look over at me and ask, *Rob, does she really hate me? Really?*"

When the laughter subsided, Rob called Pat up to the chair.

"I tried to think of what really represents Fred's personality," she said.

Rob, who took a seat next to her, shouted: "Wait a second? I've got a show stopper!" He reached into his pocket and threw a handful of pennies onto the floor in front of Fred's feet. Fred, playing along, looked frantic and scrambled from his chair to collect all the pennies and put them into his pocket.

Pat continued: "Anyway, one day Fred and I had one of our lunches where we really shared personal things with each other. During lunch, he said, *I wanna tell you something, and you tell me if I'm a terrible person for sharing this with you. You can tell me, Fred. I won't tell anybody,* I said."

After a beat, everyone roared. Pat was never good at keeping secrets.

"And so he says to me, *Every once in a while I think about this life insurance policy I've got on my wife, Kathy, and I think*—Wait! Don't laugh!—*I think what would I do if Kathy dies and I had twenty-five thousand dollars?*"

The laughter was so strong, she had to wait a minute to continue. Ron Nelson roared and shouted: "Oh Fred! Big spender! Block party! Block party!"

Pat continued: "And he said to me, *Am I a terrible person, Pat?* And I said to him, *No, you're not a terrible person necessarily*—Wait!

Wait!—I said, *So you've thought about the twenty-five thousand. You ever think about whether or not Kathy has thought about what if you died and she has a half million dollars?* And Fred comes back from lunch and asks, *Do you really think she thinks about that?*"

The room was howling. Fred grinned his sheepish grin, and Kathy was laughing. She had her own stories to tell, but her turn didn't arrive. She was merely the spouse. Next up was Paul Mac-Kinnon. He looked as always, neat and crisp, with a mustache, heavier than Frank. His brown hair covered his forehead.

"When I think of Fred, one of the memories I'll always carry with me—you bring new meaning to the word *decisiveness*. The discussions with Fred, when he comes into my office, will go something like this: *Do you think I should do it? I'm gonna do it.* And as he leaves, *I shouldn't have done it.* That follows pretty much every conversation I've had with Fred. For instance, in a staff meeting, typically every month the staff gets together and gives their outlook. *So I'll go first,* Fred says. *This month, we'll do six hundred thousand.* Frank says to Fred, *What's the real number? It's five hundred, Frank, but we're probably only gonna do four. But we'll do six anyway. I don't know why, but we will. I have a feeling.*"

After the laughter subsided again as Fred grinned with delight, Pacetta finally took the floor, with a sheet of paper in his hand. As Frank got ready to speak, Kathy thought of the stories she would have told if she'd been asked to speak. She had one prepared. She had had an experience no one else has had—childbirth with Fred. Their son, Christopher, was born a day before Fred's birthday. When she went into labor, Fred said, "Kathy, can't you hold off one more day so the baby can be born on my birthday?" So they went to the hospital, and it was four in the morning. Fred was ranting and raving. "I can't believe this. I'm exhausted! I'm exhausted! I can't believe you're doing this to me, Kathy." As the pain got worse, and she was moaning, he would look at her and say, "It isn't that bad, Kathy. You're embellishing! You're embellishing!"

But she wasn't given the chance to speak.

Frank began: "I wrote down a few notes. I spent quite a bit of time these past few weeks on this. Kathy, you know Fred. The rest of you need to know Fred. When we're going on a call to Society Bank. Just to give you a sample of the demented, warped thought processes and the things that come out of his mouth—it's incredible to believe a human being could think this way. We're in their executive board room and afterwards we're getting into the car, he says, *You know what I was thinking about when we were talking to them, Frank? No, what, Fred?* I thought he was going to say, I saw some bimbo walking downtown or whatever. But he goes, *I just thought, Imagine if your heart just stopped. I was bored with the call, and I was thinking what if my heart stopped beating, and I just slumped down.*"

The crowd was hysterical. They knew Fred as well as Frank and Kathy knew him.

"In the five years we've been together, I can't tell you how many times he's said, *Frank, you don't really know me.* I know you, Fred, I know you. So today all you hear from him is, *Frank's going to make an announcement. It's not my party.* Fred is very different. He always agitated me. He never gave me, in five years, a straight answer to anything. *You don't really know me, Frank.*"

He paused and glanced at the sheet of paper in his hand. Frank wanted to give Fred the recognition he deserved. His affection for Fred showed in his face. Pacetta had done his work with the Cleveland district, but Fred deserved much of the credit. He wanted to prove he did, indeed, know Fred.

"I get a lot of credit for what you guys do, but Fred earned the respect of all of us because Fred kept things simple. We had a theme in the district once: Let's just go get five orders. That was Fred's. Fred started that. Fred never quits. All the time. We sit, and we say he just finds a way to get it done. You tell him that, and he'll be paranoid about it. *You really are trying to get rid of me, Frank.* Fred, you're one of the best pure salesmen I've ever seen. It's an empty feeling since you left this group. You are very, very special."

Fred loved the speech. It was so simple. This was all it took. There was nothing exceptionally eloquent in Pacetta's words, nothing extraordinarily insightful. It was a good-natured, good-humored, genuinely appreciative moment of praise. There were no tricks here. No masks. He cared, and it showed. Fred beamed as Pacetta told the group how much Fred did for all of them. His life mattered. He made a difference. He was good. He needed to hear someone say these things as often as possible, and hearing them from Pacetta meant more to him than hearing them from anyone else.

Pacetta proceeded to list the numbers. He listed Fred's accomplishments year after year. Fred beamed. There were sounds of amazement in the audience, confirming what Frank was trying to show—that Fred had helped lift Cleveland to heights it hadn't attained before. Maybe there was more to life than selling, as Fred and Kathy both wanted to believe. Yet it was clear Fred would always be a salesman, and this was good, not only for him, but also for whatever company he happened to serve. There was something good and vital in the animal game, the battle, with all its trickery and guile, its winning and losing—as long as it didn't become the sum of a life, as long as it left at least a little room for something more genuine.

Finally Frank gave the stage back to Rob, who presented Fred with his gifts. Rob had taken a collection to buy the awards, and no one refused to contribute twenty or thirty dollars to the pot. He unveiled a new golf bag, new balls, new tees, new club covers, new grips, and a new ball retriever. As a joke, one of the managers presented a bag of used golf balls fished from ponds in golf courses from around the Cleveland area. Fred was known to delight in the balls he found during a game more than the score he racked up.

"This is yours, Fred," Rob said. "Touch it. Touch it. When most of us go to the tee box, we put our tee in the ground and we drive the ball and we walk on. With Fred, the difference is, he says, *Are you done with that tee?*"

"Freddie! Freddie!" the crowd chanted. "Go, Freddie! Go, Freddie!"

It was Fred's turn to speak, and he hated it. But he'd prepared himself this time.

"First of all, on a serious note, I love the bag," he said.

"You can have the cash instead, if you like!"

"This is special, it really is. Every one of the gifts—fabulous. You went overboard. This is wonderful. The waterpick—"

"It's called a ball retriever, Fred."

"I'll never forget it."

"He likes the ball retriever," Pacetta said.

"Let me just say something. I'm an emotional guy, at least I think I am."

"We don't know you, Fred," Pacetta said.

"It's been a tremendous, tremendous ride I've had. And I would not have had this successful ride if it wasn't for all the people in this room. I could try to say something special about each of you but I'm scared I might miss somebody. I've whined. I've bragged. I've boasted. And you've listened to me. We've all kept ourselves at a high, successful level the past four years. My wife, I know she's put up with me, I don't know why she does. The past four years could not have happened without the staff here today. It's been the finest group I've ever been associated with. There's an individual who has kept it together. I credit ninety-nine point nine percent of my success to that individual. I'd like to suggest all of us, as a group, come together right now—"

"And tongue kiss," Pacetta said.

"We'll talk about that later. I mean this sincerely. I'd like all of us to come together, and I'd like to hear three hip-hip-hurrays. I want three hip-hips for Frank and his magnificent staff."

The managers all gathered in front and shouted *hip-hip-hurray* three times, and everyone applauded. Rob told the group the evening's performance was concluded. Frank announced the party was just now getting started. Fred made his own pronouncement on the evening: "It's the end of an era. The end of an era."

People flow from room to room, dancing and laughing and drinking. After midnight the house becomes an island of levity and warmth, isolated and unreal. The last few hangers-on stall their departure. Around two o'clock, in the kitchen, the Huddle begins to form.

This time, Frank isn't standing in the middle. No one is reaching out to touch him. At first, only Rob, Ron, and Frank are singing, and then, one by one, the others join them. Arms thrown over shoulders, elbows interlocking, the circle grows larger, as people sway awkwardly against each other, hip to hip, shoulder to shoulder. The music of James Taylor plays softly in the family room. *My cards are on the table and there ain't nothing up my sleeve.*

Kathy joins Fred in the kitchen. They're the final couple to enter the circle. It feels good to link themselves with these other veterans. They sing in unison. For the moment, no one is selling anybody anything.

## ABOUT THE AUTHOR

DAVID DORSEY lives with his wife and two children in Rochester, New York. This is his first book.

## ABOUT THE TYPE

The text of this book was set in Janson, a misnamed typeface designed in about 1690 by Nicholas Kis, a Hungarian in Amsterdam. In 1919 the matrices became the property of the Stempel Foundry in Frankfurt. It is an old-style book face of excellent clarity and sharpness. Janson serifs are concave and splayed; the contrast between thick and thin strokes is marked.